THE UNUSUAL CHILD

THE
UNUSUAL CHILD

edited by

JOSEPH S. ROUCEK

University of Bridgeport

PHILOSOPHICAL LIBRARY
New York

Printed in the United States of America

CONTENTS

THE UNUSUAL CHILD

PREFACE

Tne rapid changes in our modern world require that the child be able to accept the maximum education which his abilities, as well as his handicaps, allow him to utilize. America acknowledges that education is a vital necessity for all children, and especially those who are "unusual" children, and that, with the proper approach, understanding, training and placement, even "unusual" children can become fully contributing members of society.

Is there a teacher who, at one time or another, does not have to deal with children who, somehow or other, become a problem because they are not ordinary pupils, and whose difficulties require help in areas with which the teacher's particular professional education has not equipped him (or her) to deal? The difficulty is that society cannot guarantee good parents or environment for every child. But this fact, in turn, imposes the responsibility on all teachers to "know" how to handle practically every problem that comes up in their classrooms. Sometimes, where the home environment is unsatisfactory, the teacher can help to meet the basic needs of all children for affection, for a feeling of belonging, for a sense of achievement and for an opportunity for creative expression. But all too often the overworked teacher must take on the added responsibility, as the laws of many states acknowledge, of serving *in loco parentis* (in place of a parent), since, in recent decades, the American family has been transferring more and more of its share of responsibilities to the school. Whether or not the teachers are expected to know the family of every pupil and discuss the child's progress with the parents, the fact remains that the family, the community and the administration of each school

1

expect the teachers to act as employers of a child-rearing agency, whose influence is carried out even beyond the framework of the influence of the family, and who, therefore, as educated specialists *must* know all about their charges.

This is, indeed, a formidable task and assignment since we live in a very complex society, and each classroom is filled with personalities which have to be handled not only as a group but also as individuals. There are always "deviates," those who are above or below the "average" intelligence, those who are always troublesome, and those who have physical, emotional, and mental difficulties. The realization of such ever-recurring phenomena has produced numerous experiments in handling "exceptionality," floods of specialized studies, and even the training of specialists. But, interestingly enough, most of the available data on the unusual child are of a relatively recent date, resulting mostly from the wide range of studies in child growth and development. In addition, there has been a definite impact from the medical contributions. The same applies to the psychologist and the educator, who have shown how children differ and what factors influence individual differences, and who have indicated programs which would satisfy the needs of each individual child. Furthermore, much has been done by statistical contributions, which show us more about the relationships, the distribution of abilities and the degree of differences, as well as the methods of measuring differences and the reliability and validity of such measurements.

But how can the average and fully occupied teacher become acquainted with all this available knowledge regarding the outstanding types of "unusual" children? Yet, paradoxically enough, each teacher should be at least summarily acquainted with it, so that he (or she) can identify the problem, learn ways and means whereby it can be handled, and refer it to authorities and specialists when necessary. The aim of this work is to present a readable and all-inclusive summary of the available knowledge about a selected number of different categories of unusual children by outstanding authorities, some of whom are college and university specialists, some "practicing teachers," and some so-

2

ciologists. The topics were picked because they concern themselves with a cross-section of those types of "unusual" children met by the average teacher, psychologist and social worker. It is true that there exist similar and perhaps more definite categories of such children; but the field is practically limitless and hence only the outstanding examples can be handled here. There is much room for individual judgment as to what is really the "unusual child."

Yet, taken together, the types handled here and the capsule descriptions of related problems cover a reasonably wide spectrum of the "unusual" children which the average American teacher may expect to meet in his daily work. Since the subject cuts across all boundaries of knowledge, several medical aspects of some subjects are also included.

Our deep thanks and appreciation to Dr. Dagobert D. Runes, Director of the Philosophical Library, for inviting the editor to inaugurate the planning of this publication and for helping to bring it to completion.

JOSEPH S. ROUCEK

University of Bridgeport.

INTELLECTUALLY GIFTED CHILDREN

Maurice F. Freehill
Western Washington State College

The development and utilization of human abilities is a matter of enduring concern to all who value the welfare of individuals and the future of society. The recent epidemic of speaking and writing in favor of intellectual excellence reflects a new profile of goals as much as a change in level of expectations. Each man and each age struggles toward greater liberty, larger security, longer life, and warmer affection. Certain eras are marked by sharper struggle with quickening pace and reforming purposes. The last twenty years have compelled both new levels of accomplishment and a concentration on selected aspects of intellectual achievement.

Many reports on the popular conversion to intellectual and academic values have been exaggerations. The public continues strong support for energetic workers, external achievements, and spectacular successes. Appreciation is given to operational men—men of action, lovers, fighters, and shrewd gamblers. It is not clear that equal acceptance is given to scholarly men—disciplined men, judgmental, quiet, and knowing. Natural scientists, the central figures in these discussions, have been acclaimed for practical technology and spectacular invention more than for scientific thought and the development of theory.

The reshaping and refocusing of attitudes concerning human abilities have been greatly influenced by urgent military needs. Adequate defense requires complex devices and capacity to outstrip an enemy in perfecting still newer equipment for attack or countermeasure. Each succeeding device depends on more sophisticated technology and more highly developed intelligence. These changes have rested the common fate in the hands of a strategic few.

The technological emphasis brought on by military concern was supported in a society characterized by material wealth, economic progress, and secular goals.[1] Since the industrial revolution, the larger rewards have been assigned to practical and industrially useful intelligence. Shrewdness brought prestige and ideas were evaluated in terms of cash returns and royalties. The society which enjoyed gargantuan satisfaction in physical comforts and abundance promoted skills which contribute to these ends. The popular definition of intelligence was made almost synonymous with applied science and business expertness. Objective knowledge and manipulative skills were emphasized while artistic sensitivity and theoretical astuteness were discounted.

An emphasis on academic outcomes should be a natural consequence of more complex social and industrial circumstances. The use of the scientific method, better communication techniques, and an enlarged fund of established knowledge have greatly accelerated the growth of new knowledge. A century ago, teachers had reasonable assurance that a major portion of what they taught would prove valid and useful throughout the student's adult life. Modern education must impart knowledge and give increased attention to students' ability for continuous, rapid assimilation, and organization of an expanding and changing body of information.

The last couple of decades brought upgrading in the labor market with increased demands for education and specialization. Specialization now involves a large proportion of the total work force and the professional and technical group is increasing at approximately three times the rate for the total working population. No end of increased requirements is in sight.

Modern technology has been accompanied by large social changes and fierce compression of the political world. The international scene changed with unruly haste. Countries which were living in a delayed Middle Ages suddenly became contemporary

6

world societies. The nation became a metropolitan society under the influence of common ideas promoted by profit-oriented and mass communication media. In his specialty the individual tends to be isolated from his political and social neighbor. The international and national problems became more complex and more remote placing new demands on intelligence and education.

New standards and goals are essential but choosing them is hazardous. There has been much talk about "toughness" but little about "thoroughness." Toughness implies intentional unpleasantness and is likely to center on peripheral or secondary requirements. The learning value of an experience is not directly related to its congeniality or uncongeniality. Some of the most significant things in our lives are learned in happy and successful moments. Others come from suffering and tragedy. Rigor for its own sake ends in rigidity and the "tough" proposals are limited to more work, a lengthened school year, a different selection of subjects, and increased teacher control. The student is assigned a passive role with established reward pattern, probably inimical to the constructive curiosity and independence so valuable to society.[2]

This era, starting roughly with World War II, has produced many hasty and uninformed proposals for modifications of education. People stirred by international anxieties and by hopes for a better national and individual future have seen education as a practical tool. Following sparse and unsystematized appraisal of schools, there have been recommendations for simple and unidimensional changes to achieve complex and confused ends.

Nearly all of the educational proposals pay particular attention to education for the intellectually gifted. Some of the proposals would promote the education of this group at the expense of the less able even though there is evidence that ever larger numbers must be prepared for technical and clerical work. Other proposals would sacrifice the individual rights of very bright children for the social good. The easy answers do not come to grips with the nature or the degree of individual differences. They assume that there is only one ability and propose a well

7

defined system of incentives to lead all students to a pre-determined goal, with the possible exception of the mentally defective. More thoughtful educational proposals embrace a greater diversity of goals and hold more generous views of ability, giving attention to talent in many fields and over a wide range in any one field.

IDENTIFYING THE GIFTED

Intellectual giftedness is sometimes defined in terms of abilities and capacities, but more often in normative or statistical fashion. Children are considered gifted if they surpass a given IQ score or fall within a designated percentage of a total population. These persons are called gifted, bright, academically able, or intellectually superior. Other terms imply both capacity and achievement. These terms include accelerated learner, talented, rapid learner, or academically able and ambitious student.

There are no very clear distinctions between labels and no very firm agreements concerning the point at which giftedness begins. Some rapid learning classes include children with IQs of 110 but 130 is probably the most common threshold figure. This score was used by Leta Hollingworth in her work with gifted children in New York. Lewis Terman, in his major work *Genetic Studies of Genius,* used 140 as a threshold and 170 for a very superior category. Many schools use 125 or 130 with a lower range added for children with unexpectedly high academic accomplishments. Percentage criteria are usually fixed at two or three per cent but there is a trend toward ten or more. Some schools consider a child gifted if he is in the top two or three per cent in one or more fields or talents. With this standard the total gifted group approximates ten per cent.

Gifted children do not come in peculiar models either bookish, bumbling, and near-sighted, or muscular, shrewd, and arrogant. Some intellectually superior children live in homes and participate in activities which fail to elicit intellectual and imaginative symptoms of ability. Others take on average "postures" in order to avoid conspicuousness or to avoid responsibilities associated with their capacity. A specific act by a gifted person is not strikingly different from ordinary behavior. The significant difference is internalized, hidden between the stimulus and the response. The gifted child responds more appropriately and on smaller clues but he walks, hammers, or smiles much like average children. Large numbers of gifted children remain undiscovered if there is no deliberate organized and sensitive search for talent.

Identification procedures geared to finding a large proportion of all existing talent must include systematic testing and observing and the tests and observations must cover an inclusive range of intelligent behavior.

A major problem in providing for orderly discovery of gifted children is the problem of defining intelligence itself. There is continuing uncertainty over whether intelligence is an unidimensional and single power or a multidimensional collection of specific capacities. Hindsight shows that intellectual abilities differentiate early. Some of these differences may be natural or congenital, some are certainly altered by social contacts and personal interests. Perhaps none are totally independent and specific talents for there is a positive relationship between skills. There appears to be a large general or *g* factor in intelligence.

The puzzle is being attacked on several fronts. In a fairly recent study of 50 pre-adolescent bright children, with Stanford Binet IQs of 150 or more, it was found that gifted children have unusual ability to synthesize and associate but no real weakness and no peculiar pattern on the Wechsler Intelligence Scale for Children.[3] Other studies show large overlap between intellectual, social, artistic, and personality factors.[4]

A number of scholars are seeking to forward the work of Thorndike and the Thurstones by more adequate definition of specific components in intellectual functions. Guilford, at the University of Southern California, is a leader in the effort to categorize functions most basic to intelligent action.[5] From a practical view, single-score tests function well with young children and for prediction of broad academic success. As students become older and tasks become more specialized, differential of category-scores add something to the unitary index of ability.

Intelligence tests have proved the most useful single criterion of intelligence. Paper-pencil tests, less adequate than individual tests, have been popular for their economy. Tests, developed to discover persons who could not profit from planned experiences, are least adequate when they measure high ability. Abbreviated tests lack "top," and standardization requirements limit the possibility for unique and imaginative responses.

Achievement test data and academic records properly play a part in the identification process. Children who do conspicuously well must have ability. The corollary is not true for achievement limitations may occur in children with outstanding ability. Intelligence is best viewed as a threshold variable or enabling quality.

Teachers consider success in certain subjects superior indications of high ability. There is merit in this, but the task components must be thoroughly understood. Routine and memorizing tasks may be "tough" but success in them is not closely related to ability. Studies show that spelling competency is a poor index of ability. Mathematics is a suitable indicator if the measured content is problem solving and application of principles and not computation alone. Probably no area of school achievement is so significant as reading. This experience is challenging and closely parallels thought itself. Intelligent children tend to become able and interested readers.

If nearly all gifted children are to be found, test data must be supplemented by thorough and organized observation. Particularly useful suggestions are found in research volumes by Leta S. Hollingworth and in the first and third volumes of the *Stanford Genetic Studies of Genius.*[6] Certain characteristics are more commonly found among the gifted but profiles or arrangements of these characteristics vary greatly from child to child.

One quality dominant in gifted children is unusual capacity to transfer knowledge or modify experience in new situations. The difficulty of each successive problem varies greatly from child to child in the degree that more or less knowledge and more or less understanding of principles is transferred into it. Transfer produces extended learning and makes for rapid solution of subsequent but related problems. This accounts for some observed precocity or learning speed. Transfer may depend largely on generalization and it is frequently observed that gifted children generalize easily and early. They talk in terms of similarities and differences and they place things in categories.

A second quality of giftedness is capacity to organize and find coherence in ideas. Any individual is uncomfortable if he cannot integrate and make sense of multiple observations. Gifted persons are peculiarly able to relate, integrate, and organize, with the result that their behavior is sensitive to peripheral knowledge and marked by directionality or perseverance.

A third characteristic, related to potential for transfer and organization, is wide-ranging interests and broad general knowledge. Bright children are eager for new activities and under desirable environmental conditions they have many play interests and knowledge over a wide range of subject matters. Terman found this broad general information to be one of the most striking characteristics of giftedness.

Observational guides should emphasize communication, language, and symbolic skills. Gifted people tend to be "symbol minded." The utilitarian quality of symbols and the challenge of abstraction combine to create interests in content such as poetry or mathematical thought. Under ordinary circumstances the gifted child is both delighted by and competent in this area.

Most gifted children have enduring interest in words. They explore, invent, and play with them. They have a particular fascination with poetry. A nine year old boy probes the mysteries of space flight and its effects on man in the following poem.

SPACE MAN?

A man is a thing
He's only so small
He's only so big
He's him—That's all.

But what is a man
   When he flies to the stars
Floating and weightless
   Then heavy on Mars?

What is man's size
   When at last he is hurled
Through the shadowy miles
   Till he's lost his own world?

Now is he a man
   Away from his earth
So far from his home
   And the place of his birth?

How does man feel
   When returning again
He's gravity-crushed
   Is the pain worth it then?

A man is a thing
   And the heavens call
So he conquers the skies
   He'll rise—and fall.

Appropriate identification processes involve many people and many observations. Essential data include those from day to day work, from specialized tests of achievement, from intelligence tests, and from observations made by both parents and teachers. Most schools make use of an observation guide or check list. These rating scales include such items as the following:

1. Is alert, responds appropriately to a wide variety of stimuli.
2. Is interested and has knowledge of many things.
3. Learns rapidly and easily.
4. Is curious and observant.
5. Generalizes and reasons.

6. Has long attention span.
7. Usually talks early and has a large vocabulary.
8. Reads more, and more complex material than his age mates.
9. Spends time on special projects such as collecting.
10. Has advanced social interests and skills.
11. Is original in drawing, story telling, or dramatizing.
12. Uses descriptive words and analogies.
13. Superior in physical development and co-ordination.
14. Tends to be self-critical and responsible.

The discovery of gifted children is a responsibility shared between teachers, administrators, school psychologists, counselors, and parents. In all cases, but especially in larger districts, there is need for an organized screening process and a co-ordinating person. The program should run throughout school life but be more intense in pre-school and primary grades so that growth rate will be maximized and maladjustment avoided.

LEARNING PRINCIPLES

Gifted learning is marked by qualitative change more than by quantitative change or accumulation. It involves a broadening, deepening, and changing of first perceptions. It moves from massive approximation to simpler orders of understanding with increased validity and accuracy of both perceptions and behavior. This deepening and systematizing creates a demand for new knowledge. The learner has a stake in the development of his own understanding and he seeks both to know and to place his knowledge in dynamic and useful arrangements.

The learner has too often been assigned a passive role, as the complex but apathetic recipient of knowledge. The "hole in the head" idea seems to assume that heads have different storage capacities and different intake rates with larger cavities having larger intake pipes. This view leads to only minor educational adaptations to differential ability. The changes are confined to rate and duration of learning and not to differences in content and method. The teacher of the gifted is expected to pour knowledge faster and slightly longer. Such adaptations are inadequate because good learners are active participants in organizing knowledge, because effective memory depends on how adequately knowledge is structured more than how often it is repeated, and because higher order learning depends on insight or the grasping of new relationships and plausible explanations.

Intuitive and insightful learning are not well understood. Psychological experiment features simple learners, signal-oriented tasks, and physical responses with neglect of complex learnings, future-oriented tasks, and symbolic responses.[7] The sharpening of intellectual purposes places greater emphasis on insight and the capacity for sudden apprehension of meaning. Intuition seems essential to but probably not sufficient for effective thought.[8] It complements rather than displaces analysis. Intuitive thought presents possible solutions which might never have reached awareness through a more formalized process. Almost simultaneously the learner depends on analytic thought to test or evaluate informed hunches. This might be called "guess and check" or "leap and test" learning.

"Leap and test" learning is not disorderly. The short-cutting and skipping are made possible by finding new order and coherence. Insightfulness would not vary in gross amount between people of equal experience and complexity if it were a phenomenon determined only by chance. Readiness for insight is not merely a matter of intelligence and age but a complicated set of relationships between what is known, the structure in which the knowledge is arranged, personal openness to relationships, and attitudinal or value commitments to new solutions.

Insight implies uniqueness in discovery but does not imply solutions which cannot be evaluated through common and analytical processes. Insight involves discovery—the personal and sudden perception of relation where none was known. There is no single door to insight and the teacher cannot prepare for a single intuitive solution. The goal is defeated rather than promoted by formalistic, atomized teaching, and beads-on-a-string curricula. Orderly, step-by-step, teacher-arranged experiences may lead to informed pupils but not to insightful and imaginative

14

scholars. Good teaching, especially good teaching for the gifted, does not exclude informing but must include helping students to new arrangements and structures. Good teaching is less orderly arranging and transmitting of pieces and more providing opportunities for students to acquire, judge, reshape, and transform knowledge in a search for increasingly adequate organization and meaning.

A search for learning models suited to able learners leads to elementary reading. About one-third of gifted children do some reading before they enter school. Their reading is thought-directed more than process-directed. They begin by telling themselves a story from pictures and incomplete clues. Gradually they move toward greater accuracy and perfection in fitting the story to the print. The early reading is a rough approximation based on limited knowledge but it is, nevertheless, whole and reasonable. This is not a progression from piece to larger piece but an increase in sensitivity to detail, ability to discriminate, and capacity to interpret with story or meaning as the organizing principle.

Good teaching for gifted learners emphasizes discovery, intuition, diversity of outcomes, personal aspects of learning, and the importance of meaning as a director of learning. Teachers may be guided by the view that learning is largely achieved through qualitative changes with each change directed toward more valid understanding and behavior. If these observations are correct, then the following suggestions may be appropriate for education of gifted children:

1. The major adaptation in subject matter for the gifted should be in complexity not in amount. Emphasis should be on conceptualization not speed.

2. Good instruction emphasizes the systematizing of knowledge.

3. The best curriculum is "spiral" so that basic ideas are revised and deepened as the learner matures.[9]

4. Lecture and laboratory instruction should sometimes be intentionally sparse and incomplete providing opportunities for intellectual leaps and insight.

5. Programs should include a relatively large portion of abstract

and symbolic thought. These learnings are one step removed from physical demonstration, handling or counting and they are among the most difficult of intellectual tasks. An adequate program for the gifted should assure competence in language, critical reading, mathematical thought, and artistic representations.

6. Informal and concomitant learning should be encouraged.

7. Many gifted children are now over-scheduled. There should be time for imagining and reflecting.[10]

8. High standards are appropriate but these should emphasize knowing, thinking, and evaluating more than memorizing, computing, and repeating.

9. Gifted learning involves errors. Bright students increase problem complexity by transferring in information, associating peripheral knowledge, and perceiving plausible solutions. They try a number of "may work" solutions. They make mistakes but they do not repeat and there is a rapid decline in error scores through a single problem. Good instruction guides the number and the severity of errors while helping the student to correct and then learn the solutions.

10. Imaginative, inventive, and exploratory projects should be included in the work of gifted children.

11. Test items should require the use of analogy, judgment of relationships, and ability to use knowledge in a new context.

12. Studies should be organized in work units or study themes so that students may be guided by overall purposes or massive ideas.

13. Early specialization is inappropriate.

14. Vocationalism should be avoided at least through the high school to assure that the student will have a wide range of possible choices.

ACHIEVEMENT MOTIVATIONS

Many gifted children who meet requirements are achieving below potential. Factors such as boredom, lack of challenge, personality defects and socio-economic conditions have been studied to find their connection with underachievement. The findings indicate that this is a depth problem not easily modified. While there is some disagreement in the findings there is general evidence that underachievement is related to psychiatric and personal problems, to inadequate environmental opportunities and to familial disinterest in academic matters. The pattern of underachievement is established early, not later than the third grade for boys and only slightly later for girls.[11]

A host of recent studies center on underachievement. One of these in the DeWitt Clinton High School in New York found differences in attitude and personality between high and low achievers.[12] Although occupational aspiration and intensity of interest were similar the anticipations of success were different. The underachievers who improved during the study were those who identified with a supportive and interested teacher and those who mastered learning skills, previously inadequate.

Motivational differences initiate early. High achieving boys expressed unconscious need for success and all achievers had stronger educational motivation.[13] Achievers indicate their fathers as the important influence in their lives and that their mothers held high aspirations for their children. It has been consistently demonstrated that college drive increases more spectacularly with parental occupational status, educational level, and social success than with basic ability.[14]

Intellectual and personality patterns bear a poorly defined relationship to achievement. A study of paired boys in the Bronx High School in New York found achievers high on numerical and verbal abilities but not above underachievers in space or abstract reasoning.[15] Achievers had stronger scientific and computational interests where the less successful had mechanical and artistic interests. Achievers' fathers were in upper occupational categories, their mothers less frequently worked out of the home and fathers were relatively better educated than mothers. No significant differences in objective health data were found but achievers had more health complaints and underachievers had more absences reported for health reasons.

Studies based on National Merit Scholars show that gifted

college students are disposed to intellectual activity, reflective thought, a cognitive approach to reality, and a positive attack on scholarly pursuits.[16] The majority, but especially the women, react preferentially to artistic over utilitarian components. The men were more socially oriented than unselected men and they were less rigid allowing for resourcefulness and originality.

Gowan summarized studies on underachievement and concluded that achievement patterns established in the elementary school were ordinarily continued.[17] Achievers had ego-strength, concern for others, clarity of purpose, effective use of time and money, reading and arithmetic skills, dominance, and socialized views. The parents troubled themselves to interest their children, imposed fairly high but not impossible standards, and were comparatively permissive.

There is consistent evidence pointing up the crucial role of interpersonal and family relationships. Teachers must conclude that impelling motivation results when a gifted student identifies with a teacher. The teacher as a model or image helps the students build scholarly identity. The teacher who will serve as communicator and model must display openness to learning and imagination.[18]

Proposals for motivating gifted students tend to reduce to meddling. The gimmicks and artificial devices are transparent to bright students. Their major motivation stems from curiosity and the need to know. It is stimulated by public values and by the child's sense of identity and purpose. The greatest stimulation comes from well organized material presented at an appropriate time by an interested teacher in a culture which values the outcomes.

The most common proposal is that scholarship should be motivated by planned competition. This approach introduces undesirable side effects but has also a more serious fault. It may be useful in simple and repetitive learning where practice is essential but it defeats complex and imaginative learning. Very competitive feelings narrow the visual and intellectual perceptions, reduce the degree of participation and openness to learning, rigidify attitudes and viewpoints, and cause the student to concentrate on immediate pragmatic outcomes. All of these inhibit leap-and-test learning.

ADMINISTRATIVE CONSIDERATIONS

Discussions about education for the gifted seem to begin and end with debate over grouping and acceleration. This is neither the first nor the most important question. Administrative plans are devices for facilitating instruction and they are properly chosen after methods and materials are selected.

The term "grouping" is now more popular than "segregation." The practice of grouping has also grown in popularity with the proponents arguing that bright companions stimulate the student, grouping provides for more adequate competition and the development of work habits, and grouping assures that gifted children will be offered more appropriate subject matter. There have been many studies including evaluations of large programs such as the Cleveland Major Work Classes. The evidence indicates some academic increments but less than is commonly supposed.

Opponents of grouping emphasize social goals. They argue that gifted children need the experience of working with others and that less able children can gain greatly from example. Modern writing scoffs at the equalitarian argument but some sophisticated scholars such as Bruno Bettelheim see imminent danger in the present attitudes.[19] He argues that the social cleavage is similar whether one sets himself apart as an attribute of color or of intelligence.

Acceleration has been less popular and many people continue to equate it with "skipping." Studies show positive results with accelerates outstripping equally able non-accelerates. These evidences are found at every level; in studies by Worchester for early school entrants, by Terman for elementary and secondary years, and by Pressey for the college level.[20] Even skipping seems successful. Apparently gifted children tolerate gaps in their experience because they have ability to relate, infer, and integrate. Studies show both academic and social success and there is very little evidence that moderately accelerated children suffer from social and physical misplacement.

It must be concluded that these devices are neither good nor bad as a rule but good or bad for specified conditions and selected purposes. The question is, under what conditions can the maximum enrichment and the greatest individuation be achieved. No arangement substitutes for good teaching.

The problems of teaching gifted children rise in part from their great variability which in turn comes from the inventive and creative range of their behavior. Such children are marked by extended knowledge, inventive responses, and complex ideas, making a gifted group, indeed heterogeneous. Some teachers assume homogeneity and offer a common fare to youngsters once grouped by ability. Such teaching is inadequate. Other teachers in classes of divergent ability may achieve greater individuation using work sheets, projects, self-monitored study, guides, and learning aids. Unfortunately, many would-be authorities believe that failure is impossible if the organization and the classification are complex enough.

Decisions about organization should involve such questions as whether or not these conditions will result in increased love of learning, ability to think, identification of talent, greater social usefulness, growing personal happiness and extended individual differences. Whatever program is selected should be articulated from level to level and from school to school. The policy should not come from an enthusiastic teacher or excited member of the board of directors but from a responsible person or committee with access to research and access to feedback from the local system.

COURSE OFFERINGS FOR THE GIFTED

Our new-found knowledge of space and atomic energy is almost paralyzing. The urgent concerns of the moment may produce a narrow perspective and concentration on immediately useful outcomes. Nevertheless, the years ahead promise a serious testing of our theories and skills in social, political, and artistic realms as much as in scientific and military strength. Schools need a broad strategy directed toward both maximum development of all children and preparation of gifted people in many fields.

Space confines this paper to near-academic outcomes but it is obvious that the personal, social, and physical development of gifted children is essential to both their happiness and the good of society. Academic outcomes are central in this development and are goals for which the school has special responsibility. A cautious view favors a fairly broad definition of the words, "academic" and "curriculum." A decision to reduce the normal range of experience for any individual must be made with the greatest care.

School offerings should: (a) exploit capacity to harmonize or find coherence, (b) promote judgement and insight, (c) provide challenge, (a) emphasize opportunities to synthesize and evaluate, (e) develop sophistication and technical excellence, (f) allow personal engagement and feeling about the content, (g) encourage divergent procedures, (h) and assure opportunities to work at different levels of abstraction. A much abbreviated list of possible suggestions might be as follows:

The student should glimpse the contemporary frontiers in several fields.

Much of the content should be covered in depth with these various aspects integrated through student inference, teacher summary, and occasional survey units.

Teach children to read maps, charts, and graphs as preparation for independent study.

Allow children to short-cut and solve problems in different ways. Encourage creative and critical writing such as editing and writing for school publications.

Choice of science units should reveal relationships among sciences.

Introduce a modern foreign language in the third or fourth grade using audio-lingual methods.

Provide for independent reading with particular wide opportunities in the social studies.

Study selected themes which run throughout literature.

PERSONAL DEVELOPMENT

It has long been held that genius and creativity are based on pathology and abnormality. Some current writers recommend the exploitation of insecurity and the development of nonconformity as essential to creative development. There can be little doubt that artistic and imaginative work involves the "depth person" and knowledge. There are striking examples where emotions have inhibited or distorted perception and there are cases where genius has been released in dreams, inebriation and madness. Apparently these conditions reduced immediately practical concerns or archaic inhibitions and allowed the person more open expression of his imagination.

It can be agreed that all learning is intensely personal, that emotions, values, and attitudes act as a filter for all that enters or leaves the mind. No thought is unmarked by personality, but the more creative and imaginative the work the more clearly it is marked by its creator. The personal organization, whatever its quality, enters into creative work, but those who have investigated the question conclude that any attempt to explain creativity as neurosis leads to incompleteness and absurdity. There is considerable evidence that regardless of field of work, creative persons are marked by common modes of thinking and considerable inner tension.[21] It is likely that only intense and zealous persons will have the daring to search the unknown and postulate new meaning.

The school contributes to the development of creativity. These functions are denied to narrowly trained persons with arbitrary disregard for other knowledge, to those who are highly success-oriented and over fearful of failure, and to those who have accumulated facts without being personally affected by a great painting or a fine poem.

22

There is evidence that knowledge and malevolence may exist together. A complete education must integrate knowledge and purposes and contribute to the values, attitudes, and sentiments of the gifted. Personal development and academic goals are not alternate choices, for the full development of one depends on the development of the other. Only the mature person can be counted on to know unscientific from scientific, unwise from wise or evil from good.

SELECTED BIBLIOGRAPHY

Abraham, Willard, COMMON SENSE ABOUT GIFTED CHILDREN, Harper & Brothers, New York, 1958, 268. This is a general text or a book for parents. It proposes some of the possible organizational and instructional adaptations.

Brumbaugh, Florence N., and Bernard Rostico, YOUR GIFTED CHILD, A GUIDE FOR PARENTS, Henry Holt and Co., New York, 1959, 182. This is a book for laymen. It will contribute to an understanding of the gifted child.

Bruner, Jerome S., THE PROCESS OF EDUCATION, Harvard University Press, Cambridge, 1960, 97. This report on a 1959 conference on teaching science provides an excellent statement of principles important in educating intellectually gifted students.

California Elementary School Administrators' Association, THE GIFTED CHILD: ANOTHER LOOK, The National Press, Palo Alto, 1958, 66. This is a practical pamphlet with descriptions of programs and suggestions for organization of schools and for teaching.

Cutts, Norma E., and Nicholas Moseley, BRIGHT CHILDREN, G. P. Putnam's Sons, New York, 1953. This is a book for parents. It will serve to increase home-school understanding.

DeHaan, Robert F., and Robert J. Havighurst, EDUCATING GIFTED CHILDREN, The University of Chicago Press, Chicago, Ill., 1957, 276. EDUCATING GIFTED CHILDREN is a readable and thoughtful text with particularly good material on community factors, motivation and special talents.

French, Joseph L., EDUCATING THE GIFTED, A BOOK

OF READINGS, Henry Holt and Company, New York, 1959, 555. This is a comparatively inclusive book of readings with editorial comment. It serves to acquaint the reader with ideas and authorities in this field.

Gardner, John W., EXCELLENCE: CAN WE BE EQUAL AND EXCELLENT TOO? Harper and Brothers, New York, 1961, 171. This is a popular contemporary effort to examine the philosophic and attitudinal problems of excellence, equality, and rewards.

Henry, Nelson B. (Editor), EDUCATION FOR THE GIFTED, 57th YEARBOOK NSSE, PART II, University of Chicago Press, Chicago, Ill., 1958. This is a collection of papers written by well known authorities. It would serve as a text or as a good review of the major issues.

Hildreth, Gertrude H., EDUCATING GIFTED CHILDREN AT HUNTER COLLEGE ELEMENTARY SCHOOL, Harper and Brothers, New York, 1952, 272. This is a description of the Hunter College Elementary School program. It is a superior source of classroom ideas.

Kough, Jack, PRACTICAL PROGRAMS FOR THE GIFTED, Science Research Associates, Inc., Chicago, Ill., 1960, 192. This book summarizes practical programs, lists authorities and consultants and describes organizations with special interests in the gifted.

Passow, A. Harry, Miriam Goldberg, Abraham Tannenbaum, Will French, PLANNING FOR TALENTED YOUTH, Bureau of Publications, Teachers College, Columbia University, 1955, 84. This is a pamphlet offering a well organized and abbreviated examination of education for the gifted. It would be suitable as the common reference for an in-service seminar for teachers.

Scheifele, Marion, THE GIFTED CHILD IN THE REGU-LAR CLASSROOM, Bureau of Publications, Teachers College, Columbia University, 1953. This brief pamphlet will be found valuable as a guide to possibilities for enrichment.

Torrance, E. Paul (Editor), TALENT AND EDUCATION PRESENT STATUS AND FUTURE DIRECTIONS, The University of Minnesota Press, Minneapolis, 1960, 210. This is a report of the 1958 Institute on Gifted Children at the University of Minnesota. It presents a range of views and interests and will help to summarize current thinking.

Witty, Paul (Editor), THE GIFTED CHILD, The American Association for Gifted Children, D. C. Heath and Company, Boston, 1951, 338. THE GIFTED CHILD is the forerunner of modern texts on the gifted. It is a multiple authored volume with chapters on most of the major issues.

MAURICE F. FREEHILL is now Director, Psychological Services and Research, Professor of Psychology, Western Washington State College. He received his early education in Alberta, Canada and has degrees from the University of Alberta and Stanford. He is the author of a number of papers and other chapters in multiple-authored books. The Macmillan Company recently published his work, GIFTED CHILDREN, THEIR PSYCHOLOGY AND EDUCATION.

NOTES

1. Barrett, William, IRRATIONAL MAN, A STUDY IN EXISTENTIAL PHILOSOPHY, Doubleday & Company Inc., Garden City, New York, 1958, 30-31.
2. Gibson, William Carleton, YOUNG ENDEAVOR, CONTRIBUTIONS TO SCIENCE BY MEDICAL STUDENTS OF THE PAST FOUR CENTURIES, Charles C. Thomas, Publisher, Springfield, Ill., 1958, 263.
3. Lucito, Leonard, and James Gallagher, "Intellectual Patterns of Highly Gifted Children on the WISC," PEABODY JOURNAL OF EDUCATION, XXXVIII, 3, Nov. 1960, 131-136.
4. Liddle, Gordon, "Overlap Among Desirable and Undesirable Characteristics in Gifted Children," JOURNAL OF EDUCATIONAL PSYCHOLOGY, IL, 4, August 1958, 219-223.
5. Wilson, Robert C., J. P. Guilford, P. R. Christensen, and D. J. Lewis, "A Factor-Analytic Study of Creative Thinking Abilities," PSYCHOMETRIKA, XIX, 4, December 1954, 297-311, and J. P. Guilford, "Three Faces of Intellect," THE AMERICAN PSYCHOLOGIST, XIV, 8, August 1959, 469-479.
6. Hollingworth, Leta S., CHILDREN ABOVE 180 I.Q., World Book Co., Yonkers-on-Hudson, 1942, and GENETIC STUDIES OF GENIUS, Stanford University Press, Stanford, California; Lewis M. Terman et al., MENTAL AND PHYSICAL TRAITS OF A THOUSAND GIFTED CHILDREN, I, 1925; Lewis M. Terman et al., THE PROMISE OF YOUTH, FOLLOW-UP STUDIES OF A THOUSAND GIFTED CHILDREN, III, 1930.
7. Allport, G. W., "Scientific Models and Human Morals," PSYCHOLOGICAL REVIEW, LIV, 4, 1947, 182-192, 190.
8. Bruner, Jerome S., THE PROCESS OF EDUCATION, Harvard University Press, Cambridge, 1960, 21-32, 53-68.
9. Bruner, Jerome S., THE PROCESS OF EDUCATION, Harvard University Press, Cambridge, 1960, 14.

10. Torrance, E. Paul, "Gifted Children," AMERICAN ASSOCIATION OF COLLEGES FOR TEACHER EDUCATIONAL YEARBOOK, 1960, 64-72.

11. Shaw, Merville C., and John T. McCuen, "The Onset of Academic Underachievement in Bright Children," THE JOURNAL OF EDUCATIONAL PSYCHOLOGY, LI, 3, June 1960, 103-108.

12. Passow, A. Harry, and M. S. Goldberg, "Study of Underachieving Gifted," EDUCATIONAL LEADERSHIP, XVI, 2, Nov. 1958, 121-125.

13. Pierce, James V., and Paul H. Bowman, "Motivation Patterns of Superior High School Students," THE GIFTED STUDENT (Cooperative Research Monograph No. 2), U. S. Department of Health, Education, and Welfare, Washington, 1960, 33-66.

14. Little, J. Kenneth, "The Wisconsin Study of High School Graduates," THE EDUCATIONAL RECORD, XL, 2, April 1959, 123-128, and Miriam L. Goldberg, "Motivation of the Gifted," EDUCATION FOR THE GIFTED (Nelson B. Henry, Ed.), 57th YEARBOOK NSSE, PART II, University of Chicago Press, Chicago, 1958, 94-95.

15. Frankel, Edward, "A Comparative Study of Achieving and Underachieving High School Boys of High Intellectual Ability," JOURNAL OF EDUCATIONAL RESEARCH, LIII, 5, Jan. 1960, 172-180.

16. Warren, Jonathan R., and Paul A. Heist, "Personality Attributes of Gifted College Students," SCIENCE, CXXXII, 3423, 5 Aug. 1960, 330-337.

17. Gowan, John Curtis, "Dynamics of the Underachievement of Gifted Students," JOURNAL OF EXCEPTIONAL CHILDREN, XXIV, 3, November 1957, 98-101, 122.

18. Bruner, Jerome S., THE PROCESS OF EDUCATION, Harvard University Press, Cambridge, 1960, 90.

19. Bettelheim, Bruno, "Segregation: New Style," SCHOOL REVIEW, LXVI, 3, Autumn, 1958, 251-272.

20. Worchester, D. A., THE EDUCATION OF CHILDREN OF ABOVE-AVERAGE MENTALITY, University of Nebraska Press, Lincoln, 1956, 17-19. Lewis M. Terman, "The Discovery and Encouragement of Exceptional Talent," THE AMERICAN PSYCHOLOGIST, IX, 6, June 1954, 221-230, S. L. Pressey, "That Most Misunderstood Concept: Acceleration," SCHOOL AND SOCIETY, LXXIX, 2027, February 20, 1954, 59-60.

21. Hammer, Emanuel F., CREATIVITY, AN EXPLORATORY INVESTIGATION OF THE PERSONALITIES OF GIFTED ADOLESCENT ARTISTS, Random House, New York, 1961, 111-115.

MENTAL RETARDATION

Clyde J. Baer

School District of Kansas City, Missouri

Children with retarded mental development have been a subject of special interest for many years. Teachers have known them in their classrooms as pupils with limited potential for academic learning, and who have presented special problems in teaching. Psychologists have known them as the focus of study in investigations of virtually every conceivable description. Physicians have known them as patients with special kinds of problems. Other children, brothers and sisters, and parents have known them, too.

The major purpose of this chapter is to discuss some of the aspects related to mental retardation as they pertain to the educational process.

CLASSIFICATION AND DEFINITION

One of the first obstacles likely to confront the teacher who has taken on the task of learning more about children with retarded mental development is the problem of terminology and the sometimes conflicting statements of definition.

Because of the widespread interest in the problem, and the variety of approaches used in studying it, efforts to develop definitions and classification systems have resulted in the emergence of varying points of view according to the area of professional discipline. The result has been the development of numerous definitions and systems for classification.

Since intellectual development is a central focus, and since the implication is that such children have "less" than average intelligence, it was only natural that one of the attempts to classify these children should be in terms of the amount of intellectual development. From this point of view, the psychometric criterion becomes of paramount utility. One such resultant classification system includes the well known terms of moron, imbecile, and idiot. The moron has been described as the child of low intelligence who is above the imbecile level, and who has some degree of educability. He is near the upper end of the range for mental retardation. The IQ range commonly associated with this term is between 50 and 70 or 75. The term imbecile is used to represent children below the moron level but above the idiot level. Persons who are included in this category are those who will be dependent upon others for support and supervision throughout their lives, but who will be susceptible to training so far as life habits and routines are concerned. The IQ range commonly associated with this term is from 40 or 50 down to approximately 20 or 25. Classification as an idiot is reserved for those persons who will require custodial care all their lives. They are not susceptible to training in life habits and daily routines. The IQ range commonly associated with this classification is up to 20 or 25 on the usual psychometric tests. The application, for educational purposes, of such classifications as are described above have been found to be generally inadequate.

It has been noted on numerous occasions that persons with identical IQ's have displayed different types of abilities, have demonstrated differential levels of achievement, have shown differences in the degree to which they have been able to achieve adjustment in adult life, and have, in short, demonstrated that although they have the same IQ they are quite different people with unique capacities and potentialities. One explanation for this is that individuals vary in the extent to which they have been able to achieve social competence. A definition for mental retardation that takes social competence into account, is that proposed by Doll.[3] According to Doll's definition, some six criteria must be met before a diagnosis may be made. According to

Doll's criteria, the individual must be (1) socially incompetent, (2) mentally sub-normal, (3) intellectually retarded from birth or early age, (4) retarded at maturity, (5) the mental subnormality must be of constitutional origin, and, (6) the condition must be incurable. The criterion of social incompetence includes also the area of occupational incompetence so that such a person would be unable to manage his own affairs as an adult. It is apparent that not all of these criteria can be applied in childhood.

Another type of classification system involves classification according to etiology. In this connection we have such terms as Benda's familial oligophrenia,[1] mental deficiency arising from physiological origins, and the Strauss classification as endogenous and exogenous.[12] Under the Strauss classification, mental deficiency acquired as a result of brain damage would be classified as exogenous, while mental deficiency associated with familial and congenital factors would be classified as endogenous. Such classifications are of great value from the point of view of the treatment and prevention of mental deficiency, but classification by etiology alone is of limited usefulness so far as the organization of educational programs is concerned.

From the point of view of providing educational services for mentally retarded children, there has been the gradual evolution of a classification system based upon degree of educability, with a strong flavor of quantitative statement based upon psychometric evaluation. There are three subdivisions under this classification: (1) the educable mentally retarded, often referred to as educable mentally handicapped, which group includes children with IQ's of approximately 50 to 75 or 80 and who are capable of profiting from instruction in basic school subjects; (2) the trainable mentally retarded, with IQ range from approximately 30 to 50, who are adjudged as being incapable of profiting from formal school instruction, but who can be trained to care for themselves physically, to communicate orally, and to become economically productive in a sheltered work situation; and (3) the custodial mentally retarded, which includes those persons who are unable to acquire self-help skills and will require permanent care. The large majority of public school programs is directed toward providing for those children classified as educable mentally retarded, although training programs for trainable mentally retarded are receiving increased attention.

Another classification system, also closely related to education, is that proposed by Rosenzweig and Long.[11] Under their four level classification the educable mentally retarded are divided into two categories, the Independent and the Semi-Independent. Their classification plan is as follows: (1) Independent (IQ 65-75) can achieve up to fourth or fifth grade level, and can be prepared for and successful in semi-skilled vocations; (2) Semi-independent (IQ 50-65) can attain second or third grade level of achievement, with some maintaining themselves through unskilled work, but with many needing help from families or public agencies; (3) Dependent (IQ 30-50) socially and occupationally inadequate in adult years, with most living in a protective situation; and (4) Custodial (IQ 0-30) needing life-long care. The authors emphasize that the IQ ranges given are a frame of reference only, with much overlapping of abilities between groups. Much depends on the supportive environment and the dynamics of behavior in making placements and in predicting future success.

IDENTIFICATION

Basic to the efficient utilization of any special program for mentally retarded children is a sound program of identification and diagnosis. A program of identification and diagnosis should include four factors: (1) an educational evaluation which will reveal the presence of educational retardation, and may provide a basis for the diagnosis of educational disabilities; (2) a psychological or psychometric examination directed primarily to the assessment of the child's level of mental development; (3) a medical examination aimed toward the disclosure of etiology and indicating medical treatment where appropriate, and (4) an investigation in the area of personal adjustment which includes inter-personal relations and personality factors.

30

Measured Achievement

Most modern school systems employ group achievement tests as part of the regular school program. A great variety of such tests is available. A battery usually includes subtests in the areas of reading, arithmetic, and language arts, and often will include tests in study skills, social studies, spelling, and science. Such tests are reasonably reliable in identifying pupils who are educationally retarded, with respect to a grade level criterion, and in assessing the amount of retardation that is present. Some of the most commonly used tests are the Stanford Achievement Test, the Metropolitan Achievement Test, the California Achievement Test, and the SRA Achievement Series. Pupil's scores on tests such as these should be incorporated as part of the educational evaluation.

Measured Intelligence

Attempts to measure intelligence have had a long and colorful history. In the early years of this century Alfred Binet and Thomas Simon produced the forerunner of the present Binet test. The original commission had been to devise and prepare an instrument that could be used in determining which children should start to school and which should not. Eventually they produced an instrument scaled according to chronological age, and this instrument came to be known as an intelligence scale. Since that time numerous other instruments have been developed to serve as devices to estimate intelligence. Some have continued the age scale technique, others have not. Built for use with one individual at a time, and used largely as clinical instruments, these scales require a substantial period of formal training plus supervised practice in actual test situations before the individual is competent to employ the instrument.

With the advent of World War I, and the need to test many thousands of men, the demand for group tests of intelligence became apparent and urgent. The use of an individual intelligence test would mean that the testing of thousands of men would be a long, time consuming, laborious process, but if these same men could be tested with a group instrument, the time necessary for examining them would be greatly reduced. Under the pressure of national need, psychologists soon produced group intelligence tests.

Group intelligence tests have come to be widely used in the school systems of the nation, and are the kind of test that the teacher is likely to encounter as one aspect of the regular school program. With a few hours preparation in general testing procedures, and the specific directions for the test to be used, these group tests can be administered by teachers without special training in the area of psychometrics. Such tests are often considered as indicators of scholastic aptitude.

Children are referred for special study when someone concerned with their welfare has noticed that the child is not progressing the way they think that he should in mental, social, or educational growth. In the school setting it is usually the teacher who makes a referral. She makes this referral based upon her knowledge of the child's failure to make normal progress in school, which is usually associated with low scores on group achievement tests and low scores on group intelligence tests. Because poor progress in school, low scores on achievement tests, and low scores on group intelligence tests may result from many factors ranging from a sensory defect such as poor hearing or poor vision, through specific educational disabilities, to the child who is unable to utilize his intellectual potential because of emotional disturbance, it is important that these children be referred for individual study before a diagnosis of mental retardation is made. One of the actions that the psychologist is likely to take, upon receipt of the referral, is to provide for the administration of an individual intelligence test. Because of the importance usually accruing to these instruments, some of the most commonly used ones are described below in some detail.

Probably the instrument most commonly used as a test of individual intelligence is the Revised Stanford-Binet Intelligence Scale.[13] Based upon the original Binet Scale brought to the United States from Europe, it has undergone a series of revisions, the latest of which was produced in 1960. Elements of the previous forms, L and M, were brought together to produce the 1960 LM Form.[14] The basic approach to the measurement of intelligence used in the Binet is the age scale. The scale is composed of a series of items at each age level, and of increasing difficulty as the age level goes up. Subjects at each age level are then tested with the scale, and performance at each age level noted. These values then become the basis for the norm structure. With this kind of a scale it is possible to examine an individual and to assess the age level which his functional level of performance most nearly resembles. Age levels on the Binet begin at age 2 and ascend in half-year intervals until age 5, at which point the intervals become one year. Above year 14 the intervals are Average Adult, and three levels for Superior Adults. In administering the Stanford-Binet, the basal age is obtained by identifying the age level at which the subject answers every item correctly, then progressing upward until the child misses every item at an age level. By adding the month value of every item answered correctly above the basal age to the value for the basal age, the mental age is obtained. The mental age is then divided by the chronological age, and multiplied times one hundred, to yield the IQ. There are six subtests at each age level. The actual content of the scales involves a great variety of items. Many attempts have been made to classify these items into more meaningful form. The classification developed by Porteus illustrates one of these, and has proved helpful in the analysis of test performance. He classified the tests as follows:

1. *Memory.* These include memory span for digits, sentences, commissions, items read in a story or news paragraph, pictures, and designs—21-½ tests.

2. *School Attainments.* There are four and one-half tests involving school attainments—four of arithmetic and the "Reading and Report" test.

3. *Verbal Ability.* These are tests of vocabulary, verbal comprehension and expression, description, definitions, verbal reasoning, rhymes, word associations, and verbal classifications—32 tests.

4. *Common Knowledge and Comprehension of Practical Situa-*

tions. These include similarities, picture interpretation, picture absurdities, problems of fact, and esthetic comparison—19 tests.

5. *Practical Judgement and Abilities.* These are tests of manipulative skill, drawing, form board, planning, induction, and ingenuity—20 tests.[10]

The items included under the different headings named above occur at different points throughout the scale. Hence, since no one person will cover all of the age levels included in the scale, his performance in each of the areas is sampled according to the number of age levels in which items are attempted.

Another clinical instrument in common usage is the Wechsler Intelligence Scale for Children.[16] This test also yields IQ scores, but the approach to the measurement of intelligence is different from that used in the Binet. In the Wechsler, various subtests have been developed and the IQ is obtained from the extent to which an individual score deviates from a central tendency for his chronological age. When an IQ is obtained in this fashion it is known as a deviation IQ, and mental age is not involved in its extraction. The WISC is an example of a type of test which combines both verbal and performance intelligence tests. Three IQs are obtained; one IQ for the performance scale, another for the verbal scale, and a third as the full-scale IQ. The verbal scale is composed of six subtests entitled General Information, General Comprehension, Digit Span, Arithmetic, Similarities, and Vocabulary. The performance scale includes subtests identified as Picture Arrangement, Picture Completion, Block Design, Object Assembly, and Coding or Mazes. Digit Span and Mazes are considered as supplementary tests to be used when time permits, or as alternate tests when some other part of the scale is invalidated. The interpretation of this instrument involves a qualitative analysis of the performance of the subject on each of the subtests for each of the two parts.

Although the two tests described above are probably the most commonly used instruments, there are many other excellent tests available.

There are many test situations where the psychologist is confronted with the need to obtain information concerning measured intelligence, but where the subject is unable to respond to the usual verbal test of intelligence. Such situations usually occur where the subject has auditory, visual, or physical impairment. It might also occur when a child has a foreign background, with resulting deficiency in language ability. To satisfy the testing needs in these situations, various kinds of instruments have been developed. Prominent among these are the performance tests. An example of this type of instrument is the battery of tests included in the Arthur Point Scale of Performance Tests. For children with auditory impairment, there is the Nebraska Test of Learning Aptitude for Young Deaf Children and the Ontario School Ability Test. In addition, Hayes has made an adaptation of the Binet for use with the blind.

Personal Adjustment

Another aspect usually investigated by the psychologist includes the area of personal adjustment. Here most rewarding outcomes have been obtained from the application of the projective instruments. Two of the most commonly used instruments in this connection are the Rorschach and the Thematic Apperception Test. The Rorschach Ink Blot Test is composed of ten unstructured ink blots. Some of the blots contain chromatic colors while others are presented as shades of black and white. The subject's response to each blot is analyzed in terms of specific criteria. The Thematic Apperception Test includes a series of relatively unstructured pictures that are given to the subject one at a time. He is then asked to make up a short story about each picture. These stories are then examined in terms of certain criteria and inferences concerning the personality structure of the individual are made.

As was the case in the measurement of intelligence, there are many other excellent instruments available which will satisfy these purposes.

In the assessment of social maturity the Vineland Social Maturity Scale is widely used.[4] Unlike the instruments discussed previously, the Vineland does not involve direct response from

the subject. Instead a person in the child's immediate environment is asked to render judgment according to certain kinds of
things the child is able to do. Beginning at the zero to one age
level, the scale continues through to age 25 plus. Like the Binet,
the Vineland is an age scale. A single score, known as the social
quotient and abbreviated SQ, is obtained. With the SQ it is
possible to compare the social maturity of any child with the
social maturity of other children at any specified age level within
the range of the scale.

Medical Diagnosis

Another important element in the identification and diagnosis
of mentally retarded children is the medical examination. In
some cases the mental retardation may be associated with certain
medical conditions. This information is important in developing
the prognosis for the case, and in planning the educational program. In some cases the medical condition associated with the
retardation may be susceptible to medication. In those instances
the program should take into account any arrangements necessary
for medical treatment. In other instances the associated medical
condition may be of a type that will become progressively more
severe. This also is important information in thinking about an
educational program.

Before leaving the area of identification and diagnosis, some
note should be taken of other aspects in the measurement of
intelligence. All of the tests cited earlier are the type of tests that
result in the extraction of a single index, the IQ. However, it has
been noted on many occasions that intelligent behavior is the
resulting manifestation of the function of various components.
The application of the statistical technique of factor analysis in
studying intelligence has resulted in the identification of several
factors which are viewed as components of intelligence. According to Guilford,[7] more than forty factors have been reported and
it is likely that numerous others will be identified. The utilization of the factorial approach in the study of intelligence offers
promise in a more rich and complete understanding of the facets

of intelligence as they function in producing intelligent behavior. This approach helps to explain why individuals with identical IQ's may tend to show varying abilities in different areas of operation. One example of a test based upon the factorial approach is the SRA Primary Mental Abilities Test.[15] In this test the measurement of intelligence is divided into five separate subtests, each of which is based upon a factor extracted as the result of a factor analysis. The parts of the test include Verbal-meaning, Space, Reasoning, Number, Word fluency, Memory, Perceptual Speed, and Motor. With the exception of Memory Ability, all of the above named factors are included in one of the batteries of the SRA Primary Mental Abilities. After the tests have been administered and scored, the separate subtest scores are extracted and a profile constructed. A formula is also provided by which the different subtest scores can be combined to form a total score. The SRA Primary Mental Abilities is a group test.

INCIDENCE

Attempts to study the prevalence of mental retardation have been handicapped by difficulties in definition and measurement. If educable mentally retarded pupils are defined according to the IQ range of 50 to 75 or 80, obtained on the Binet or WISC, the expected percentage of such pupils ranges from approximately five or six per cent to as much as eight to ten per cent. However, such a definition has not been uniformly applied, with the result that estimates of prevalence have shown substantial variation. It has been a generally held belief that approximately two to four per cent of the school population needs special service. This would be consistent with the opinion held generally by educators, that of the pupil population approximately one-half of the children identified as educable mentally retarded on the basis of intelligence test scores would be in need of special class placement.[5] The incidence of children classified as trainable has been studied, with the general finding that these children comprise less than one percent of the population.

SPECIAL CLASSES

Most mentally retarded children will be found in one of three settings: (1) in regular classes, (2) in special classes, and (3) in residential schools. In addition, a few will be found on homebound programs, and a few more in special day-schools.

Organization

Special classes for mentally handicapped children provided within the framework of the regular school have been in existence for many years. However, since World War II, great impetus has been given to the development of these classes. Special classes have most often been established in the elementary school, with primary and intermediate divisions. In recent years there has also been increased attention directed toward special classes in the secondary schools. In the elementary schools, pupils selected for special class placement usually work with the teacher on an all-day, every-day basis. In the secondary schools, organization is often on a block-of-time schedule. A maximum number to be enrolled per class section is usually specified, and in many states there is provision for some state reimbursement of funds spent in operating classes which meet the state requirements.

Selection of Pupils

The selection of children classified as educable mentally handicapped for inclusion in the special classes usually revolves around three considerations. The first of these is an examination of whether or not the child is progressing according to what might be expected in terms of his measured potential to achieve. In order to satisfy this criterion there must be some prediction of what the expected achievement would be, and some measurement of what the achievement actually is. The second consideration revolves around the relationship that obtains between the child and his peers. In the great majority of cases pupils of this type have met with frequent failure in their school experience. Children react to these failures in various ways. In some instances they may react with aggressive behavior which leads to poor relationships with the other members of the class. In other instances these children may withdraw to the extent that they are virtually unnoticed by the other members of the class. Still a third adjustment occurs when the child can accept his plight and maintain good relationships with the other class members. In some cases the child may not show the maladjustive behavior in the school setting, but may demonstrate such behavior outside the school to the extent that he becomes a problem to his parents and in the community. This last described condition is the third consideration. When the child is able to achieve at the expected level, is able to maintain good relationships with his peers, and is not an undue problem in the community or at home, then this child is ordinarily left in the regular class. On the other hand, if he is not achieving to the expected level, if he exhibits poor relationships with his peers, or if his behavior in the community is such that he is a problem, then he is a likely candidate for special placement.

Objectives

Statements of objectives for programs for mentally handicapped pupils usually consist of three elements: (1), social adjustment, (2), personal or emotional adjustment, and (3), occupational competence. Kirk and Johnson[8] have expanded these objectives into statements of specific aims which[9] are quoted below:

1. They should be educated to get along with their fellow men; i.e., they should develop social competency through numerous social experiences.

2. They should learn to participate in work for the purpose of earning their own living; i.e., they should develop occupational competence through efficient vocational guidance and training as a part of their school experience.

3. They should develop emotional security and independence in the school and in the home through a good mental hygiene program.

4. They should develop habits of health and sanitation through a good program of health education.

5. They should learn the minimum essentials of the school subjects, even though their academic limits are third to fifth grade.

6. They should learn to occupy themselves in wholesome leisure time activities through an educational program that teaches them to enjoy recreational and leisure time activities.

7. They should learn to become adequate members of a family and a home through an educational program that emphasizes home membership as a function of the curriculum.

8. They should learn to become adequate members of the community through a school program that emphasizes community participation.[8]

Statements of aims and objectives such as those quoted above help to shape the curriculum and the organization of the special program.

CHARACTERISTICS

Numerous attempts have been made to describe the characteristics of educable mentally retarded pupils. Physically, most mentally handicapped children do not show marked deviation from the normal child. They vary in height and weight and other physical characteristics much as do normal children. Generally they are not expected to deviate markedly with respect to motor development, but a recent study[6] of the motor characteristics of the mentally retarded indicates that the amount of motor retardation of the educable retarded child is greater than had previously been supposed, although the organization and development of motor abilities tends to occur in much the same way as in normal children. Because of this relatively normal physical appearance and development, the educable mentally retarded child is often viewed with impatience, rather than with the sympathy and understanding usually accorded to more severely retarded children. This helps to emphasize that their primary deviation is in the area of intellectual growth where the development is significantly retarded.

With respect to the type of characteristics more closely associated with school success the educable mentally retarded pupil is usually very poor in ability to organize, he cannot draw generalizations based upon the abstraction of specific elements from different situations, nor can he apply principles learned in one connection to other specific situations. His social skills are largely dependent upon the kind of training he has received and the experiences that he has had. And, since repeated investigations have demonstrated consistently that these children tend to live in low social-economic, culturally deprived areas, it is likely that the social training will have been of the most meager type.

CONSIDERATIONS IN TEACHING

When the child enters a special class, the receiving teacher should receive information about his level of mental operation, the extent of educational retardation, a description of his adjustment, and, where appropriate, a statement about etiology and prognosis. Information of this type has significance to the teacher in developing the educational program for the child with respect to the content areas and in the way in which she will deal with him.

One of the pieces of information that the teacher would usually receive is the score on an intelligence test. The IQ may serve as an indicator of the rate of mental growth, and as such, may function as an indicator of the child's academic potential. When the teacher is given the IQ and the chronological age, it is then a simple matter to obtain the corresponding mental age. When the mental age has been obtained it may serve as a tentative indicator of the general level of mental operation, and, as such, may be translated into educational content, materials, and teaching procedures appropriate for that age. The word "tentative" must be stressed, and a word of caution introduced because of the imperfect correlation that exists between IQ and school achievement, and because of the frequently reported discrepancy between test and non-test performance. Such discrepancies occur when a child's performance in problem solving behavior is different than would have been predicted from the test result. It has been noted [9, 11] that with mentally retarded subjects it is more likely that the children will perform better in non-test situations than in test problem solving situations. It is also noted that for the normal child the obverse quite often obtains. This helps to emphasize that the assumption that the test behavior is a representative sample of that individual's problem solving behavior is often unwarranted. This point is also related to the factorial approach to the study of intelligence discussed earlier. Another important consideration is the interaction of emotional and intellectual factors in shaping behavior.[2] In summary, while the intelligence quotient can serve as a very useful aid, it must be interpreted with care and caution.

The extent of educational retardation is usually indicated by the results made on achievement tests when considered in conjunction with expected level of achievement and grade level standards. Sometimes these tests may also include diagnostic sections which will give a clue to the teacher as to any areas of specific educational disability. This, in turn, may provide the spring board for the academic teachings. In cases where the use of an achievement test has been inappropriate, the teacher may approach this problem with the use of graded materials of which there is an abundant variety.

Through exploration of the child's attitudes, and of his motivation structure, the teacher may be helped in deciding how to work with the individual child. Working with aggressive, acting-out children is quite a different matter from working with withdrawn children.

Some of the teaching methods used with normal children are applicable in classes for educable mentally retarded children. However, those of a verbal and abstract nature are largely inappropriate. The first important ingredient in teaching educable mentally handicapped pupils, as in all good teaching, is to develop a need for the concept that is to be taught. This may be done through the use of an experience unit or an activity within the classroom, or related in some way to every day experience. After the child has developed the need for learning, the concept may be taught. When it is taught it must be taught in a concrete fashion, using many materials and illustrations. After the concept has been taught there must be provision for practice. At first this should be in the same form and with the same materials in which the concept was taught. The third step is to expand the application of the new learning into everyday life experiences. In this way the learning assumes a functional, meaningful character. The concepts to be taught must be carefully developed and provided in a step by step sequence. These children will take longer to learn and will require more repetition than normal children. The teaching plan must be developed step by step, and must be highly organized. Since the mentally handicapped child has extreme difficulty in applying learning in new situations, the concepts taught must be taught in many specific situations, and integrated with other areas of the curriculum.

And last, but far from least, it is essential that the teacher study each individual child to discover what he *can* do before she studies what he *can't* do. This will help to preserve contact with the child as an individual personality, entitled to as much careful consideration as any other child.

SELECTED BIBLIOGRAPHY

Carlson, Bernice Wells, and David R. Ginglend, PLAY ACTIVITIES FOR THE RETARDED CHILD, Abingdon Press, New York, 1961. Describes various play activities for use with retarded children, with specific directions, leading to successful participation.

Cruickshank, William M., and G. Orville Johnson (Editors), EDUCATION OF EXCEPTIONAL CHILDREN AND YOUTH, Prentice-Hall, Inc., Englewood Cliffs, 1958. Excellent chapters on the education of mentally handicapped children, and the training of mentally deficient children.

Kirk, Samuel A., and G. Orville Johnson, EDUCATING THE RETARDED CHILD, Houghton Mifflin Co., Boston, 1951. General reference for education of mentally retarded children, with description of specific teaching procedures in various content fields.

Masland, Richard L., Seymour B. Sarason, and Thomas Gladwin, MENTAL SUBNORMALITY: BIOLOGICAL, PSYCHOLOGICAL, AND CULTURAL FACTORS, Basic Books, Inc., New York, 1958. Grew from a survey, sponsored by National Association for Retarded Children, to study the causes of mental subnormality, and aimed ultimately at preventive measures. Analyzes and discusses each area indicated in title with reference to mental subnormality.

Perry, Natalie, TEACHING THE MENTALLY RETARDED CHILD, Columbia University Press, New York, 1960. Discusses various considerations in the teaching of severely retarded children. Emphasizes home-school relationships, developmental aspects, some skill areas, group work and school-community relations.

Sarason, Seymour B., PSYCHOLOGICAL PROBLEMS IN MENTAL DEFICIENCY, Harper and Bros., New York, 1953, second edition. Intensive discussion of psychological problems associated with mental deficit. Comprehensive coverage.

Stacey, Chalmers L., and Manfred F. DeMartino (Editors), COUNSELING AND PSYCHOTHERAPY WITH THE MENTALLY RETARDED, The Free Press, Glencoe (Ill.), 1957. Collection of papers relating to various aspects of counseling and psychotherapy. Primarily directed toward professionals in the field.

Strauss, Alfred A., and Laura E. Lehtinen, PSYCHOPATHOLOGY AND EDUCATION OF THE BRAIN-INJURED CHILD, Grune and Stratton, New York, 1947. Identification and discussion of certain problems associated with brain injury, plus principles and techniques of instruction in arithmetic fundamentals, reading, and writing.

CLYDE J. BAER, Ed. D., Director, Department of Research, School District of Kansas City, Missouri, since 1955. Formerly, Supervisor of Psychological Services in Kansas City, and public school teacher in Missouri and Kansas. He has served as visiting professor at the University of Kansas, Bowling Green (Ohio) State University, William Jewel College, University of Kansas City, and as lecturer in extension service for Central Missouri State College. Member of Research Committee, Council for Exceptional Children, and contributor to REVIEW OF EDUCATIONAL RESEARCH.

NOTES

1. Benda, Clemens E., "The Familial Imbecile or Oligo-encephaly as a Morbid Entity," AMERICAN JOURNAL OF MENTAL DEFICIENCY, XLIX, 1944, 32-44.
2. Bower, Eli M. and Holmes, Jack A., "Emotional Factors and Academic Achievement," REVIEW OF EDUCATIONAL RESEARCH, XXIX, No. 5, 1959, 529-544.
3. Doll, Edgar A., "The Essentials of an Inclusive Concept of Mental Deficiency," AMERICAN JOURNAL OF MENTAL DEFICIENCY, XLVI, 1941, 214-219.
4. ——, THE MEASUREMENT OF SOCIAL COMPETENCE, Educational Publishers, Inc., 1953.
5. Dunn, Lloyd M., and Rudolph J. Capobianco, "Mental Retardation," REVIEW OF EDUCATIONAL RESEARCH, XXIX, No. 5, 451-470, 1959.
6. Francis, Robert J., and G. Lawrence Rarick, MOTOR CHARACTERISTICS OF THE MENTALLY RETARDED, Cooperative Research Monograph No. 1, Office of Education, U. S. Department of Health, Education, and Welfare, Washington, 1960.
7. Guilford, Joy P., "The Structure of Intellect," PSYCHOLOGICAL BULLETIN, LIII, 1956, 267-293.
8. Kirk, Samuel A. and G. Orville Johnson, EDUCATING THE RETARDED CHILD, Houghton Mifflin Co., Boston, 1951.
9. Masland, Richard L., Seymour B. Sarason, and Thomas Gladwin, MENTAL SUBNORMALITY: BIOLOGICAL, PSYCHOLOGICAL, AND CULTURAL FACTORS, Basic Books, Inc., New York, 1958.
10. Porteus, Stanley D., THE PRACTICE OF CLINICAL PSYCHOLOGY, American Book Corp., 1941, as quoted in Mautner, Hans, MENTAL RETARDATION, Pergamon Press, New York, 1959.
11. Rosenzweig, Louis E., and Julia Long, UNDERSTANDING AND TEACHING THE DEPENDENT RETARDED CHILD, Educational Publishing Corp., Darien (Conn.), 1960.
12. Strauss, Alfred A., and Laura E. Lehtinen, PSYCHOPATHOLOGY AND EDUCATION OF THE BRAIN-INJURED CHILD, Grune and Stratton, New York, 1947.
13. Terman, Lewis M., and Maud A. Merrill, MEASURING INTELLIGENCE, Houghton Mifflin Co., Boston, 1937.
14. ——, STANFORD-BINET INTELLIGENCE SCALE, Houghton Mifflin Co., Boston, 1960. (Manual for the third revision, Form L-M).

15. Thurstone, L. L., and Thelma Gwinn Thurstone, SRA PRIMARY MENTAL ABILITIES, Science Research Associates, Inc., Chicago, Ill., 1949 (Manual).

16. Wechsler, David, THE WECHSLER INTELLIGENCE SCALE FOR CHILDREN, Psychological Corporation, New York, 1949 (Manual).

THE EMOTIONALLY DISTURBED CHILD

Clarence C. Sherwood
Columbia University
and
Sylvia Sherwood
C. W. Post College

Although there seems to be general agreement in the field of psychology—at least on the descriptive level—as to the definition of "human emotions," there is great variation in the literature in the definition and use of the concept "the emotionally disturbed." Rage, fear, disgust, anger, jealousy, excitement, pleasure, elation, love—all these and others—are treated without question as emotions in most texts in psychology which deal with this topic. This degree of agreement does not exist, however, when it comes to the definition of the "emotionally disturbed." Some texts carefully avoid mentioning the concept directly even when they discuss topics generally included by others under the reading of "emotional disturbance." Nor is there general agreement, even among those who do use the concept, as to the subject matter to be included. At one extreme the concept "the emotionally disturbed" is used to refer specifically to behavior dominated by the visceral component of the human organism. At the other extreme it is an all inclusive term referring to a broad range of personality and behavior disorders. In some studies "the emotionally disturbed" includes such types as brain damage, schizophrenia, neurosis, and hyperacting-out. In others, this same category will include cases of "acute separation anxiety," "impaired object relations," and "the seriously rejected child." As an example of the most generalized use of the term, the United States Children's Bureau in its publications summarizing *Research Relating to Children* has indicated that— for purposes of classification, at least—it regards the concepts "emotional disturbance" and "personal disturbance" as virtually synonymous.

There is also confusion between descriptive categorizations of "types of emotional disturbance" and theories or assumptions about the cause or causes of emotional disturbance. For example, in some categorizations the "type" refers to an emotional disturbance on a *descriptive* level—enuresis, school phobia, etc.; in others the "type" reflects a presumed *cause* of emotional disturbance—the *rejected child;* and still others represent a combination of both the causal and the descriptive—*separation anxiety,* for example. For a clearer understanding of emotional disturbance, it is important to distinguish between the concepts used to describe the variety of types of observable behavior *descriptive* of the state of and type of emotional disturbance from the concepts used to *explain* the occurrence of emotional disturbance. The former requires concise and clear definition so that observed behavior can be reliably categorized; the latter requires scientific "testing"—in other words, verificational producers.

Given the observed hodge-podge of definitions of types of behavior, and the degrees of severity and degrees of significant behavior impairment considered by different authors under the heading of "emotional disturbance," it should be recognized that whatever definition is selected it must of necessity be arbitrary. Although there are surely other ways to disentangle these definitions and approaches in the use of the concept "the emotionally disturbed," it seems meaningful to distinguish four aspects of this conceptual problem:

(1) *Disturbance in overt emotional expression.* This refers to the directly observable component which within an over-all analysis may be viewed as symptoms of a more basic underlying emotional disturbance. Disturbances on this overt level can be

viewed as either: (a) excesses, or (b) deficiencies of emotional expression.

(2) *Basic, underlying disturbance.* Focus here will be almost exclusively on two basic sets of concepts: (a) conflict and anxiety —generally held to be the most widely prevailing as well as the most generalized basic underlying category of emotional disturbance, and (b) the inadequate internalization of value systems —those sets of ideas (conscience, super-ego, etc.) which integrate the individual's internal motivation system with the patterns and needs of the social groups with which he interacts.

(3) *Adaptive non-adjustive mechanism,* particularly those presumed to be involved in the reduction or avoidance of anxiety. And finally,

(4) *Etiological considerations.*

PATTERNS OF EMOTIONAL DEVELOPMENT

To facilitate an understanding of disturbance in emotional expression, a summary of the process of normal emotional development is included here:

The emotional responses of infants tend to be few in number and highly generalized. The most generalized and earliest expression of emotion is *excitement.* The more specific emotional patterns distinguishable at the earliest ages (by the time the infant is two months old) are *distress* and *delight* (displeasure and pleasure). Both are expressed by the very young infant through relatively undifferentiated, whole-body activities. The two basic activity patterns related to emotional expression are *adience* (tendency to move toward or continue) and *avoidance* (tendency to move away or terminate). That is, as the baby begins to perceive the world around him he learns that there are some unpleasant situations which he can handle through *avoidance* or withdrawal whereas other situations can be handled through an *adience* mechanism. Emotional development thus tends to become differentiated in terms of these two activity patterns. Within this framework, for example, distress is *excited avoidance;* delight, *excited adience.* Anger can be seen as an

49

adience response, one which, according to Shaffer and Shoben, becomes differentiated as a result of the learning and stereotyping of responses involving emotion and struggling, perhaps first experienced by the infant in connection with the feeling of being restrained by clothing, bed covers, and adult holding. Fear, on the other hand, can be seen as an *avoidance* pattern of activity, becoming differentiated as a result of distress responses involving excited emotion plus impulses to avoid, withdraw, or flee. Thus, through the developmental process of differentiation, other emotions emerge: elation and affection from delight; anger, fear, disgust from distress.

From the above it can be seen that as the individual matures and begins to perceive experiences in the context of his social world, more and more emotions become differentiated, including shame, remorse, affection, jealousy, etc. To feel "shame," for example, requires an unfavorable self-evaluation as part of the emotional pattern. Particularly for the more complex emotions, it is now generally recognized that it is impossible to completely disentangle a purely emotional component of human activity from other components, such as the "purely intellectual" activities. It is also now agreed that these (the emotional and the intellectual) do not represent the bad and the good in us, but that any kind of behavior may have emotional components. Nor is emotional behavior to be construed as synonymous with disorganized behavior. From this point of view emotion can be seen as one dimension of behavior, becoming developed at the same time as and functionally to an individual's performance, perception, and thought. Sargeant lists five distinct aspects of a total emotional reaction: perception of a stimulus; interpretation of a stimulus; an organic or visceral reaction; a feeling state; and toward expression of muscular or glandular activity (smiles, frowns, tears, etc.).

DISTURBANCES OF OVERT EMOTIONAL EXPRESSION

If "fear," "love," "affection," "shame," "remorse," etc. are properly identified as "normal" emotions, at what point does emotional expression or lack of expression indicate emotional disturbance? A meaningful behavioral clue to "emotional disturbance" is the frequency and intensity of emotional response. Emotional disturbance is characterized by a greater or lesser frequency and/or intensity of emotional response than can be normally expected from the situation. Of course, some degree of emotional disturbance, at least on occasion, is a common feature of the behavior of everyone.

From this point of view, the emotionally disturbed child persistently manifests either greater or less than normal frequency and/or intensity of emotional reaction. For example, after having been angered in one situation an ordinary individual will tend to be somewhat more susceptible to anger for a subsequent period of time. After a while, however, his susceptibility tends to disappear. For the emotionally disturbed child, for whom anger responses are characteristic, susceptibility to anger will tend to persist for an extended period of time. For the severely emotionally disturbed child it may represent a more or less persistent and permanent characteristic of his personality. The same principle applies to all other types of emotional responses—including excesses or deficiencies in fear, jealousy, etc.

From observations and experimental studies by psychologists of emotional developmental processes and from sociological and anthropological studies of normative behavior in different classes and societies, it can be seen that the "under" or "over" expression of emotions as compared with "normal" emotional behavior can be further discussed in terms of its "absolute" and "relative" aspects.

An absolute—as opposed to a relativistic—definition of normal emotional expression assumes that, just as there is a normal "healthy" body temperature for human beings regardless of ethnic background, cultural standards, etc., there is a normal "healthy" level of emotional expression which serves as a standard against which judgements of emotional disturbance can be made.

Normal emotional expression, relativistically defined, refers to characteristic behavior generally observed of individuals within a specific social context and generally considered appropriate. By implication, emotional disturbance can be measured by, or is a function of, the extent of deviation—whether apathetic or hyperactive—from the range of what is accepted as normal and acceptable behavior for the given society. This point of view takes into account the empirical observation that different societies exhibit different emotional "habits," and that deviation from these normative emotional patterns are considered "abnormal" by the society. Societies, for whatever historical reasons, differ with respect to which emotions are considered to be "natural" and which emotions are considered proper for various categories of persons and for the various situations. For example, in many societies different normative prescriptions or "allowed behavior patterns" exist for women as compared with men, the young as compared with the old, the soldier as compared with the poet. Moreover, behavior which is considered emotionally disturbed in one society may be considered acceptable and adaptive in another.

Many psychology texts dealing with the problem of emotional disturbance discuss it in absolute terms. There are studies, for example, which indicate the way in which an unsatisfactory fetal environment may produce an infant who is hyperactive and irritable, and who can be described as emotionally disturbed at birth. Further support of the notion of "absolute" emotional imbalance can be found in the studies of Spitz who found that babies who received little emotional interchange had a significantly higher death rate, were less able to solve problems, were less able to master bodily functions, had poorer perception and manipulative abilities, had poorer memories, had poorer social relations, and generally acted in an agitated or in an apathetic manner as compared to children who were not emotionally "starved."

On the other hand, a close inspection of the ways in which peoples in different parts of the world habitually handle emotional problems indicates that very often judgements as to absolute emotional disturbance may become distorted by ethnocentric considerations. In China, for example, voices are raised only when an individual is angry and when he has lost control of his emotions. Thus what might be considered an abnormally disturbed and angry reaction by a visitor from China to an American home when the American host, raising his voice in enthusiasm as his guest departs, declares, "I'm so glad you could come!," is considered by his American host as a perfectly fitting, proper, polite and friendly expression. Likewise a South American visiting this country for the first time may consider North Americans—citizens of the Northeast region of the United States in particular—to be an emotionally disturbed lot, stiff and withdrawing. As the visitor from South America steps up to ask a North American passerby a simple question concerning directions, the latter is likely to appear uncomfortable, perhaps even alarmed, and to step back physically before answering the question. The North American may think, as well, that the South American is an odd, aggressive individual, peculiarly insistent on close contact. Neither may realize that his judgment is being influenced by cultural considerations since studies have shown that physical distances between conversing individuals vary from society to society. The average distance is likely to be less by half a foot or more in Latin America than in the United States.

The particular significance of this type of analysis becomes apparent on a practical level for professionals of one socio-economic or ethnic background when they deal with children from another socio-economic or ethnic background with different patterns of emotional expression. Unless the behavior is evaluated in terms of the normative behavior of the group involved, a teacher or a social worker, for example, may incorrectly come to the conclusion that almost all the children in the group are emotionally disturbed. The children considered most healthy by an outside observer may, in fact, be most disturbed from the point of view of fitting in with the needs and patterns of the society in which he is being socialized. When such a situation is misjudged, and the observer takes what he considers are appropriate steps to remedy the situation, he may, instead, actually contribute toward producing emotional disturbance.

Keeping in mind the fact of cultural variations in expectations concerning the expression of emotions, normal emotional expression may be distinguished from emotional disturbance in that the normal is (a) usual, expected, and predictable in the socio-cultural context, (b) appropriate, both individually and, again, culturally, and (c) of relatively short duration.

It should be noted that the notions of absolute and relative criteria of emotional disturbance are alternative ways of viewing the problem, but are not necessarily contradictory. Although as emphasized above, the observer must be very careful in making judgments about emotional disturbance on the basis of observed expressions of emotion, it is possible under certain circumstances to view even entire cultural patterns as manifestations of emotional disturbance. That is, there is the possibility that the normative prescriptions within a given society may be such that they facilitate or create anxiety producing situations. This in turn may result in the majority of the society becoming emotionally disturbed in an absolute sense, whether or not the behavior is recognized as "disturbed" by the given society. The point is that mere differences in intensity and/or frequency of expression do not provide a sufficient basis for judgments of emotional disturbance. In an absolute sense, the issue is how the expressive patterns function for the individual in terms of problem solving and emotional growth.

CONFLICT AND ANXIETY

All children, in the process of growing up in an interpersonal, socio-cultural milieu, encounter many emotionally challenging situations. The variety, frequency, and intensity of these situations will vary from child to child, and for that matter will vary among various cultures and sub-cultures. Fromm feels that a basic emotionally challenging situation for the child centers around his fear of and submission to parental authority, which he describes as irrational—as opposed to rational—authority. Rational authority is based on competence, whereas irrational authority is based on power and the fear and awe which it elicits. The child's impulses—many relating to parts and functions of the body—are suppressed through the irrational power of the parent, and guilt concerning those functions are built into the child. This guilt coerces the child into submission.

In attempting to identify, evaluate, and understand emotional pathology, the child's behavior can be viewed as attempts to adapt to a series of tension-producing situations. The distinction between adaptive and adjustive behavior is important here. The "adaptive" responses of the "well-adjusted" child are, by definition, both satisfying (tension reducing) and appropriate: simultaneously socially acceptable, problem solving, and non-problem-creating. Adaptive, non-adjustive responses may be temporarily satisfying for the individual, but are unlikely to meet any of the other criteria: They are inappropriate both socially and functionally and, in addition to failing to solve problems, are likely to create additional ones.

A key concept at this point is *anxiety*. As Sullivan has emphasized in his analysis, every human being apparently has the capacity to experience anxiety. This very unpleasant experience is utilized by all cultures, some more than others, in its efforts to make a social being out of human animals. Anxiety is closely related to the emotion of fear, distinguishable mainly in terms of the nature of the evoking stimulus. Fear is evoked by an existent external stimulus; anxiety by a future, anticipated situation as a function of a perceived quality of self.

The concept of "the self" is currently regarded as an extremely important one both in terms of an understanding of general personality development and of the concept of anxiety. The self refers to the organization of perceptions of one's own qualities, abilities, impulses, relationships to others; learned anticipations that one will accept or be accepted, reject or be rejected, etc. The most generally held view of the relationship between anxiety and the self is that anxiety arises where there is a threat to the integrity of the self system; where, as May has put it, some value which the individual regards as essential to his existence and security as a personality is threatened. Fears develop on the basis of the security pattern which the individual has developed; anxiety results when this security system itself is threatened. Sullivan has also emphasized the prime significance of the concept of self in understanding anxiety but believes that the self-system is organized to minimize or avoid anxiety.

A major significance of anxiety to adjustment is found in the fact that whereas emotions such as fear and anger contain commitments to action—flight or attack—anxiety does not. Anxiety represents distressful excitement without a specific adjustment function. This absence of a specific commitment to action gives anxiety a prominent place in maladjustment.

Anxiety is also closely related to conflict, involving apprehension and dread of the future arising from a conflict of one's own impulses. A person in conflict is unable to find a solution to his problem. A child, for example, dependent upon his parents but rejected by them, may develop a conflict involving his attachment and hostility relationships with them. Another example is frustration. A usual emotional response to it is anger, expressed behaviorally through aggression. Frustration is thus seen to be one type or category of stimuli giving rise to emotional response and expression. When a motive pattern (a motivated behavior sequence) is blocked by some obstacle, physical or social, an emotional reaction pattern is triggered off. However, aggression is only one possible emotional reaction to frustration. Regression —the reverting to an earlier, less well organized behavior—is another common reaction. Thus, if the socialization process is successful in teaching the child to inhibit aggressive responses, but the child has learned no appropriate, acceptable, substitute behavior patterns, he may then become anxious.

Therefore, the identification of emotional disturbance involves an examination of the child's successes and failures in handling the anxiety producing situations presented him by his society. These situations range all the way from the relatively common but very intense threat of loss of parental love and protection to the equally common threats involved in peer group interaction. These threats may be augmented by actual, anticipated, or even

56

unrealistically imagined "experiences" such as abandonment, separation due to illness, etc.

It is important to emphasize at this point that the encountering of a conflict or crisis is not in and of itself pathological. It is the nature of the solution—or lack of it—of the crisis, which marks it as pathological or as a developmental step to further emotional growth. If, when confronted with a conflict and its attendant anxiety, the child can deal with it openly and realistically, a contribution will be made to the basic personality foundations from which is gradually built the healthy, maturing, adult character.

DEFENSE MECHANISMS

However, many children, without the requisite internal emotional skills, are unable to find such healthy solutions of internal conflicts. Instead, the child begins to find ways of dissociating his conflict from awareness through what are called mechanisms of defense.

These adaptive, non-adjustive response systems can be seen to be operating at two reasonably distinct levels: (1) the reduction of the anxiety evoked by the situation or "reminders" of it; or (2) the prevention of the experiencing of anxiety, or what Sullivan has called the "uncanny emotions,"—awe, dread, loathing, and horror—associated with these situations. The primary process is escape, escape from anxiety.

An elementary psychological step in this direction is "denial to others." This pattern easily develops into "denial to self," including the process of rationalization. The latter consists of turning anxiety into "real fear," the irrational into the rational. Weaknesses are turned into admirable qualities, base motives are described as worthy ones.

Another common means of "escape" is withdrawal. The child, in order to avoid any possibility of encountering an anxiety provoking situation, avoids participation completely. Withdrawal is, in a sense, a more general form of what may exist on more specific levels, inhibitions. Flight into illness, hysterical symptoms such as paralysis, blindness, etc., are additional examples of escape mechanisms.

The most severe forms of withdrawal are found in the group of serious mental illnesses called schizophrenia. Some of the generally agreed upon descriptive symptoms of schizophrenia include: inappropriate emotional responses; inability to communicate; loss of interest in normal activities; and bizarre speech and motor patterns. However, it should be noted that although schizophrenia has been discussed above as a defense pattern, some current research indicates that its relationship to defense systems may be quite complicated. For example, Heilbrun found that schizophrenic daughters tended to more accurately predict the responses of their mothers on the Schaefer-Bell *Parent Attitude Research Instrument* than did normal daughters, with the latter perceiving their mothers to be less authoritarian than their actual responses. The research suggests that distortion may be an adjustive device present in normal individuals and relatively absent in schizophrenics. Heilbrun calls this "benign delusion," and hypothesizes that schizophrenia is partially a function of inadequate systems of defense, that schizophrenics do not employ defenses to deal with negative affect toward parents.

Thus it can be seen that excesses and/or deficiencies in the overt expression of emotions—whether mild or severe—function as symptoms of or mechanisms in emotional disturbance. In this regard, direct observation of children and their emotional expression patterns is an important tool facilitating the diagnosis of emotional disturbance.

Some of the more common as well as fundamental patterns of disturbance of emotional expression are: exaggerated anger, manifested behaviorally through aggression and involving bursts of undifferentiated destructive excitement; exaggerated fears or phobias, differing from ordinary fear or apprehension in that they are related to conditions or experiences which would not ordinarily evoke fear responses; acute depression, a state of exaggerated sadness and hopelessness extending over unusual periods of time in which the individual remains unmotivated by

58

what would usually be motivating conditions and events; mania, exaggerated elation and excitement, persisting over time and usually unrelated to variations in the experiences and fortunes of the individual; and, apathy, an emotional dullness—deficiency in emotional expression—involving absence of joy, grief, concern for others, etc., and also unusually unrelated to the variations in the experiences and fortunes of the individual.

These patterns of emotional disturbance may be seen to function in relation to two important components of an individual's emotional development: (1) an individual's competence and emotional "adjustment" in handling his own developed needs regardless of how well these needs fit with the needs and functioning of groups in which the individual participates; and (2) an individual's competence and emotional "adjustment" in handling group and societal needs, specifically in handling social interactional problems. This latter dimension includes both "appropriate" behavior patterns in solving interactional problems as well as insight into his relationships with groups in which he interacts. In other words, given the kinds of situations in which the individual is involved—his own *private* "mental" and "emotional" world, and his "life-space" made up of other individuals, groups, and societal demands in his social world—both components are of significance in discussing the "emotionally disturbed" individual, for an individual can be emotionally disturbed *privately, societally,* or both. And, it should be pointed out, the two components are intricately interrelated. For example, persistent deviation from normative patterns, by affecting the way in which the individual is reacted to by others, may affect his picture of self, possibly calling forth additional non-adjustive behavior mechanisms.

INADEQUATE INTERNALIZATION OF VALUE SYSTEMS

Of special significance to an understanding of what has been referred to as societal disturbance is the notion of "inadequate internalization of value systems," which was listed as a basic underlying disturbance at the opening of this chapter.

As was pointed out previously, the newly born child exhibits undifferentiated emotion in the form of generalized excitement. It is only as he matures and gains social experience that his actions begin to become differentiated. Certainly the "interpretive" aspect of emotions can emerge only as the individual begins to build up a set of attitudes and values. The particular attitudes and values the individual will incorporate, how he connects these attitudes and values with concrete goals, and whether he is emotionally healthy or disturbed in adapting his responses to goal achievement is intimately tied to the cultural milieu and his personal social interactional experiences. The child experiences societal demands through his interactions with others. The specific norms, the intensity of interaction, how he is treated—whether emotionally starved or loved, whether accepted or rejected, etc.—will determine: the range of attitudes and values for potential acceptance or rejection; which in this range he will accept and which he will reject; the goals he is likely to set up; and his capability for integrative behavior in achievement of these goals. Integrative behavior here refers to behavior responses which allow the individual to either reduce tension or continue opportunities for feelings of pleasure at the same time that he is solving problems without creating further problems of present or future distress.

The child is likely to incorporate as part of his response system (internalize) values of individuals with whom he strongly identifies. Therefore the content of the norms which the child does incorporate will depend upon the significance to him of the individuals with whom he interacts—including family, peer group, teachers, etc.—the extent to which he differentially associates with individuals who are significant to him, and the extent to which these significant individuals are able to communicate to him what in fact their values are. It is through these interactions that the child begins to internalize societal norms. If there is an effective affectional tie between parent and child as well as effective communication, the child is likely to strongly identify with his parents, incorporating into his response system their set of values. In any case the content of the social norms which do become internalized in the individual, the super-ego (conscience) in Freudian terminology, sets the framework for the individual's emotional evaluation of his own behavior patterns.

Should there be a conflict between certain emotional needs or even basic drives and other values and attitudes incorporated into an individual's response system—his superego requirements—and should the individual be unable to handle the problem in an integrative fashion, the individual then becomes emotionally disturbed. He may express this disturbance through excess emotional expression such as aggression, temper tantrums, etc., or he may withdraw into a shell of inaction, expressing his disturbance in the form of deficiency of overt emotional expression.

Should an individual *fail to internalize norms,* although the individual will not experience internal conflict or anxiety with respect to the "appropriateness" of his behavior responses, emotionally he will appear cold and unsympathetic—insensitive to the rights of others; devoid of shame or remorse; devoid, in fact, of the psychological component, the learning aspect, of emotional development. Such an individual, descriptively classified as the *psychopath,* gives free expression to his primitive impulses without a sense of responsibility or obligation to others around him. He is bent on the immediate satisfaction of felt needs, without heed to future consequences. In this sense, he doesn't seem to learn from experience. Such an individual may be very clever and even "cunning"; he will not be hampered by anxiety or neurotic behavior patterns, but he is nevertheless emotionally disturbed in his handling of social-interactional patterns and societal needs; his response patterns do not fit with societal demands. An individual who fails to internalize a set of norms which governs his behavior is not disturbed in his own "private" mental world, but rather he is emotionally disturbed on the "societal" level.

SUMMARY AND CONCLUSIONS

Up to this point we have dealt with disturbance in overt emotional expression, the basic underlying disturbance of conflict and anxiety, adaptive non-adjustive mechanisms, as well as the basic underlying disturbance of inadequate internalization of value systems. Etiological processes have been discussed in connection with each of the above topics. From the foregoing, the following can be seem:

Excesses and/or deficiencies in overt emotional expression can be used as clues in the diagnosis of emotional disturbance. Interpretations of expressive behavior should be made against a background of normative prescriptions for the given group from which he comes.

The cultural milieu and the social groups with whom the child interacts are importantly related to the etiology of emotional disturbance: (1) The culture increases or decreases the likelihood that various "challenges" will confront the child. (2) It determines how these challenges will be "handled" and presented to the child by the child's environment. (3) It provides a content of normative prescriptions within which the child must operate. (4) The normative pressures applied by the culture as to how the child is supposed to handle such experiences affects his emotional responses and development.

When an individual does internalize a set of societal values but is unable to handle the conflicts among them as they relate to his needs and experiences, anxiety results. The more an individual's efforts are devoted exclusively to dealing with the anxiety rather than the problems about which the anxiety has risen, the more emotionally disturbed the individual.

When an individual fails to internalize a set of societal values, his behavior is unlikely to include the variety of responses needed to fit the demands of the groups with whom he interacts; and the individual is emotionally disturbed on the societal level.

A child's behavior, then, may be analyzed and evaluated in terms of "variety," "balance," and "integration." From this point of view the emotionally disturbed child may be deficient in the *variety of his emotional response repertoire,* may evidence *lack of balance*—that is, may be dominated by one or a few emotional patterns or absence of them—and/or his response system may be *non-integrative.* Thus the psychopath can be described in terms of a deficiency of emotional expression, particularly with respect to interpretive, self-evaluative emotional response; consequently he exhibits a lack of variety and balance in emotional expression. From the point of view of society his behavior is non-adjustive and non-integrated. The persistently aggressive child whose behavior can be traced to basic anxiety can be seen as well to fit the criteria of emotional disturbance on virtually all the above counts: in this case *excess* of emotional response, lack of variety and balance, inappropriateness of response, and thus non-adjustive and non-integrated.

It should be noted at this point that, difficulties in diagnosis notwithstanding, techniques for the identification of emotional disturbance are much more advanced than techniques for doing something about it. Certainly it has been recognized for some time that there is great need for research in this regard as well as a need for specially trained therapists for consultation with parents and schools as a first step in dealing with the emotionally disturbed child. In the case of parents, adult education needs to be emphasized to further their understanding of the dynamics of emotional disturbance as well as to urge them to seek "help" when needed and to take advantage of services available to them. Oftentimes, however, the root of the emotional disturbance of the child is the emotional disturbance of the parents. Many such parents are not receptive to help by trained therapists; they have no understanding of, nor do they desire to understand the dynamics of their own behavior patterns as it relates to the emotional development of their children.

When the emotionally disturbed child becomes of school age, however, the school becomes involved in his care, and must somehow deal with him. Rubin and Simson have suggested that there is value in having specially trained teachers to deal with such children in a "clinically-oriented" classroom. According to them there are indications that a setting involving a special educational program which provides an atmosphere adjusted to the child's readiness to gain satisfaction from learning *may have significant therapeutic value.*

But for the school more problems arise in dealing with the *less* severely emotionally disturbed child than with the *very severely* disturbed child. The severely disturbed child is both more easily recognized and a case for immediate referral for psychiatric help. The dividing line between the "severely" and the "less severely" emotionally disturbed child is, of course, an arbitrary one, and it is likewise essential that the teacher have an understanding of the symptoms and the dynamics of severe emotional disturbance. But it is the child who is emotionally disturbed enough to be noticeable, whose behavior may be disruptive to the class, but whose disturbance is not serious enough for him to be eligible for specialized psychiatric treatment with whom teachers are more likely to be left on their own.

Oftentimes emotional disturbance may first become apparent in the school situation. When the child enters school the new demands placed upon him may bring about anxiety and reveal immaturity not apparent in the family setting. Certainly the school and the cultural values attached to it is one of the major situations confronting the child during his growing-up period. Therefore, in order to reduce the likelihood that a child will become emotionally disturbed as a result of the way in which challenges in the school situation are presented to him, and the pressures applied governing successful achievement, it is important that the teacher and other professionals dealing with the child be aware of the norms of the group from which the child comes, the dynamics of anxiety and anxiety-producing situations, and the relationship of inadequate internalization of values to emotional development.

But the school is not the only source, nor necessarily the primary source for tension-producing situations, and the child may come to the classroom in an already emotionally disturbed state. What does the teacher do with him when the child becomes disruptive to the class? The teacher may send him home with a note to his parents. But if the parents are the primary source of the child's anxiety, parental participation may only aggravate the child's disruptive behavior. What does the teacher do then? A usual procedure is to refer the child to the Assistant Principal. If the Assistant Principal cannot put the fear of God into him, the child is sent to the Principal. If the Principal can't deal effectively with him, the child may then be referred to a school psychologist or perhaps a local casework agency. If the psychologist or psychiatric social workers in the casework agency are burdened with very heavy case loads the child may be put on a long "waiting list," or if it is considered that the child's behavior is not serious enough to warrant specialized professional attention, the psychologist or agency may send the child back again to the teacher, where the procedure starts all over again. The child is shuttled back and forth, missing classwork, being sent from one anxiety-producing situation to another. The point is, that unless care is taken that actions are directed at positive change, the teacher and others dealing with the child may actually accentuate and contribute further to his emotional problems, eventually succeeding in producing a more seriously emotionally disturbed individual. One suggestion is to train teachers in techniques such as those Wineman reports have been used in camp work with emotionally disturbed children. Staff members were told to seize opportunities in their daily interactions with children to interpret behavior *on the spot* privately to individual children and to suggest socially more desirable behavior.

Certainly what happens to the child in his interaction situation in school will contribute importantly to his emotional as well as intellectual development.

SELECTED BIBLIOGRAPHY

Children's Bureau, U. S. Department of Health, Education, and Welfare. RESEARCH RELATING TO CHILDREN. Washington, D. C. Research workers studying problems of growth and development, psychological, emotional or environmental factors, special education and health services are asked to register their research projects with the Clearing House for Research of the Children's Bureau. These reports of ongoing studies are abstracted and published periodically.

Fromm, Erich, "Individual and Social Origins of Neurosis," AMERICAN SOCIOLOGICAL REVIEW, IX, 1944, 380-384. A basic statement of a modification of Freud's theory of the origin of neurosis. Fromm's thesis is that it is not the sexual rivalry between child and parent but the child's conflict about fear of and submission to parental authority which is at the root of neurosis.

Hall, Jr., Edward T., "The Anthropology of Manners," SCIENTIFIC AMERICAN, CXCII, 1955, 84-90. A well written article dealing with the unconscious habits and attitudes which differentiate peoples, and their implications for cross-cultural interaction situations.

Heilbrun, Jr., Alfred B., "Perceptual Distortion and Schizophrenia," AMERICAN JOURNAL OF ORTHOPSYCHIATRY, XXX, 1960, 412-416. An empirical study of schizophrenic daughters and a control group of normal daughters comparing their responses about their mothers on the Schaefer-Bell Parent Attitude Research Instrument. The very provocative conclusions suggest that schizophrenia may be a function of inadequate systems of defense rendering the individual unable to deal with negative affect toward parents.

Horney, Karen, THE NEUROTIC PERSONALITY OF OUR TIME, W. W. Norton, New York, 1937. A pioneering statement by one of the most prominent of the Neo-Freudians. In particular, it challenged orthodox Freudian theory by substituting cultural for biological assumptions concerning the basis of neurosis.

Jersild, Arthur T., CHILD PSYCHOLOGY, Prentice Hall, New York, 1946. One of the standard texts on child psychology. Includes a thorough discussion of the development of the emotions with an extensive description of the emotions of anger, fear, jealousy, pleasure, affection and sympathy.

May, Rollo, THE MEANING OF ANXIETY. Ronald Press, New York, 1950. A clearly written review of theories of anxiety with an analysis of the difference between normal and neurotic anxiety.

Nash, John, "Some Thoughts on the Question of Neurosis," BULLETIN OF THE MARITIME PSYCHOLOGICAL ASSOCIATION, VIII, 1959, 9-19. Advances the thesis that the concept of neurosis is unnecessary. Instead of behavior disturbances as symptoms of a neurosis, views them as learned responses. Suggests two categories: the learning of socially undesired responses; and, the failure to learn socially desired responses.

Rubin, Eli Z., and Clyde B. Simson, "A Special Class Program for the Emotionally Disturbed Child: A Proposal," AMERICAN JOURNAL OF ORTHOPSYCHIATRY, XXX, 1960, 144-153. Emphasizes the role of the school in both the development of emotional disturbance and as an opportunity to identify it. Suggests that special classes for the emotionally disturbed may have significant therapeutic value.

Sargent, S. Stansfeld, SOCIAL PSYCHOLOGY, Ronald Press, New York, 1950. A basic text in social psychology which places special emphasis on the importance of cultural factors. "Social role," "ego-development," "ego involvement," and "the self" are key concepts in the analysis.

Shaffer, Laurence F., and Edward J. Shoben, Jr., THE PSY-CHOLOGY OF ADJUSTMENT, Houghton Mifflin Co., Boston, 1956. Standard, widely used and well-written text on adjustment which emphasizes the concepts of motivation, learning, anxiety, and defense mechanisms. The last section is devoted to a thorough discussion of the mental hygiene movement and applications of mental hygiene principles and practices.

Sontag, Lester W., "War and the Fetal-Maternal Relationship," MARRIAGE AND FAMILY LIVING, VI, 1944, 16. Summarizes what is known about maternal-fetal relationships. Suggests hypotheses concerning conditions in the fetus which affects emotional development and which have implications with respect to war and the fetal-maternal relationship.

Spitz, Rene A., "The Role of Ecological Factors in Emotional Development in Infancy," CHILD DEVELOPMENT, XX, 1949, 145-155. A condensed report summarizing the findings of several empirical investigations conducted by the author concerning infants and their emotional development in the first few years of life.

Sullivan, Harry S., THE INTERNATIONAL THEORY OF PSYCHIATRY, W. W. Norton, Inc., New York, 1953. A penetrating, but difficult to read, analysis of the nature of anxiety with an emphasis on the relationship between anxiety and the personality. Represents one of the major theoretical works concerning the development of the self through interaction with others.

Wineman, David, "The Life-space Interview," SOCIAL WORK, IV, 1959, 3-17. Description of a technique developed by Fritz Redl in camp work with emotionally disturbed children wherein staff members make on-the-spot interpretations of behavior to the children.

CLARENCE C. SHERWOOD. Ph.D. in Sociology, Graduate School of Arts and Science, New York University, 1955; specializing in social psychology and criminology. Presently, Director of the Crime Prevention Program for Morningside Heights, Inc., and special lecturer in criminology at Columbia University. Has previously taught at New York University, Brooklyn College, The College of the City of New York, and Bellevue Hospital. Has a number of publications in such journals as THE JOURNAL OF CORRECTION, SOCIOLOGY AND SOCIAL RESEARCH, PERSONNEL AND GUIDANCE JOURNAL, JOURNAL OF EDUCATION, GROUP PSYCHOTHERAPY.

SYLVIA SHERWOOD. Ph.D. in Sociology, Graduate School of Arts and Science, New York University, 1955; specializing in psychology and juvenile delinquency. Presently, Assistant Professor of Sociology and Social Psychology, C. W. Post College. Has previously taught at Brooklyn College, Adelphi College, and Hofstra College. Has a number of publications in such journals as THE JOURNAL OF ABNORMAL AND SOCIAL PSYCHOLOGY, AMERICAN SOCIOLOGICAL REVIEW, PERSONNEL AND GUIDANCE JOURNAL, SOCIOLOGY AND SOCIAL RESEARCH, JOURNAL OF EDUCATION.

68

THE SPEECH HANDICAPPED

Albert T. Murphy

Boston University

INTRODUCTION

Speech handicaps constitute or contribute to crucial disruptions to harmonious interpersonal relationships and to feelings of self-esteem. For this reason it is unwise to regard a child's impaired speech without also looking for the meaning of the speech defect in terms of its significance for social interaction and in relation to the speaker's perception of himself. The speech of the communicatively disordered child, as of any person, will vary in accordance with the degree to which he feels accepted or rejected, worthy or unworthy. In the simplest of speech defects, psychosocial factors may play an important part, in relation not only to the maintenance, but to the alleviation of the problem as well. And in cases of speech disorders caused primarily by physical or intellectual deficits, psychosocial influences are often even more conspicuous. Finally, many speech handicaps are caused by emotional disruptions emanating principally from friction in child-adult relationships.

Speech disorders may be caused or maintained by breakdowns at one or more of three main sources. Analogically, we may liken these disrupted or disruptive foci to a television circuit, wherein we have a transmitter, a specific channel, and a receiver. Disruptions at any of these points will interfere with efficient communication. In the speaking process, the transmitter is the speaker, and disruptions—physical, intellectual, emotional—may occur within him. The receiver is the listener; if the listener reacts to the speaker in a consistently harsh, suppressive, or inconsistent manner, the speaker's comfort and efficiency may very well be disturbed. The channel can be likened to the setting in which the speaking occurs; one can recall without difficulty how the nature of speaking varies in relation to whether the speech behavior is occurring at home, in school, at work, during leisure, before a strange audience, or in solitude. In any case, the speaking circuit always includes the effects of interpersonal dynamics, including those cases in which the basic flaw is in the transmitter, the child. Because this is so, we must continually emphasize the criticality of attitudes within both child and adult, and attempt to improve basic attitudinal relationships, for it is in this way that the tending elder, such as the teacher, can make the greatest contribution to the speech welfare of children and youth. What follows constitutes an introductory primer of basic facts about the more common speech disorders and their treatment; however, the presentation of such facts is to be regarded in the light of one simple but important assumption: where children with speech handicaps are concerned, attitudes are more important than facts.

WHEN IS SPEECH A HANDICAP?

Ordinarily, speech pathologists consider speech to be defective when it is deviant enough to create unusual concern in either speaker or listener, or otherwise disrupts oral communication. Quite often a child is judged by an adult as having a speech defect, when the child himself is unaware of or unconcerned about the behavior. Many times, speech which would be considered normal by experts, is considered inadequate by perfectionistic elders. On the other hand, a child may have normal speaking ability according to his elders, but be quite unsatisfied himself about his speech performance, sometimes to the point of chronic emotional upset. Then again, the writer has known naturally articulate, gifted youngsters who purposely spoke more slovenly and less grammatically, for they found that speech which

70

was "too good" handicapped them in being accepted by peers.

Estimates of the number of persons having speech disorders, then, vary according to identification criteria or survey procedures used. However, figures vary as a function of age, sex, intelligence, emotional status, and physical condition, in addition to speaking situations and cultural milieu tapped. In the most significant survey of incidence of speech disorders available in one source, Milisen concluded that twelve to fifteen per cent of elementary and four to five per cent of secondary school children had seriously defective speech, all types considered.[1] Non-organic (functional) articulation defects constitute the majority of such disorders, while stuttering and voice disorders together comprise about two per cent of the total school population. As is true in other categories of exceptionality, boys have more speech and language deficiencies than girls, with stuttering providing an excellent example, boys outnumbering girls about six to one.[2,3]

FUNCTIONAL (NON-ORGANIC) ARTICULATION DISORDERS

The degree of success with which a child produces all of the culturally required speech sounds consistently and accurately is referred to by speech pathologists as *articulation* ability. Templin found that girls achieve ninety per cent ability by about age seven years, while boys do not reach this level of speech maturity until about a year later.[4] It can be concluded, for example, that adults searching for perfectly articulated speech in pre-school or first-grade children are being premature in their expectations. Articulation disorders may range in severity from a mild deviation in a single phoneme to complete unintelligibility. Young Ellen omits sounds: she says "daw" instead of "doll" and "innerbed" for "gingerbread." Lou substitutes one sound for another: he says "fum" rather than "thumb" and "wail-woad" for "railroad." Johnny distorts sounds: when he tries to say "lock" he says "ilyock." And George has two or more of these errors: he says "yack a lantuh" instead of 'jack-o'-lantern" and "evva" when

71

talking about a "feather." Teachers can do much for such children through a little extra attention in phonics or many phases of the oral language program. Helping the child to hear the difference between his production and a more desirable articulation of the defective sound may be the crucial step. Increasing the amount of successful oral participation aids greatly. Songs and games which stress the defective sounds are helpful. Suggestions such as these and many more of a specific nature are in books written for such purposes, a representative selection of which is given in the Selected Bibliography at the close of this chapter.

Ideally, however, a school speech therapist should be available to diagnose the more severe problems, provide appropriate treatment, and work together with the teacher in terms of therapeutic classroom procedures. For behind the most seemingly simple speech defect may lie a configuration of causal factors properly necessitating the time and competence of a certified speech specialist. FitzSimons, for example, comparing seventy first-grade children having functional articulation problems with a matched group of non-speech-impaired children, found that the speech defective group had experienced significantly more abnormal birth conditions, earlier weaning and toilet-training, and significantly more habit and conduct disorders (eating problems, destructiveness, fears, jealousies, nervousness, disobedience, shyness, and thumbsucking).[5] Often, in such cases, psychologically oriented speech therapy is indicated.[6, 7]

STUTTERING

Speech pathologists have conducted a great amount of research in stuttering and among the observations and conclusions having general agreement in speech science are the following: (1) one child in about 150 children stutters to a handicapping degree; (2) about six or seven boys stutter for every girl who stutters; (3) the vast majority of stuttering problems begins before the child becomes a fourth-grader; (4) parents who have stuttered are more likely to have a child who will stutter, evidently primarily through a cultural transmission rather than a genetic one; (5) the child's stuttering will tend to range from severe to mild, usually in relation to fears or anxieties associated with certain situations or people; (6) the personality patterns of stutterers range from neurosis to apparent normalcy; (7) most stutterers achieve more vocal fluency while reading aloud, speaking in chorus, or singing; (8) stutterers, as a group, do not reveal physical differences which can be associated causally with the disorder, or which consistently differentiate them as a group from the non-speech-handicapped; and (9) in cases where stuttering behavior has been persistently present for three or more years, secondary manifestations such as eye-rolling, odd posturings and gestures, and facial grimaces tend to appear.[8, 9, 10, 11]

Theories as to the origin of stuttering are developed primarily on the basis of factors relating to (1) constitutionality (2) learning, and, (3) psychogenicity. Constitutionalists hold that stuttering's origins can be understood best through an analysis of such variables as hereditary influences, cortical dominance processes, physiological perseveration phenomena, blood chemistry and allergy findings.[12, 13] However, the amount of research of a contrary indication available is considerable.[14, 15, 16]

Learning theorists regard stuttering as learned behavior occurring in essentially normal persons. Sheehan regards stuttering as an approach-avoidance conflict between opposed urges at various operational levels; for example, the urge to speak and the urge to be silent due to the fear of stuttering. The conflict is resolved by actually stuttering, thus reducing the fear accompanying the anticipation of stuttering, thus, the stuttering is continually reinforced. The speech block, says Sheehan, may also represent a conflict between meeting or avoiding a threatening situation, expressing or inhibiting unacceptable feelings, and accepting or rejecting various social roles.[17] Johnson believes that stuttering results when parents who may be anxious label the child's normal vocal non-fluencies "stuttering"; the parents (and child) come to regard and act toward the child in terms of what he has been named. In attempting to avoid stuttering the child

73

grows more apprehensive, further complicating the stuttering, and further eliciting parental reactions.[18] Johnson's viewpoint has been labeled "Semantogenic." Wischner believes that stuttering is linked intimately to anxiety and that possibly both are learned behaviors.[19] Acquired anxiety causes the person to escape discomfort, successful escape behavior being reinforced because of anxiety-reduction. The stutterer may be silent but the urge to speak is so strong that he will try different ways of speaking, the least burdensome of which will tend to persist. A considerable amount of objective data is available as support for many of the views of the learning theorists who, therapywise, tend to blend speech correction techniques with a generous portion of psychotherapy in their treatment of individuals who stutter.

Psychogeneticists emphasize early developmental experiences and the psychodynamics of contemporary interpersonal relationships. Here, as in all theories concerning the origins of stuttering, much research has been done and needs to be done. While the majority of available evidence is in the form of clinical case studies, a considerable body of supportive data based on recognized clinical assessment techniques is available. One research project representative and supportive of the psychogenic view was executed by Despert, who studied fifty stuttering children between the ages of six and fifteen years and their parents via projective tests, case histories and clinical observations.[20] The majority of the children were judged to be socially maladjusted even prior to the onset of stuttering. Fifty per cent revealed early compulsive manifestations. Seventy-four per cent revealed a variety of intense fears and anxiety dreams. The large majority of the mothers were found to be domineering; seventy-two per cent of them were overanxious, especially regarding feeding and physical health. They tended also to be overprotective, oversolicitous and compulsively perfectionistic. Sixty-two per cent of the mothers and forty-two per cent of the fathers were found to be "definitely neurotic." Although space prevents reporting other such studies, the interested reader has much literature at his disposal. The writings of Travis,[21] Barbara,[22] and Murphy and FitzSimons[23] might well serve as a survey of typical psycho-

74

dynamic theories and therapies being utilized today in the service of stuttering children.

The present author's view, presented in book form elsewhere, is presented briefly here.[24] Stuttering's origins lie in the matrix of early socialization processes, its tap-roots being interlaced closely with and part of the dynamics of the parent-child relationships. When unusual frustrations or failures occur in the child's attempts to complete successfully the successively arduous verbal and non-verbal developmental tasks society places before him, disruptions in self-regard, self-differentiation and self-integration occur which are experienced by the child as anxiety. Anxieties may occur in relation to non-verbal tasks, such as toilet-training, but through generalization and other learning processes, may become associated with other developmental tasks such as learning to speak fluently. Seeking self-protection, the child develops self-defensive behavior such as projection, repression, and denial. When the pressures of struggling to integrate societal or parental requirements with personal inner reality become too great, a self-disintegration in the form of an oral self-defensive symptom occurs which is called stuttering. Persisting initially as a consequence of anxiety, eventually the child comes to acquire specific conscious fears, one of which is the fear of stuttering; focussing more attention on the speech symptom and attempting to control the blocked or broken words, the child develops associated mannerisms, such as grimaces and other "break-through" gestures. In some cases, stuttering behavior may persist because it is somehow rewarding, attention-getting or convenient as a scape-goat focus for inadequacies. It may become self-perpetuating because of extra- or intro-punitive needs. All such manifestations may be in addition to or quite independent of anxiety promptings. Regarded in these ways, perhaps it is not too metaphorical to say that the stutterer is an artist, an author really, and his stuttering is his story, his autobiography. His stuttering tells us that unusual self-defensive processes are at work, and that the person is striving not only to protect himself, but to prove and improve himself also. The stuttering is an audible record of his past history; it speaks of how much he has been able to blend inner drives with outer demands; it gives us an idea of what the person thinks of himself and of how he thinks others regard him. In such ways he is an artist, but with two significant differences. First, *he* is his own "creation" and, second, whereas the true artist can communicate his images, the stutterer tries to communicate false images and, in so doing, blemishes and weakens his own self-image, thereby contributing all the more to his speech symptom.

CLASSROOM AID FOR CHILDREN WHO STUTTER[25]

Teachers, because of daily opportunities over a long period of time to observe the child's behavior, often are the best speech field-workers. Although often frustrated by large numbers of pupils, inadequate materials or facilities, and scanty or non-existent specialist resource personnel, their sincere attempts to nurture the communicative ability of their charges often spell the difference between good adjustment and maladjustment for the speech handicapped child. During a decade of working with classroom teachers, the writer has found that teachers who are most helpful to children who stutter are those who are more likely to make such statements as the following:

(1) "I suggest that the parents consult a speech therapist or child psychologist."

(2) "I think of his stuttering as being tied in with his feelings rather than as just simply a speech defect as such."

(3) "I try to accept him as he is; not as I think he ought to be."

(4) "I try to hear him out whenever and for as long as I can."

(5) "I find that if I can reduce demands a bit, that he speaks better and although I discipline him as I do the others, I try to emphasize that although I dislike what he did, I still like him."

(6) "If he stutters severely, I try to switch his attention and the class's, to something else, so that our thoughts won't linger on the stuttering; and I'll try to shift to one of his strengths, too, whenever I can."

On the other hand, teachers who, without realizing, may hinder the attainment of greater speech fluency in the stutterer are likely to make such statements as these:

(1) "I ask him to take a breath and start over."
(2) "I give him 'tongue-twisters' to practice."
(3) "I say the word for him whenever he's having difficulty and encourage him by suggesting that he 'take it easy'."

We see that the stress in the latter instances is on the mechanics of the speech production *per se,* rather than on the feelings involved. It is as though the teacher were saying, *"What is happening?"* when she might be asking to better avail, *"Why is this happening?"*

VOICE DISORDERS

Speech pathologists work with a large number of children and youth whose voices impair their interpersonal relationships. Voices which are too high or too low in pitch level, excessively loud or weak, nasal, hoarse, breathy, or monotonous in pitch, volume, or rate may be acceptable in certain theatrical personalities, but are liabilities for most other persons. Both organic and psychological aberrations may produce such symptoms, although, in the majority of cases, emotional determinants seem to be the primary factors. And, indeed, the reader can recall how his own voice changes in accordance with such emotional states as sorrow, anger, joy, excitement, sincerity, apprehension, and apathy. Voice disorders having a physical basis most often stem from hearing loss and pathologies or structural anomalies of the oral, nasal, or laryngeal cavities. Often, there is no clear division between the predominantly organic vs. predominantly psychogenic or functional voice disorders. Organic disorders usually are complicated by psychosocial stresses, while chronic voice disorders of psychogenic origin may lead to the development of organic damage. The voice change in boys and, to a smaller degree in girls, at the onset of puberty is a somewhat different matter. The sudden lowering of the pitch of the voice (boys, about an octave; girls, about three tones) is due to a rapid growth of the larynx making it difficult for a time to maintain control of fine vocal muscle movements governing pitch. Attempts to compensate create additional tension resulting in a pitch level even higher than the pre-puberty voice pitch. Except in cases of excessively persistive "breaking" or falsetto voice, the adolescent vocal change is a normal transitory voice phenomenon and does not warrant special treatment beyond the supportive effort needed to neutralize the adolescent's feelings of consternation or embarrassment.

Because voice disorders require a sound differential diagnosis and carefully selected therapeutic techniques, the help of a voice specialist is indicated. Teachers who notice a child with a voice disorder which persists for longer than a month or so can serve the child well by attempting to refer him to the school or community speech therapist who, in turn, usually arranges for an ear, nose and throat medical examination before initiating therapy. The speech therapist will work together with the teacher by considering classroom techniques which may alleviate the vocal impairment. The teacher will try to provide the therapist with descriptions of the child's behavior in the classroom, for this may have important implications for therapeutic approaches used by the speech specialist. Although space limitations preclude more than an introductory discussion of these disorders, the works of Perkins[26] and of Moore[27] will prove rewarding to the reader. A list of sources providing helpful background information and specific suggestions for helping children with voice disorders in the classroom situation will be found at the end of this chapter.

SPEECH AND VOICE DISORDERS
IN EXCEPTIONAL CONDITIONS

There is an irony in disability; it is that one handicap tends to beget another. The child who is mentally retarded stands a better than average chance of having speech or voice problems; so, too, with the cerebral-palsied child, the hearing handicapped child, the culturally displaced child or the emotionally disturbed child. Conversely, gifted children, for a great many reasons (intellectual, physical, cultural), have a better chance of having fewer speech or voice disorders. As we move downward on the scale of intelligence, for example, the incidence of oral communicative disorders rises. Among children with intelligence quotients below seventy-five, from fifty to eighty per cent are likely to have speech or voice disorders. In those with I.Q.'s below fifty, the acquisition of the first spoken word (occurring at nine to fourteen months in normals), may not take place until three to five years of age or more, while spoken sentences tend to be five years or more delayed. Children below thirty in I.Q. may not speak at all. At all levels, organically defective children tend to be more seriously impaired than familial retardates. Speech pathologists are wary, however, of attributing the speech disorders solely to the intellectual deficit, just as they consider it unwise to attempt to make too precise an estimate of a child's intelligence purely on the basis of his speech or language facility. For in groups of children having high proportions of hearing loss, visual deficiencies, physical impairments, and adjustment problems, all of which are found more commonly in children of lower intellectual ability, the whole gamut of possible contributing factors must be taken into account in any effort to understand the basis for and plan the treatment of the communicative inadequacy.[28]

Children with oral organic anomalies include those with cleft palate, hare-lip, overbite, underbite, and various other abnormal conditions of the teeth. Speech defects produced by such irregularities sometimes become more intractable as a consequence of emotional involvements stemming from the physical deviation;

79

for example, feelings of embarrassment or self-pity due to unfortunate cosmetic effects influence the child's maturation and efficiency in communicating. Most children with palatal clefts will have experienced at least several operations prior to the first grade. In addition, most will have experienced difficulty in eating during infancy and many will have had ear problems traceable to the palatal condition—an above average number will have a hearing loss, probably of mild degree. All such factors will influence speech and voice status and choice of therapy procedures, requiring that the aid of a qualified speech clinician be sought. The speech therapist attempts to help the child to learn to reduce the degree of nasality, usually the outstanding voice symptom; special exercises, the development of compensatory movements, and intensive ear training are stressed. In addition, procedures to improve faulty articulation are employed, for the child probably has difficulty in producing correctly such sounds as *b, p, d, f, s, sh, ch, j*, and *k*. Efforts to minimize facial grimaces and to increase pitch and loudness variation (doing so often helps to improve articulation and voice quality) are made. Obviously before a teacher attempts to work specifically on speech with these children, consultation with a speech specialist is most desirable.[29, 30, 31]

Among cerebral-palsied individuals, speech and voice handicaps are extremely common, for here is a disability, usually congenital, in which there are not only neuromuscular impairments resulting in paralysis, incoordination or weakness of the speech mechanism, but also often intellectual, sensory and psychic deficiencies. Few of these children will be seen in regular classroom situations, even though the number being so placed is increasing slowly. Speech pathologists provide voice, articulation, fluency and auditory training, and supportive counseling or release therapy with children and youth so handicapped; in addition, parents are counseled.

Speech rehabilitation, though difficult because of the severity of the primary disability and its associated disorders, has been administered with excellent results to thousands of these children.[32]

There are some children in whom sensory ability, emotional adjustment, motor ability, speech mechanism functioning and intelligence appear to fall within normal limits, yet who are unable either to understand, or to formulate or to express spoken language. This disorder has been termed "aphasia" or "dysphasia" and presents very special problems in diagnosis and treatment. The disorder is attributed by many workers to a non-physically handicapping brain injury; others maintain that the behavior may occur in the absence of brain damage. The picture is further clouded because of the similarity of many of the behavior characteristics of these youngsters to other exceptional groups such as autistic children (childhood schizophrenics). The number of classroom children who have learning problems possibly ascribable to a marginal dysphasia is probably not inconsiderable, although valid evidence is lacking. Discussions by speech pathologists of this fascinatingly perplexing disorder are available to the interested reader.[33, 34, 35]

THE TEACHER AND THE SPEECH HANDICAPPED CHILD

Sometimes the entire burden of satisfying a child's speech or other special needs is left squarely up to the teacher with rarely an assist from others. The school system may have neither a speech therapist nor a community speech and hearing clinic to call upon. In such cases, the teacher, in addition to fulfilling her basic task of instruction, finds herself alone trying to understand and help the child who cannot speak adequately. As Murphy and FitzSimons have stated:

> In the life of a child, the teacher's importance may be second only to that of the child's parents. School life ranks next to family life in its influence upon a child's development. In terms of the actual beginning of a child's speech problem, the teacher's role may be completely non-existent. Yet, the teacher remains a key person who can regulate the emotional and the communicative comfort of children.

. . . It is the teacher who creates the emotional environment in which the child is called upon to make extra
familial peer relationships. It is the teacher who creates
the emotional environment in which the child must strive
to attain academic achievements which are consistent with
his intellectual capacity. It is the teacher who compounds
feeling-learning relationships which contribute to the
child's feelings of either self-acceptance or self-inadequacy.
It is the teacher who establishes an emotionally comfortable
classroom climate which can help children who have speech
handicaps to reduce anxiety, and concomitantly, increase
speech ease and fluency.[36]

In identifying and aiding children with speech disorders, the
teacher may be able to: (1) Listen carefully to the children's
speech in class, at recess, or in the cafeteria, noting any deviations
and variations from one setting to another; (2) Collect background information from the parents or previous classroom
teachers; (3) Provide a variety of speaking situations which will
make possible a more accurate description of the child's speech;
(4) Consult references which will provide specific suggestions
for helping speech-handicapped children in classroom situations
(see the Selected Bibliography at the end of this chapter) ; (5)
Attempt in more serious cases, to have the parents make an
appointment for an evaluation at the nearest source — even a
day's trip to a hospital or University clinic may be a wise investment in terms of the possible benefits to the future adjustment of
the child. The American Speech and Hearing Association annu-
ally publishes a list of names, addresses, degrees held, positions,
and certification status by city and state of all members (available from the Association, 1001 Connecticut Avenue, N. W.,
Washington 6, D. C.) .
    In the majority of cases, the classroom teacher will best serve
handicapped children, not in terms of specific speech procedures,
but on the basis of a sensitive, nurturant interpersonal relationship with the child as both interact throughout the school year.
For the child, the teacher will attempt to counter his feelings of
inadequacy; she will create a feeling of belongingness; she will

attend to his needs for achievement; she will try to provide successful speaking experiences; acceptantly, she will hear him out; she will set the tone of the classroom by virtue of her own tolerant and accepting attitudes and reactions. She will be wise to recognize that, with speech handicapped children, a teacher's attitudes are more important than specific methods or materials. For whether or not a child wants to speak more adequately has a great deal to do with the nature of the emotional relationship existing between child and teacher. This is especially true for speech handicapped children. Speech is social behavior of a most intimate and powerful kind. A speech handicap is a social handicap. Children with speech disorders are rather commonly ostracized or belittlingly mimicked by peers; sometimes they have been rejected in school and community; they have become self-rejecting in their realization that they do not satisfy the desires of parents and teachers; on the basis of their speech defects, they have been regarded as "queer," "sissies," or "stupid" and have served as objects of pity or as scapegoats. The thorns of their crown have consisted of stereotyped perceptions and attitudes of rejection.[37] In this light, it is not unreasonable and unprofitable to consider many speech-handicapped persons as members of minority groups, comparable in self-regard, attitude, and proneness to prejudice to those who are minority group members because of religion or race.

There is little doubt that thousands of youngsters with speech or voice handicaps have received their greatest nurturance and stimulus to speech improvement from classroom teachers. With children more severely disturbed communicatively, the services of specialists well-trained in the diagnosis and treatment of speech and voice disorders is needed. For others less involved, the teacher can be the key, not only through ways of doing, but even more, through a special way of *being*.

SELECTED BIBLIOGRAPHY

Berry, Mildred F., and Eisenson, Jon, SPEECH DISORDERS: PRINCIPLES AND PRACTICES, Appleton-Century Crofts,

Inc., New York, 1956. A thorough survey of all types of speech and voice disorders, their diagnosis and treatment.

Eisenson, Jon (Editor), STUTTERING: A SYMPOSIUM, Harper and Brothers, Publishers, New York, 1958. Six leading theorists present their own theories and therapeutic approaches in stuttering.

FitzSimons, Ruth M., and Murphy, Albert T., LET'S PLAY HIDE AND SEEK, Expression Company, Publishers, Magnolia, Massachusetts, 1959. An easel of ten large pictures containing scores of hidden objects: designed for speech correction or phonics training for all children. Kit also contains manual and workbook representative of materials speech therapists use.

Irwin, Ruth B., SPEECH AND HEARING THERAPY, Prentice-Hall, Inc., Englewood Cliffs, New Jersey, 1953. Presents essential information in organizing and administering public school speech correction programs.

JOURNAL OF SPEECH AND HEARING DISORDERS (AND) RESEARCH, Interstate Printers and Publishers, Inc., Danville, Illinois. Quarterlies. The official Journals of the American Speech and Hearing Association, 1001 Connecticut Avenue, N. W., Washington 6, D. C.

Johnson, Wendell, et. al., SPEECH HANDICAPPED SCHOOL CHILDREN, Harper and Brothers, Publishers, New York (rev. ed.), 1956. Surveys the common speech and voice disorders in a way most practical for regular classroom teachers.

Johnson, Wendell, CHILDREN WITH SPEECH AND HEARING IMPAIRMENTS: PREPARING TO WORK WITH THEM IN THE SCHOOLS, U. S. Office of Education, 1959 (Bulletin No. 5).

Mayper, Lois, et. al., HANDBOOK FOR SPEECH IMPROVEMENT, KINDERGARTEN, GRADES ONE TO SIX, New England Speech Association, 332 Bay State Road, Boston, 1956. This booklet contains well-tested materials for use by classroom teachers working toward improved oral communication in their classrooms.

Murphy, Albert T., "The Speech Handicapped, "REVIEW OF EDUCATIONAL RESEARCH, XXIX, 1959, 553-565 (Chapter 9). Reviews important research in speech and voice disorders for the period 1953 to 1960.

Murphy, Albert T., and FitzSimons, Ruth M., STUTTERING

AND PERSONALITY DYNAMICS, The Ronald Press Company, New York, 1960. Presents a psychodynamic view of stuttering plus psychotherapeutic procedures such as counseling, play therapy, creative dramatics and puppetry, including verbatim reports. One chapter is devoted to the teacher and the stutterer.

Pronovost, Wilbert L., THE TEACHING OF SPEAKING AND LISTENING IN THE ELEMENTARY SCHOOL, Longmans, Green and Company, New York, 1959. Clearly detailed methods of teaching by means of illustrative lessons using appropriately graded materials drawn from elementary subject matter areas.

Scott, Louise B., and Thompson, Jack J., SPEECH WAYS, Webster Publishing Company, St. Louis, 1955. A guidance approach to oral communication in the middle grades.

Scott, Louise B., and Thompson, Jack J., TALKING TIME, Webster Publishing Company, St. Louis, 1951. Similar in content to SPEECH WAYS and geared to the lower grades.

Travis, Lee E. (Editor), HANDBOOK OF SPEECH PATHOLOGY, Appleton-Century-Crofts, Inc., New York, 1957. Written by twenty-seven of America's leading speech pathologists, this volume stands as a fair representation of the current knowledge in the area of the speech handicapped.

Van Riper, Charles, and Butler, K. G., SPEECH IN THE ELEMENTARY CLASSROOM, Harper and Brothers, New York, 1955. This little book presents practical suggestions for the classroom teacher.

ALBERT T. MURPHY, Professor of Speech Pathology and Special Education and Co-Director, Speech and Hearing Clinic, Boston University, and Speech Pathologist of the Massachusetts Memorial Hospitals and the Joseph P. Kennedy Memorial Hospital, received his M.A. and Ph.D. degrees from the University of Southern California; is the author of STUTTERING AND PERSONALITY DYNAMICS (Ronald Press, 1960) and numerous other publications and clinical materials.

NOTES

1. Milisen, Robert, "The Incidence of Speech Disorders," in HANDBOOK OF SPEECH PATHOLOGY (Travis, Lee E., Editor), Appleton-Century-Crofts, New York, 1957. Chapter 7, pp. 246-266.

2. McCarthy, Dorothea, "Language Development in Children," in MANUAL OF CHILD PSYCHOLOGY (Carmichael, L., Editor), Second Edition, John Wiley & Sons, Inc., New York, 1954. Chapter 9, pp. 492-630.

3. Templin, Mildred C., CERTAIN LANGUAGE SKILLS IN CHILDREN, University of Minnesota Press, Minneapolis, 1957.

4. Templin, Mildred C., "Speech Development in the Young Child: 3. The Development of Certain Language Skills in Children," JOURNAL OF SPEECH AND HEARING DISORDERS, 17, 1952, 280-285.

5. FitzSimons, Ruth M., "Developmental, Psychosocial, and Educational Factors in Children with Nonorganic Articulation Problems," CHILD DEVELOPMENT, XXIX, 481-489.

6. Murphy, Albert T., and FitzSimons, Ruth M., "Music Therapy for the Speech Handicapped," ELEMENTARY SCHOOL JOURNAL, LIX, 1958, 39-45.

7. Murphy, Albert T., "Counseling Students with Speech and Hearing Problems," PERSONNEL AND GUIDANCE JOURNAL, XXXIII, 1955, 260-265.

8. Reid, Loren D., "Some Facts About Stuttering," JOURNAL OF SPEECH DISORDERS, XI, 1946, 3-12.

9. Murphy, Albert T., "The Speech Handicapped," REVIEW OF EDUCATIONAL RESEARCH, XXIX, 1959, 553-565.

10. Berry, Mildred F., and Eisenson, Jon, SPEECH DISORDERS, Appleton-Century-Crofts, New York, 1956.

11. Van Riper, Charles, SPEECH CORRECTION, Prentice-Hall, Inc., Englewood Cliffs, New Jersey, 1958.

12. West, Robert, "An Agnostic's Speculation About Stuttering," In STUTTERING: A SYMPOSIUM (Eisenson, Jon, Editor), Harper & Brothers, New York, 1958, 167-222.

13. Hill, Harris, "Stuttering: II. A Review and Integration of Physiological Data," JOURNAL OF SPEECH DISORDERS, IX, 1944, 289-324.

14. Knott, John R., Correll, Robert E., and Shepherd, Jean N., "Frequency Analysis of Electroencephalograms of Stutterers and Non-Stutterers," JOURNAL OF SPEECH AND HEARING, II, 1959, 74-80.

15. McCroskey, Robert L., "Effect of Speech On Metabolism," JOURNAL OF SPEECH AND HEARING DISORDERS, XXII, 1957, 46-52.

16. Williams, Dean E., "Masseter Muscle Action Potentials in Stuttered and Non-Stuttered Speech," JOURNAL OF SPEECH AND HEARING DISORDERS, XX, 1955, 242-261.

17. Sheehan, Joseph, "Conflict Theory of Stuttering," in STUTTERING: A SYMPOSIUM (Eisenson, Jon, Editor), OP. CIT. 121-166.

18. Johnson, Wendell, et al., SPEECH HANDICAPPED SCHOOL CHILDREN, Harper & Brothers, New York, 1956, pp. 202-300.

19. Wischner, George J., "Stuttering Behavior and Learning: A Preliminary

Theoretical Formulation," JOURNAL OF SPEECH AND HEARING DIS-
ORDERS, XV, 1950, 324-335.

20. Despert, J. Louise, "Psychosomatic Study of Fifty Stuttering Children,"
AMERICAN JOURNAL OF ORTHOPSYCHIATRY, XVI, 1946, 100-113.

21. Travis, Lee E. (Editor), HANDBOOK OF SPEECH PATHOLOGY,
Appleton-Century-Crofts, New York, 1957.

22. Barbara, Dominick A. (Editor), PSYCHOLOGICAL AND PSYCHIA-
TRIC ASPECTS OF SPEECH AND HEARING, Charles C. Thomas, Springfield, Illinois, 1960.

23. Murphy, Albert T., and FitzSimons, Ruth M., STUTTERING AND
PERSONALITY DYNAMICS, New York, Ronald Press, 1960.

24. Murphy, Albert T. and FitzSimons, Ruth M., OP. CIT.

25. Adapted from Murphy, Albert T., FitzSimons, Ruth M., and Pronovost,
Wilbert L., DOES YOUR PUPIL STUTTER?, Boston University Speech and
Hearing Center, Boston, 1956.

26. Perkins, William, "The Challenge of Functional Disorders of Voice."
In HANDBOOK OF SPEECH PATHOLOGY (Travis, Lee E., Editor), OP.
CIT., pp. 832-877.

27. Moore, G. Paul, "Voice Disorders Associated with Organic Abnormalities." In HANDBOOK OF SPEECH PATHOLOGY (Travis, Lee E.,
Editor), OP. CIT., pp. 653-706.

28. Matthews, Jack, "Speech Problems of the Mentally Retarded." In
HANDBOOK OF SPEECH PATHOLOGY (Travis, Lee E., Editor), OP.
CIT., pp. 531-551.

29. Van Riper, Charles, and Irwin, John V., VOICE AND ARTICULA-
TION, Prentice-Hall, Inc., Englewood Cliffs, New Jersey, 1958, pp. 164-217.

30. Koepp-Baker, Herbert, "Speech Problems of the Person With Cleft-
Palate and Cleft Lip," In HANDBOOK OF SPEECH PATHOLOGY, OP.
CIT., pp. 597-607.

31. Bloomer, H. Harlan, "Speech Defects Associated with Dental Abnormalities and Malocclusions." In HANDBOOK OF SPEECH PATHOLOGY,
OP. CIT., pp. 608-652.

32. Denhoff, Eric, and Robinault, Isabel, CEREBRAL PALSY AND RE-
LATED DISORDERS, McGraw-Hill Book Company, Inc., New York, 1960.

33. Monsees, Edna K., "Aphasia in Children: Diagnosis and Education,"
VOLTA REVIEW, 1957, 392-401, 414.

34. Mykelbust, Helmer R., AUDITORY DISORDERS IN CHILDREN,
Grune and Stratton, New York, 1954.

35. McGinnis, Mildred, et al., "Teaching Aphasic Children," VOLTA
REVIEW, LVIII, 1956, 239-244.

36. Murphy, Albert T., and FitzSimons, Ruth M., STUTTERING AND
PERSONALITY DYNAMICS—Play Therapy, Projective Therapy, and Counseling. Copyright 1960, The Ronald Press Company, OP. CIT., p. 471.

37. Murphy, Albert T., "Attitudes of Educators Toward the Visually
Handicapped," THE SIGHT-SAVING REVIEW, XXX, 1960, 157-161.

CRIPPLING CONDITIONS AND SPECIAL HEALTH PROBLEMS

Jean Louise Bloom

Federation of the Handicapped, New York

INTRODUCTION

Over the past thirty years, there has been a gradual decrease in the number of children attending special educational programs because of infectious diseases, cardiac and other special health problems. Some of the diseases seen by the teacher in 1930 have almost completely disappeared; others, which were considered long-term chronic illnesses involving an extended hospital stay, now require relatively short-term hospitalization or treatment at home. Because of these recent gains in scientific and medical knowledge, children who previously required educational services in the hospital are now more in need of home instruction programs or special health conservation classes within the regular school facility. As funds being spent for scientific research by government and private agencies increase, we can expect a change of emphasis in the types of problems and programs currently experienced by the special educator. Trends over the last two decades indicate that larger numbers of children with congenital anomalies, cerebral palsy, and other neurological disorders are surviving birth and childhood because of anti-microbial therapy, better procedures for surgical intervention, and more concerted efforts at early case finding. These same strides in the field of medicine have brought about a decrease in the formerly crippling, chronic, infectious diseases such as tuberculosis and rheumatic fever. It is to be hoped that these trends will continue as more and more youngsters enter into programs of preventive medicine.

Although there are many different kinds of crippling conditions which might be discussed in this chapter, the most common types of special health problems of school children are rheumatic fever, congenital anomalies, asthma-hay fever and tuberculosis. It is these disabilities which will be presented, as well as a section on multiple disabilities. Also, regardless of the type of disability, there are certain educational methods of handling students with special health problems which are common to all. By way of summary, these "rule of thumb" procedures will also be presented.

COMMON CARDIAC CONDITIONS OF CHILDREN

Current thinking in the field of cardiology emphasizes what the cardiac child can do rather than what he cannot do. In the total population, less than one percent of all children are born with congenital heart defects. However, in order to better understand the scope of the problem, it will be necessary to present some morbidity figures as well as a brief summary of the types of cardiac defects. In a survey of select groups of crippled children attending special and hospital classes in New York State (not including New York City) during the 1956-57 and 1957-58 school years, there were between 622 (1957-58) and 757 (1956-57) children classified as having rheumatic, congenital and other heart diseases according to Fenton and Connor.[1] Abramson points out that 14.8% of the students enrolled in the 1958-59 school year, in the Home Instruction Program with the New York City Board of Education had heart and circulatory disorders or rheumatic fever.[2]

CONGENITAL ANOMALIES

The most common heart defects are patent ductus arteriosus, Tetralogy of Fallot, coarctation of the aorta, valvular pulmonary

89

stenosis or septal defects. A patent ductus arteriosus is an open passageway between the pulmonary artery and the aorta. All babies are born with this opening, but these two arteries should normally close within several weeks after birth. When this does not occur, the blood needed to nourish other body tissues is shunted back to the lungs. As a result, the body may become undernourished and the heart must work harder to pump life-sustaining blood through the body. The Tetralogy of Fallot is a name given a combination of four defects; essentially this is a defect which prevents enough blood from getting to the lungs to be oxygenated, thus starving body tissues. Youngsters with this defect are known as "blue babies." Coarctation of the aorta is a constriction or narrowing of the aorta which causes a diminished blood supply to some organs and tissues of the body. Valvular pulmonary stenosis is a sticking or malfunctioning of the valve at the entrance of the pulmonary artery. This anomaly reduces the flow of blood from the right side of the heart to the lungs where oxygenation occurs. A septal defect occurs when a baby is born with an opening in the wall of the heart which separates the right and left chambers thus causing the blood to circulate improperly, and creating malnourishment of the body cells.

Most of the research and experimentation being carried on in the area of congenital defects lies within the scope of the medical profession and the physicist. The Blalock operation for "blue babies" is well-known to most of us now. However, many new types of corrective surgery are being devised for some of the other anomalies. It should be noted that all defects cannot as yet be corrected by surgery, and that each child must be evaluated individually to determine whether the condition can be corrected by surgery. The physicists have greatly enhanced the physician's ability to perform heart operations by contributing such devices as the heart-lung machine and special valves to replace the defective ones in the child's body. Other operations use special devices to arrest heart action while the defect is sutured or while part of the vessel is removed and then sewed together. With ever increasing knowledge of and experimentation in human physiology and in the realms of physics, we can anticipate that

90

many conditions which are now considered hopeless will be able to be corrected in the near future. This should mean an increasing diminution of congenital heart defects and heart degeneration resulting therefrom.

The family of the child with a heart defect will need special help and support. They will need to know how to help the child live within the physical restrictions of the disability while encouraging the youngster to become as independent as possible. When this fine balance cannot be effected a "cardiac cripple" may result. If surgery is contemplated there will be a great need to help allay the fears of both parent and child.

After successful surgery, a major adjustment needs to be made on the part of both the parent and child. Help will be needed to encourage the family to resume a normal way of life and to encourage the child to live a normal life. The educator, too, may find it difficult to accept a once ill child as normal. After years of illness and limitation this is no mean task.

If the defect has been only partially corrected, the youngster may still be somewhat limited in physical activities and need a modified classroom program. Planning for the future of the "limited" youngsters must begin during the high school years or even earlier. The child will need special vocational guidance in the school or from a private agency so that he can be directed toward occupations that will not expose him to heavy physical exertion or an unhealthy environment. If the child is to be guided into occupations meeting those requirements, he must continue school as long as possible; therefore, program modification which would entail extending the total number of school years may be required. However, demands must be put on the child to perform at a competitive level within these modifications; otherwise the youngster is being done an injustice.

RHEUMATIC FEVER

Much of the heart disease of childhood is a result of rheumatic fever which is most common between the ages of five and fifteen.

Rheumatic fever is a far greater overall problem than congenital heart disease. It is still the leading cause of death in the 5-19 yr. age group. Although morbidity statistics are inadequate, the reported surveys reveal a rate of 2 to 4 cases of established rheumatic heart disease per 1,000 school children.[3]

The onset of rheumatic fever is associated with attacks of hemolytic streptococcal infections and is therefore of public health importance. There is evidence that the control of these infections, which are spread from person to person by contact, reduce the incidence of rheumatic fever. The disease also is associated with the lower socio-economic groups where damp, crowded, unhygienic living conditions are most prevalent. This overcrowding would seem to foster the rapid spreading of respiratory and streptococcal infections. There is evidence of familial tendencies as well as some evidence that hereditary factors also play a part in the contraction of the disease.

Rheumatic fever is often difficult to recognize because it simulates a variety of other diseases and because there is no specific test for diagnosis. However, we do know that the disease is preceded two or three weeks before the attack of rhumatic fever by a sore throat. Early signs, though vague, may be poor appetite, pallor, failure to gain weight, pains in arms or legs or inflamed and swollen joints. Occasionally, the child is irritable and may cry easily or develop nervous habits or twitching.

Most physicians feel that the child's heart is affected during an acute attack of rheumatic fever and that a considerable number of patients are left with a damaged heart. In some cases the damage disappears later but, in others, signs or symptoms of cardiac damage may gradually develop. The "damage" which occurs is a result of the inflammation of one or both valves on the left side of the heart. The healing process or scarring may prevent the valve from opening and closing properly thus interfering with the normal blood flow. Sometimes the disease process leaves the heart muscle permanently damaged. Nonetheless, the greatest danger in rheumatic fever usually comes from repeated attacks.

Some of the clinical factors important for the teacher to know are:

1. There is difficulty in diagnosing rheumatic fever and rheumatic heart disease because of its insidious onset.

2. There is a recurrent tendency of the infection and difficulty in evaluation of heart murmurs.

3. There is a prolonged period of sub-acute infection and convalescence.

4. Chronic heart damage often results from the disease.

5. Many cases of cardiac insufficiency as a result of rheumatic fever occur in young and middle adulthood—a time when maximum earning power and family responsibilities are greatest.

Each of these medical problems will require a different approach in planning and working with the child.

Several years ago, in one New York State County (Lewis), a special community oriented program was set up for children suspected of having cardiac disorders. These youngsters received a diagnostic evaluation by several cardiologists. Evaluation encompassed and was concerned with the integration of information about family history, psycho-social adjustment, and educational progress. On the basis of the evaluation, coordinated recommendations were made to the home, school and community. Such procedures kept all concerned informed about the positive aspects of "cardiac conditions," what "limitation" meant in regard to each child, and how and when to handle some of the problems resulting from these health conditions. A similar study has just been completed as a joint effort of the New York City Board of Education and New York City Department of Health on The Function of Adolescents with Cardiac Limitations Enrolled in New York Secondary Schools. The findings will not be available until June 1961, but will no doubt offer valuable, up-to-date information on how to handle the educational problems of children with cardiac limitations.

Other studies which contribute to our knowledge and control of rheumatic heart disease are the number of medical studies being conducted in prophylaxis or the use of chemo-therapy to prevent recurrence of attacks. These are of importance because the teacher has a responsibility for seeing that the child is taking medication as advised by the physician and also in being alerted to the possible symptoms of recurrence. Some medical studies are being conducted on cardiac output, which deals with the amount of energy expended by the heart in various types of activities. This type of research offers concrete evidence of the kind of activity the child can be requested to perform during the various stages of illness. For example, such a project at the University of Minnesota Medical School pointed out that cardiac output was slightly lower while sitting in a chair or on the side of the bed with the feet supported than when lying supine (flat on the back). For those working with youngsters still in bed, this fact should help in planning school work and activities which can be carried out in these two positions. Another factor growing out of the study is that use of hand motions increases cardiac output very little while standing increases cardiac output by 60 to 70%.[4] As a result of this study and others, the doctors may now make specific recommendations for gradual increase of activities which would help increase physical strength but which would offer no undue physical hardship.

In a preliminary report of a Seven Year Pilot Study of Vocational Counseling for Children with Heart Disease or a History of Rheumatic Fever, the problems are summarized as follows:

1. Because of the limited social experience and impoverished cultural background of these children it is difficult to make full use of community resources which might ordinarily be tapped in order to give them a broad perspective of work and training opportunities.

2. As they return to the challenges of a competitive environment from the very protective environment of the hospital or convalescent home, there is a tendency to give up rather than to fight the difficulties which they find there.

94

3. Not only are these children inexperienced in travel about the city but in many cases they have a distorted fear of it. From a counseling point of view, therefore, they are not getting the normal exploration of activities which boys and girls of their age usually have.

4. Excessive records of absence seem to be a pattern in the histories of these children. This seems to be directly related to another problem, namely overprotective parents who, after a period of illness, are so fearful of recurrence that they are overcautious with regard to school attendance and travel in inclement weather.

5. As a group, the school records of these children are not on a level commensurate with their ability.

6. The most striking problem is the very inadequate educational background which these children present as a basis for their secondary and advanced education.

7. There was a great deal of anti-social behavior of various kinds ranging from truancy to prison offenses.

8. It was necessary at times to ask the clinic for special consideration of the general medical picture (physical reexamination) because the counselor felt that no school or job success was possible unless better general health was achieved.

9. The very complicated family situations of which these children are a part interfere in many instances in the final success of the counseling process.

10. In many instances where special programs in school seemed necessary, the counselor found them extremely difficult to arrange even though full interpretation had been given.[5]

These studies would seem to indicate the need to revise our attitudes toward the educational process of the rheumatic child in school. The old approach of long-term bed rest and physical restriction is now considered outmoded. Dr. Brownell, who has been involved for many years with studies of children with rheumatic fever, states: "Infinitely more harm has been done children with rheumatic heart disease through overrestriction of physical activities than has been done by failure to limit them sufficiently."[6] Children who are deprived of normal school activities including sports are laboring under a severe handicap. Undue restriction may promote invalid reactions which seriously affect the acquisition of an adequate education and, in turn, propagate serious deficiencies affecting the planning of realistic vocational goals utilizing the highest abilities of which the youngster is capable.

Feinstein[7] in reporting a study which followed varying degrees of heart disease for 21 years after the initial attacks of rheumatic fever found that restriction of physical activity did not appear to favorably or unfavorably influence the progression of heart disease. He did find, however, that there was a higher incidence of undesirable psychosocial effects in the restricted group. For the special educator, this would mean that, although physician's recommendations must be followed, wherever the question of "to limit or not to limit" is left to the interpretation of the school personnel, "not to limit" should be the rule. However, each case must be individualized and the personality of the student taken into consideration; for example, the physically lazy youngster may need no limitation while the very active, tense student may need to have some limitations placed on his activities. Excessive fatigue, shortness of breath or blueness are guides to when and to what extent a child must be limited in activity. Many youngsters with more severe cardiac involvement are aware of their physical needs and limitations and automatically adjust themselves to these demands.

Most children who have had rheumatic fever do best in the regular classroom situation. They may need such modifications as special bus transportation, elevator passes, ground floor classrooms (where no elevators exist), extra sets of books—one for home, one for school, attendance dispensations, and somewhat modified physical education programs. For a minority, special health classes may be necessary because of the need for more health supervision, or a balanced schedule of classes, exercise and rest, or because of lack of suitable plant facilities, such as elevators. In some instances special guidance and interpretation will be needed for the parent, and in most instances, special vocational planning will be necessary early enough to teach the student, in addition to the basic skills and knowledge generally disseminated by the teacher, good work habits, how to conserve energy and how to handle competition. Special abilities should be recognized and help should be given to encourage the child to discover his limitations and work within them. The teacher has an added responsibility for helping the child become integrated socially, to help allay his fears, and to help him achieve some modicum of personal satisfaction while putting demands on the child to produce the best work of which he is capable. Only as a last resort should the youngster be placed on home instruction.

COMMON CHRONIC RESPIRATORY AILMENTS

Respiratory ailments constitute one of the leading causes of time lost from work or school. It is estimated by the National Tuberculosis Association that at least 15% of all people with chronic health problems have a chronic respiratory ailment.

ASTHMA—HAY FEVER

Asthma-hay fever affects 48 out of every 1,000 persons according to a 1957-58 National Health Survey.[8] It is more common in children than in adults, and much more common in boys than in girls. This same survey showed that asthma-hay fever caused 21,379 restricted-activity days and 8,543 bed-disability days within the under 15 year age group.[9]

The cause of asthma remains somewhat obscure; however, it is thought that the cause can be both congenital and psychosomatic and that it also has some relationship to infections. The allergens, substances giving rise to allergic conditions, are usually inhaled with the air or ingested with food. When these substances are inhaled they are more likely to give rise to respiratory reactions such as asthma or hay fever. Difficulty in breathing results because of swelling or spasm in the lower part of the respiratory tract. Because of the swelling or spasm the watery discharge from the mucous membrane remains in the air sacs and the patient is literally "drowning in his own juice."

Asthmatic children may need special attention from the teacher. The attacks cause difficulty in breathing, and this would automatically limit play activities or other school work during the attack. More severe attacks may necessitate absence from school so that special help should be given to the youngster to aid him in keeping up with his school assignments. In some cases, the attacks occur at night or in the early morning hours and are severe enough to interfere with sleep. Rest periods at school would then be advisable. Chronic lateness may also result from such nocturnal attacks. However, because each child is different, it would be well to check with the child's doctor before working out an adjusted school program.

There are few research reports dealing with the asthmatic that are of direct concern to the teacher. From several psychological studies and a limited one being conducted on a small group of homebound asthmatic high school students in a pre-vocational evaluation research project at Federation of the Handicapped in New York City, it would seem that there is a strong psychological component in the development of asthma in children. This information points out that the mothers of these youngsters lack "motherliness" or warmth and understanding of the baby and feel little sense of gratification in caring for the child. From this, it is hypothesized that the child's relationship to the mother becomes ambivalent, fearful and angry. Because this first social relationship is impaired, later interpersonal relationships are damaged and the child exhibits inhibition, lack of spontaneity, and mistrust in his dealings with other people. Educational implication would be that the youngster be assigned to a male teacher or to a warm, understanding, motherly woman.

Psychological testing of these homebound asthmatic youngsters has shown that most of them have a potential for high average or above average intellectual functioning. It is found, however, that they are underachievers and need gentle but firm prodding

98

to help them produce grades of which they are capable. An individual intelligence test, such as the Wechsler Bellevue, shows that they have higher manipulative skills than verbal skills. The reason for this would seem to be that because the child is tied up emotionally he is unable to express himself verbally. Therefore, the teacher may have an inaccurate appraisal of the student's intellectual functioning if the test which measured the IQ was one of the verbal, paper and pencil type. Also, the child might be observed to have difficulty in forming relationships with peer groups and may need special counseling for this problem. Special vocational guidance should be offered because of the limitation of the types of jobs available as well as places where the youngster may be employed.

TUBERCULOSIS

Tuberculosis, although decreasing in incidence during the past two decades, is still a health problem needing special consideration because of the nature of its communicability. It is caused by the tubercle bacillus and infection in the school age population is of importance because of the danger of recurrence in later life as well as the immediate hazard of the disease. Tuberculosis is spread most commonly by personal contact with a person who has an "active" case of the disease. Many people become infected with the TB bacillus as young children but do not develop clinical symptoms of the disease because of the body's ability to build up defenses against it. This is not a guarantee that tuberculosis will never develop into a clinical case later in life because sometimes stress and deprivation of a physical or emotional nature may lower the body's defenses against the possibility of reinfection. If the initial or primary infection has taken place, a tuberculin test would reveal a positive reaction.

Many youngsters, because of the concerted effort to eliminate or prevent tuberculosis, have had tuberculin tests or x-rays. Some of them have positive tests or x-rays. The children whose tests or x-rays are positive, as well as the children who have someone in the home with the disease, should be allowed to participate in

99

all normal activities of school life. However, periodic check-ups by a physician should be encouraged. Again, because of the focus on preventive medicine, Lincoln and others are studying the use of chemotherapy on children with primary lesions. For children having primary lesions, chemotherapy would seem to reduce the incidence of TB meningitis and may prove to reduce the likelihood of breakdown later in life from the secondary infection which actually produces the "active" case of tuberculosis.

The child with active tuberculosis should not be in the regular classroom but at home or in the hospital under the care of a physician. The chronicity of the disease sometimes necessitates a long period of convalescence with a gradual resumption of activity and educational plans. The doctor, of course, will determine when the child is ready to resume educational pursuits, and to what extent. Physicians feel that, if there is no toxemia present, it is far better for the youngster's general morale and total rehabilitation that educational activities begin as early as possible. The doctor's recommendations will be assigned on a gradually increasing basis as the child's work tolerance increases. The teacher assigned to work with tuberculous children need not be fearful of infection if they have a positive tuberculin test and continue to have periodic chest x-rays. With the use of many of the new drugs, the sputum is rendered negative within a short period of time thus reducing the communicability of the disease.

When a child is ready to return to school from the home or hospital, the school program should be arranged only after consultation with the physician, since physical activities may need to be limited for some time and arrangements may need to be made for supplemental nutrition. The teacher should remain on the alert for signs of fatigue or recurrent respiratory infections and see that the child is sent to the school nurse or physician who then may want to adjust the educational program.

MULTIPLE DISABILITIES

There are students who are being taught in Special Health classes or on Home Instruction who fall into the group known as the multiply disabled. The exact number of these students is unknown because physicians, health departments and school boards have classified them under the major disability only. They are a group about whom little has been written, but if we believe that each child in a democratic society is entitled to the fullest realization of his potentials personally, socially, educationally and vocationally, then more work needs to be done with this group. The job of helping these youngsters achieve some modicum of satisfaction will fall primarily to the teacher, the social worker and the vocational counselor.

In a research and demonstration project for homebound high school students in New York City, the question arose as to why youngsters with seemingly slight physical or emotional disabilities were being taught at home. In reviewing the case load for the school years, 1959-60 and 1960-61, it was found that many of these youngsters had complicated physical disabilities which not only involved ambulation or hand-arm coordination, but severe visual-perceptual or speech difficulties as well. A large proportion (34 out of 47 in 1960-61 school year) [10] had emotional problems which ranged from anxiety and depression to severe schizophrenia requiring group or individual psychotherapy. Some were mentally retarded in addition to the physical and/or emotional disability, and others had a combination of all three. In many instances, the disability noted on the school record was of minor importance in the planning of the school program or in indicating the problems which the school personnel would need to handle.

According to the New York City Board of Education, all youngsters who were educationally homebound as of June 1959, were, on an average, one year behind in reading and two years behind their regular classmates nationally on standardized tests.[11] The implication of these facts is manifold and involves the entire "team" working with these handicapped youngsters. Also, (1) that better, more thorough and adequate diagnoses are necessary from the medical personnel; (2) that ancillary services, such as social case work and/or psychotherapy are necessary to enable these youngsters to achieve the fullest potential of which they

101

are capable; and (3) that the teacher is ill-equipped to deal with these children because of inadequate information in the school records thus making realistic program planning almost impossible. Unless teachers of these youngsters have an adequate background and understanding of the problems involved, it would be open to question as to whether they are able to provide maximum educational opportunity.

From this author's experience in the project to date, and from the fact that the research population approaches an intellectually normal IQ distribution, it would seem that the teacher is reluctant to put competitive demands on these pupils; and because of the emotional involvement with the child and his family, the teacher continues to handle the pupil by feeling sorry for him and letting him get away with doing as little as possible. In some instances it has been admitted that grades are gratuitous. It should not be, but evidently is, necessary to state the fact that such attitudes and practices ill-equip these youngsters for their role in the adult world. If the child has any possible vocational potential, what employer will hire a person who is not able to produce his best or retain an employee who feels that, because he is disabled, he should not be required to put forth the same effort on a job as the non-disabled worker.

The teacher and social worker then can and must do something to help this group of children. The multiplicity of handicaps requires the full use of community resources—public and private. The teacher must be able to develop skill in identifying educational problems and in becoming aware of factors interfering with the learning process. If the problems are beyond the scope of the teacher, referrals must be made to another person who can cope with them. It may even be necessary for the instructor to learn to use the skills and knowledge contributed by the other team members—in science, medicine, social work, psychology, and vocational rehabilitation—and to apply these techniques in planning the curriculum of the disabled child. Again, the importance of cooperating with and utilizing the services of all community agencies and of the entire "team" cannot be overemphasized.

102

THE ROLE OF THE EDUCATOR
IN SPECIAL HEALTH PROBLEMS

"Human development is a consequence of learning and experience. Disruptions in flow of normal experience lead to disruptions in development. One major cause of impaired experience is disability. When this occurs, it may be expected that certain essential life goals appropriate for the individual at his stage of development will be thwarted. This thwarting will have important consequences for subsequent development. The developmental tasks of young people are much the same for all—disabled or not. Typical ones include learning to talk, to control the physical environment, to get along with others, to build a philosophy of life, and to establish career patterns. However, the disability often serves as a barrier to successful completion of these tasks. Failure to complete them results in retardation and creates a need for remedial and therapeutic measures."[12]

It is with this total development that the special educator is charged. The teacher must provide the opportunities that the other aspects of the student's life do not provide owing to the fact that he is disabled. This is a heavy burden for the educator to bear but one that can be most gratifying.

There are certain "rule of thumb" measures which can help in the education of all handicapped youngsters.

1. Whenever possible, integrate the disabled child into the regular school curriculum and modify activities as needed. If this cannot be done, set up special health conservation classes within the regular school system. Only as a last resort and when the above two plans are impossible, should the child be given home instruction.

2. Know the medical limitations of the disabled student and work within the physician's recommendations.

3. Help the youngster to grow socially and emotionally as well as physically. This may mean using other members of the "team" to accomplish this total growth.

4. Be aware of the symptoms of the child's disease and make

referrals to the school nurse or physician or to the child's doctor if any of the following symptoms develop and continue for a period of time—pallor, weight loss, nose bleeds, poor appetite, low or persistent fever, twitching of face, arms or legs, pains in the extremities, abdomen or joints, persistent cough, listlessness, or inattention.

5. Know the normal reactions of children during illness and convalescence. After the acute phase of illness, the youngster will want to become active immediately and this may not be desirable. Some limitation of activity may still be recommended by the physician.

6. Some youngsters, after a long term illness, may be afraid of socialization and have anxiety about resuming normal activity. It will be necessary for the teacher to help in the desensitization process that must occur for the child to overcome being a "cripple." He may need special help in learning how to get along with peers and in groups.

7. Above all, remember that the educational objectives are the same for any child. The goals must be set according to aptitudes and abilities considering only those limitations which must be imposed by the special health problem.

8. Help foster the child's personal development through encouraging him to think independently, become self-reliant and self-confident, and establish an adequate self-concept. He must learn to accept the limitations of his disability and learn to use his *abilities*.

9. Help toward becoming economically self-sufficient by directing him toward sound vocational goals and by placing demands on him to produce his best work in a competitive situation. Anything less will produce a youngster who is a passive recipient of life and will ill prepare him for a role personally, socially, and vocationally, in the adult world.

SELECTED BIBLIOGRAPHY

A HANDBOOK FOR PROGRAMS IN RESPIRATORY DISEASES, National Tuberculosis Assn., June 1960.

Abramson, David A., A STUDY OF THE HOME INSTRUC-
TION PROGRAM, Bureau of Educational Program Research
and Statistics, New York City, Board of Education, No. 156,
June 1960.

Brownell, Katherine Dodge, "Community Aspects of Rheumatic Fever," THE BULLETIN of St. Francis Hospital, Roslyn,
New York, January 1954.

Brownell, Katherine Dodge, "The Rheumatic Child in School,"
THE HEART BULLETIN, IX, July-August 1960, 71-74.

CHILDREN WITH SPECIAL HEALTH PROBLEMS, Report from National Tuberculosis and Health Assn., 1953.

Cruickshank, William M. and Johnson, G. Orville, EDUCA-
TION OF EXCEPTIONAL CHILDREN AND YOUTH, Prentice-Hall, Englewood Cliffs, 1958.

DEMONSTRATION AND RESEARCH PROJECT FOR
THE EFFECTIVENESS OF A COMPREHENSIVE PRE-VO-
CATIONAL PROGRAM IN ENHANCING THE READINESS
OF PHYSICALLY AND EMOTIONALLY HANDICAPPED
HIGH SCHOOL STUDENTS FOR VOCATIONAL TRAIN-
ING AND EMPLOYMENT, Federation of the Handicapped,
New York, Annual Reports I and II and an unpublished study of
a group of Asthmatic Adolescents, 1959, 1960.

EXTENT OF RESPIRATORY DISEASE, National Tuberculosis Assn., Division of Research and Statistics, C-799, April
12, 1960.

Fenton, Joseph and Connor, Frances P., "Children with Crippling Conditions and Special Health Problems," EXCEPTIONAL
CHILDREN, XXV, September 1958-May 1959, 257-262, 277-278.

Frampton, Merle E. and Gall, Elena D., SPECIAL EDUCA-
TION FOR THE EXCEPTIONAL, Vol. II, Porter Sargent,
Boston, 1955.

HEART DISEASE IN CHILDREN, American Heart Assn.,
rev. April 1959.

Kubicek, William G., Kottke, Frederic J., Danz, Jean N., "Cardiac
Demands of Rehabilitation: Variability of Metabolic and Cardiac
Demand in Hospital Activity," UNIVERSITY OF MINNESOTA
MEDICAL BULLETIN, XXVIII, December 1956.

Lawrence, Edna M., A SEVEN YEAR PLOT STUDY OF
VOCATIONAL COUNSELING FOR CHILDREN WITH
HEART DISEASE OR A HISTORY OF RHEUMATIC

FEVER, Vocational Advisory Service, New York City, December 1956.

Lincoln, Edith M., "Indications for Treatment of Primary Tuberculosis in Children," BULLETIN OF THE NEW YORK ACADEMY OF MEDICINE, XXII, July 1956, 509-516.

Rusalem, Herbert, "The Habilitation Role of the Special Educator," REHABILITATION LITERATURE, XX, December 1959, 355-361.

JEAN LOUISE BLOOM is Coordinator of a Special Pre-Vocational Research and Demonstration Project for Homebound High School Students at the Federation of the Handicapped, New York. She received both her B.S. degree in Nursing and her M.Ed. in Guidance and Counseling from the University of Maryland, as well as a Professional Diploma in Rehabilitation Counseling from Teachers College, Columbia University. She formerly was Director of Rehabilitation at the Queensboro Tuberculosis and Health Association and has held various teaching positions at Hunter College in New York and at the University of Maryland in Baltimore, Maryland. She is a contributor to the recently released United States Office of Vocational Rehabilitation Textbook on Comprehensive Rehabilitation Services to the Homebound Disabled.

NOTES

1. Fenton, Joseph and Connor, Frances P., Children with Crippling Conditions and Special Health Problems, EXCEPTIONAL CHILDREN, XXV, Sept. 1958-May 1959, 257.

2. Abramson, David A., A STUDY OF THE INSTRUCTION PROGRAM, Bureau of Education, Div. Program Research and Statistics, N. Y. City Board of Education, No. 156, June 1960, 13.

3. Brownell, Katherine Dodge, "Community Aspects of Rheumatic Fever," THE BULLETIN of St. Francis Hospital, Roslyn, N. Y., January 1954, 29.

4. Kubicek, William G., Kottke, Frederic J. Danz, Jean N., "Cardiac Demands of Rehabilitation," UNIVERSITY OF MINNESOTA MEDICAL BULLETIN, XXVIII, December 1956, 12.

5. Lawrence, Edna M., A SEVEN YEAR PILOT STUDY OF VOCATIONAL COUNSELING FOR CHILDREN WITH HEART DISEASE OR A HISTORY OR RHEUMATIC FEVER, Vocational Advisory Service, N. Y. City, December 1956, 4, 7.

6. Brownell, Katherine Dodge, "The Rheumatic Child in School," THE HEART BULLETIN, IX, July-August 1960, 72.

7. IBID., 71.

8. EXTENT OF RESPIRATORY DISEASE, National Tuberculosis Assn., Div. of Research and Statistics, C*799, April 1960, 10.

9. IBID., 12.

10. DEMONSTRATION AND RESEARCH PROJECT FOR THE EFFECTIVENESS OF A COMPREHENSIVE PRE-VOCATIONAL PROGRAM IN ENHANCING THE READINESS OF PHYSICALLY AND EMOTIONALLY HANDICAPPED HOMEBOUND HIGH SCHOOL STUDENTS FOR VOCATIONAL TRAINING AND EMPLOYMENT, Federation of the Handicapped, 2nd Annual Report, 5.

11. IBID, First Annual Report, p. 53.

12. Rusalem, Herbert, "The Habilitation Role of the Special Educator," REHABILITATION LITERATURE, XX, December 1959, 356.

HEARING PROBLEMS IN CHILDREN

E. W. Johnson

Otologic Medical Group, Los Angeles, California

NATURE OF THE PROBLEM

Hearing losses in children produce communication defects. The hearing loss and its severity, together with its time of onset (whether congenital or adventitious), will largely determine the adjustment or maladjustment of the child to a hearing world.

Almost any hearing loss that involves both ears will have its effect upon the speech and language development of the child. A very slight loss may result in only a small amount of defective speech. A severe or profound loss will completely block normal development of speech. The development of speech sounds and their formulation into meaningful words is dependent upon the ability to hear those speech sounds as spoken by others and to monitor those sounds produced by one's self. The hearing child between his first and second birthday attaches a certain amount of significance to the speech of others, and experiments with vocalizing many speech sounds himself. During this period, he strives to produce meaningful words. Between the second and the fifth birthdays, there is rapid growth of speech and language so long as he can hear the speech of others and can monitor his own efforts at reproduction. Without this ability to hear, or with an imperfect hearing mechanism, the child may be discouraged in his babbling efforts and in the attempt to formulate meaningful words. Therefore, in any case of retarded speech development there is reason to investigate more fully the possibility of a loss of hearing. This does not imply that all retarded speech is due to hearing impairment. Retarded speech may be caused by any one of a number of conditions, including mental deficiency, emotional trauma, aphasia, as well as a defective hearing mechanism.

A loss of hearing in one ear will not, in itself, result in retardation of speech. A total impairment of one ear will have little or no effect on acquisition of speech sounds and development of language, providing the other ear is normal. This is not to say that a child with unilateral hearing will have normal responses to speech in all situations. On the contrary, this child will have difficulty understanding some parts of speech wherever there is high-level background noise. The raucous playground, the noisy lunchroom and the roar of traffic all present special problems of discrimination of speech for the child with unilateral hearing loss. Fortunately, however, one normal ear is enough to develop normal speech and language.

It is not neccessary nor is it advisable to wait for the normal period of time required for development of speech and language to question the possibility of hearing loss. Through careful observation and through the use of gross tests, the parents are often able to discern the lack of response to sound stimuli at a very early age. In early infancy, a failure to respond to normal environmental sounds may indicate a hearing loss. The child that instantly reacts to light stimuli but makes no apparent response to noises in the nursery may arouse the parent's suspicion of hearing impairment. Simple tests such as loudly calling the child's name, clapping the hands, shaking a rattle, or hitting two pans together, may give some indication of lack of response to sound. Care must be taken that such gross tests are administered outside of the visual field of the child. If the child does not turn toward the source of the sound or if there is no eye blink or physical reaction noted when the sound is made, it may indicate a loss of hearing.

CAUSES OF HEARING LOSS IN CHILDREN

The cause of a hearing loss has an important bearing on the type of impairment that results. At the risk of over-simplification, it is convenient to categorize types of loss as primarily sensori-neural or primarily conductive. In order to understand the meaning of these two terms, it is necessary to consider briefly the function of the normal ear. The ear is divided into three parts: an external ear, a middle ear, and an inner ear. (See Figure 1.)

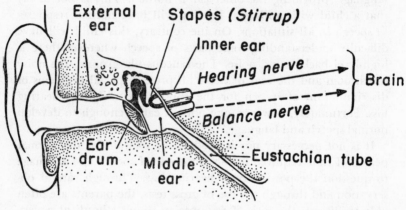

Figure 1.

All of these parts must perform their normal functions to produce accurate hearing. Acoustic stimuli must be transmitted from the sound source by means of sound waves that pass through the canal of the external ear and set the ear drum into vibration. The bony chain of three small ossicles attached to the drumhead at one end and to the footplate of the stapes at the other end transmits the energy of the sound vibrations to the inner ear fluids. The result of the sound impulses striking the ear drum is activation of the fluid filled inner ear and the consequent firing of the nerve impulses. These nerve impulses are then transmitted along a complex neural pathway to the brain and are there interpreted as sound. If there is some impairment of the hearing mechanism affecting the external or the middle ear, the resulting problem is called a conductive hearing loss. If the lesion, however, involves the inner ear and/or the neural pathways to the higher centers of the brain, this is

110

generally termed a sensorineural hearing loss. Sometimes there may be problems in the middle ear and in the inner ear resulting in a mixed type hearing loss, partly conductive and partly sensorineural in nature. Most conductive type hearing losses are amenable to surgical or medical treatment. Children with this type of loss are also very good users of a hearing aid in most cases and present relatively simple problems of rehabilitation. On the other hand, the perceptive or nerve type of loss is not suitable for surgery at the present time. Individuals with this type of loss often have difficulty in using a hearing aid and present far greater problems of rehabilitation.

Fortunately the most common cause of hearing loss in children is a conductive problem that is remedial through medical and surgical treatment. A blocking of the external canal by impacted ear wax, or infections or effusions of the middle ear can often be corrected with complete restoration of hearing through treatment. There are other types of conductive hearing losses in children that are congenital in origin. Certain anomalies that are developmental in nature may cause malformations of the middle and external ears. A child may be born without an ear canal or outer ear. In such cases, there is very often a normally functioning inner ear. Through surgery a new pathway may be created to the inner ear so that hearing may be restored. In some instances, there may be a normal external ear but a congenital abnormality of one or more of the little ossicles of the middle ear. Again this may be satisfactorily managed through surgery in many cases. In all of the conductive cases enumerated above, if the hearing cannot be restored after adequate medical treatment or if surgical procedures are not desired, a well fitted hearing aid together with speech reading and correction of deviate speech sounds will normally result in excellent rehabilitation of the child.

Sensorineural hearing losses in children may be due to a number of causes, most of them congenital in origin. In many instances, it is extremely difficult to pinpoint the cause of the hearing loss. In most cases of this type, some residual hearing is present. Fortunately, the child who is unable to respond to any sound

111

stimulus is very rare. In most instances, the residual hearing present in the congenitally impaired young child will remain essentially unchanged throughout life. In a few cases, however, there is progressive loss of hearing resulting in diminution of hearing levels related to the maturation of the child. In some instances, although there is no marked hearing loss at birth, there is apparently an hereditary weakness that makes these individuals susceptible to further hearing loss in later life. Such susceptibility may account for hearing losses due to excessive noise exposure. This may also account for many of the sudden losses associated with certain types of infection including measles, mumps, etc.

Another fairly common cause of congenital perceptive loss is a disease known as erythroblastosis. This disease is the result of the incompatibility of the infant's blood with the mother's blood (the Rh factor). This may cause cerebral palsy, lesions of the central nervous system (including the hearing centers in the cortex) as well as impairment in the inner ear itself. In some instances, premature birth, especially if associated with lack of oxygen (hypoxia) may result in severe perceptive hearing loss. Another common cause of perceptive loss in children is maternal viral infections during the first three months of pregnancy. It is a well known fact that German measles is very often the cause of developmental changes in the fetus including impairment of the organ of Corti (inner ear) and resulting in a perceptive loss of hearing.

There are further categories of perceptive loss in children that are adventitious rather than congenital in origin. Examples in this group are losses due to spinal meningitis, and viral infections that result in high fevers and/or convulsions. Prognosis for rehabilitation in this group is dependent upon the age of the child at the onset of the disease. If language and speech are well established prior to the illness, the chances are much better for maintaining good speech and for more normal language development. If the illness occurs before speech has developed, the problems are comparable to the habilitation problems of the congenitally deaf child.

112

MANAGEMENT OF HEARING PROBLEMS

The preceding discussion has been concerned with different types of organic hearing loss and their various causes. While it is true that deaf children will fail to respond to speech and auditory stimuli, it does not follow that all children that fail to make such responses have actual organic losses. In some instances, young children will recognize sound and speech but are unable to speak themselves or may have greatly retarded or infantile speech. Many of these children are suffering from early emotional trauma and should be referred to qualified speech therapists and child psychologists for proper management of their problems. A related problem known as psychic deafness is one in which the young child rejects all auditory stimulation, even at high intensity levels, although the hearing mechanism is functioning without impairment. Again this type of problem must be referred to the child psychiatrist or clinical psychologist. Sometimes a mentally deficient child is presumed to have a hearing loss. These youngsters are very slow to develop motor functions and slow to integrate speech and environmental sound and, therefore, slow to develop speech patterns.

There is another large group of children that has only been briefly mentioned up to this point. Some of these may be considered to fall within the definition of organic hearing loss since the lesions may occur in the auditory-neural tract running from the endorgan of hearing up to the higher centers. In most instances, however, it would appear that the lesions are in the cortical centers resulting in certain types of language disorders stemming from damage to the brain itself. This problem may manifest itself as (1) an inability on the part of the child to comprehend the spoken word, (2) an inability to use speech (3) an inability to use language in any meaningful way, or (4) a combination of these difficulties. These children are able to hear speech sounds as such but the signals are received in a jumbled fashion and they are unable to integrate the sound impulses into any meaningful pattern. These children are often mis-diagnosed as perceptive losses involving the endorgan of hearing and are presumed to be deaf. It is possible in some situations that there is both a loss of hearing in the periphery organ as well as along the auditory tracts or in the cortical centers. It would appear likely that many of the children that have been considered essentially perceptively deaf have at least some degree of central nervous system involvement as well.

In order to successfully rehabilitate this child, it is essential that as accurate a differential diagnosis as possible be made of the problem. This is sometimes a very complex and difficult task. Ideally a team approach should be made involving the otolaryngologist, the audiologist, the pediatrician, the neurologist, the speech therapist, the child psychiatrist, and the clinical psychologist. Obviously not all children who present the same complaint of lack of speech need be subjected to this inter-disciplinary evaluation. Careful observations of the behavioral patterns of the child may give some clues as to the true nature of the difficulty. Problems other than organic hearing loss may be suspected in a child who exhibits traits such as bizarre emotional behavior, insensitivity to tactual sensations and disregard of gestures. On the other hand, if the child's vocalization is non-rhythmic and non-melodious, if he is sensitive to vibration, and if he tends to watch faces and interpret gestures, there is reason to believe he has an organic hearing loss. The remainder of this chapter will be devoted to consideration of remedial steps for this child with either conductive or perceptive impairment of the hearing mechanism.

In the great majority of conductive-type hearing problems, careful otologic management will result in normal hearing for the child. In those cases that are not amenable to medical or surgical treatment, or where treatment has not restored normal hearing, the child may be rehabilitated relatively easily. This is accomplished through the use of properly fitted hearing aids together with the guidance and counseling of a clinical audiologist. A purely conductive hearing loss will rarely exceed a level of forty to forty-five decibels. Good hearing aids, particularly if binaural fitting is employed, will be able to shift the hearing level to within an essentially normal range. There will, of course, be an interval of time necessary to learn to adjust to the use of a hearing aid. The guidance and counseling necessary to make this adjustment can best be facilitated through a trained audiologist. If there are some deviate speech sounds present, it may also be necessary to obtain the help of a speech therapist. So far as the conductive loss is concerned, however, the rehabilitation problem is usually a relatively simple matter and the prognosis for excellent adjustment in a hearing world is very good indeed.

The habilitation of the congenitally perceptive impaired child is a much more complex and lengthy procedure. Success of habilitation is dependent upon the type of the loss (that is to say the pattern of residual hearing) and the severity of the loss. To make this discussion meaningful, it is necessary to define terms simply and to explain the audiogram.

The human ear is capable of distinguishing a tremendous number of pitch differences. Whether we hear a sound as low pitch, medium pitch or high pitch is dependent upon the number of vibrations of the sound wave in a given unit of time (one second). Thus, a sound wave that consists of only a few cycles per second is perceived as a low-pitch sound and a wave that vibrates many times per second is recognized as a high-pitch sound. It is essential that we differentiate the terms "pitch" and "frequency." Pitch perception is a psychological phenomenon whereas frequency is a physical measurement of the rate of vibration of the molecules transmitting the sound waves. We hear "pitch" and not "frequency". A normal ear is capable of detecting as few as approximately twenty vibrations per second up to approximately 16,000 vibrations per second. Only a small part of this vast range is of importance as far as speech is concerned. Most audiometers used to test hearing loss are capable of presenting a pure tone at intervals of an octave or one-half octave from 125 cycles per second through 8,000 cycles per second. The frequencies that are normally tested on the audiometer are 250 cycles through 8,000 cycles. The areas of greatest importance so far as speech is concerned are the frequencies of 500, 1000, and 2000 cycles per second. These three frequencies are often referred

115

to as the speech frequencies. If the child hears well at these three frequencies, he will usually understand speech well and will be able to develop good speech and language. It is very important, therefore, to have a frequency by frequency record of the hearing loss of the child in order to determine the problems of habilitation.

The second dimension of hearing that we are concerned with in plotting the audiogram is the intensity at which the signal must be delivered in order for the child to just barely hear the sound stimuli. Most audiometers are calibrated to deliver a signal at varying intensity levels from minus ten to plus one hundred. The term "intensity" applies to a physical measurement of acoustic pressure. The child does not hear the "intensity" of the tone but rather its psychological counterpart that we call "loudness." It is important to realize that the zero line on the audiometer is not an absolute zero but represents the point where a large number of young adults could just barely perceive the tone produced by a given amount of acoustic energy.[1] Since this is an average figure, there are some better than average and some poorer than average that must be considered within normal brackets. Therefore, minus ten to approximately plus fifteen on the audiometer is considered essentially normal hearing. It is also important to realize that the steps on the audiometer are not linear but are logarithmic. Consequently, the amount of energy involved in making the change from zero to five is vastly different than the five db step from forty-five to fifty, etc. Since a logarithmic progression would be very difficult to express in easily understandable terminology, a method of showing the relative steps on the audiometer called the decibel, was employed. It should be remembered that the ratio from zero to one hundred decibels is not a relationship in terms of one to one hundred but is more in the nature of one to one million. It can be readily understood that the tremendously greater increments of acoustic pressure necessary to reach the child with a severe loss who responds only at the outer limits of the audiometer, will vastly increase the problem of adequately fitting the child with hearing aids. It was pointed out, a moment ago, that normal hearing youngsters may

116

fall anywhere from minus ten to approximately plus fifteen decibels. If they fall in the range from plus fifteen to approximately thirty decibels, they will not have normal hearing but will be able to get by in most situations without very much difficulty. Thirty decibels is often regarded as the outer limit of serviceable hearing. In other words, a loss greater than thirty decibels requires the use of amplification in order to communicate in an essentially normal fashion. Losses that fall between thirty decibels and approximately seventy decibels may usually be fitted adequately with a hearing aid provided the loss is fairly equal throughout the frequency range. If the child has normal hearing in the low tones and then drops off sharply through the middle of the speech range and into the higher frequencies, many more problems will be encountered in the use of an aid. Losses of hearing that fall between the seventy decibel level and the one hundred decibel level will greatly increase the problems of using an aid and will require the use of speech reading, auditory training and speech correction.

Children with a hearing loss that follows a ski drop pattern, with essentially normal hearing in the lower part of the speech range and a steep drop-off through the middle and higher frequencies, will hear some parts of speech perfectly well and will not hear at all, other parts of speech. These children will hear all of the vowel sounds and perhaps some of the consonant sounds, while other consonant sounds will be inaudible (particularly the voiceless consonants). Since they cannot hear the consonants, they will not learn to reproduce the sounds without the expert attention of the speech therapist. They will also experience considerable difficulty in understanding the teacher's speech. This is particularly true if she turns her back to write on the board, or frequently moves around the room, and deprives them of the opportunity of speech reading. They will hear many sounds loudly enough, particularly background noises, and some of the parts of speech. They will, however, have considerable difficulty in differentiating certain sounds and will not understand speech, unless they can also employ speech reading. Until fairly recently there were very few hearing aids available that could do much, if any, good for this type of hearing loss. During the past year, a number of aids have been developed with relatively little amplification in the low tones and greatly increased amplification in the higher frequencies that seem to be promising for many of these children. It is essential to provide auditory training, speech reading and speech correction for these children in addition to a carefully selected hearing aid.

Many children with congenital perceptive losses that fall within the moderate to severe range (thirty to seventy-five decibels) may be fitted with hearing aids. If they are also provided with adequate instruction in speech reading they may be able to function on an essentially normal communication basis. Many of these children if given parental help plus outside tutoring in speech, are able to keep up with the normal educational program of hearing children.

When the hearing loss exceeds seventy-five decibels, problems of habilitation are tremendously increased. It is a rare occasion when the sound field threshold for speech can be shifted more than forty to forty-five decibels by a hearing aid. Very often the shift in threshold will be more in the nature of thirty decibels. One can see, therefore, that if the speech threshold unaided is seventy-five decibels or greater, an ideal hearing aid fitting would still leave the child short of what we term the serviceable limits of hearing. With this group of children, it is essential that we have (1) carefully selected hearing aids, (2) auditory training to assist with sound differentiation and to help in adjusting to the use of the aid, (3) trained teachers of the deaf to assist with speech reading and speech correction. As we approach the outer limits of the audiometer, the messages transmitted through the hearing aids become more sketchy and less effective, the problems of teaching speech are increased and greatly prolonged, and the prognosis for effectve communication becomes less and less.

The next group that concerns us is the group of congenitally deaf children who give no response to any frequencies tested with the audiometer even at maximum levels of amplification, or the profoundly deaf children who have only small islands of residual hearing. These children may respond at only two or three fre-

118

quencies at the outer limits of the audiometer. Fortunately, the first mentioned group is very rare. Nearly all profoundly deaf children will respond at least at one or two frequencies within the limits of testing equipment.

Children with such minimal residual hearing are obviously limited in the use of a hearing aid. The help that they can receive from a hearing aid is much different from the gains to be expected for the child with hearing responses at all frequencies through the speech range. Some of these children with tiny islands of hearing may still get a part of certain speech sounds (the vowel sounds) but will not be able to pick up other parts of speech (consonants) or understand words or phrases by hearing alone. These children are primarily dependent upon their ability to speech read and without development of this ability will remain a world apart from their hearing playmates.

This is not to say that these children should not wear hearing aids. On the contrary, it is extremely important that they wear aids to prevent them from living in a world of isolation. In spite of the fact that the hearing aids will not reproduce speech as we know it, they receive many clues through the hearing aid that enable them to become better speech readers. Furthermore, the constant bombardment of environmental sound makes them more a part of everyday living situations. Instead of withdrawing into a lonely life of isolation, they are more easily included in normal family relationships and experiences. In addition, the use of hearing aids helps with the monitoring of their own voice. It also helps these children to develop better rhythm patterns of speech.

The final group that merits our attention is the group of adventitious perceptive losses. Help for this group varies greatly depending upon the age of the child when inflicted with the disease or illness causing the hearing loss. If the onset of illness is prior to the development of speech and language and if the resulting loss is severe or profound, then habilitation steps must follow the program outlined above for the profoundly deaf congenital loss. If the disease is at a period following the development of language and speech and is severe in nature, the audiologist and the speech therapist assume the main role in rehabilitation. Every effort is made to utilize whatever residual hearing there is through carefully selected hearing aids. As soon as this first step is accomplished, the major emphasis is then placed upon maintaining the speech and language that had developed before the illness. The danger is that the child who is unable to hear consonant sounds will after a period of time no longer be able to reproduce them either. The teaching of speech reading is absolutely essential for good communication for these children. This will be a never ending process that must be followed throughout their school careers. The adventitious perceptive loss that is mild or moderately severe, may of course, be reached through properly fitted hearing aids and through the other steps of rehabilitation as mentioned previously.

In all the foregoing discussion, there has been considerable emphasis placed on the use of well-fitted hearing aids. There are differences in hearing and differences in the ways in which hard-of-hearing children will use the different aids. It is important that a trained clinical audiologist give guidance in the selection of the best aids possible for the individual child with his particular hearing loss. It is also the opinion of this author that there are many advantages in using two hearing aids (true binaural hearing) for most children, with the possible exception of the youngsters with sharply sloping ski-drop losses. There are no carefully controlled studies to either confirm or deny this thesis. This is a clinical judgment based on working with many children over a period of years. There are some generally accepted facts applicable in most instances. We do know that in most cases the use of carefully selected binaural aids will result in a favorable shift of the speech threshold by anywhere from six to twelve decibels over the use of a monaural aid. We know also that it is essential to have two approximately balanced ears in order to locate the source of sound. Location cannot be determined with one ear alone. Consequently, monaural use of aids, in ears that are relatively balanced without amplification precludes the possibility of sound localization. It would appear, however, that the use of binaural aids has many additional advantages related to the ability to pick out the speech signal from a background of noise. Obviously, we do not live in a silent world; we live in a noisy world. With classroom noises, outside street and traffic noises and many other noises competing with speech, it is vitally important to insure as much clarity as possible for the speech signal. We want to provide hearing impaired children with every advantage to aid in the development of speech and language. The application of true binaural hearing means two separate microphones, amplifiers and receivers and not a Y-cord with two receivers from a single instrument. The Y-cord arrangement splits the incoming signal between the two ears and may be of some advantage in some cases, but it is not delivering true binaural hearing.

No mention has been made of the ideal time to begin working with the child. It should be emphasized that the time should be as early as is feasible depending upon the nature of the problem. In the case of the adventitious loss, the rehabilitation process should start as soon as it is possible following recovery from the illness. In the case of the congenital loss, some steps may be taken at a very early age level. In some instances, hearing loss may be confirmed in the child of a very few months, up to his first birthday. This is not too young to begin the use of hearing aids provided a differential diagnosis can be made. The important point is that it should be established beyond a reasonable doubt that this is a hearing loss and not some other problem. Once this can be ascertained, it is not necessary to wait until we can get threshold measurements to put on hearing aids. It is enough to know that the loss is mild or severe or profound to procede with binaural hearing aids. It is especially important that the hearing aid be available to the child during the early phases of babbling and vocalization and during the first attempts at beginning speech. If he is able to hear his own voice as well as the voices of others, he will be encouraged to continue the vocalization. This child will develop much more rapidly than the youngster who does not have the hearing aids until after the normal period of babbling and early speech development has passed.

The nursery school teacher or the elementary teacher faced

with the problem of lack of speech or defective speech may well raise the question of possible hearing impairment in the child. Most public school systems, at least in the larger communities, provide for a program of hearing testing. These tests are usually screening tests rather than threshold measurements of hearing. If a child fails to pass the simple screening tests, or if there are any questions regarding the responses to the tests, professional consultation should be utilized. Referral to an Otologist or oto-audiological center is the first step in the rehabilitative process. Subsequent referrals to the various specialists for a careful differential diagnosis may be indicated in some cases. Once the diagnosis has been made and the habilitative or rehabilitative process started, there are several ways in which the classroom teacher can lend valuable support.

In the first place, a knowledge of the type and severity of the loss will give some indication as to the length and degree of difficulty of the remedial steps involved. If a hearing aid is about to be introduced for the first time, the teacher can pave the way to general class acceptance by discussing the use of the hearing aid *before* the child brings it to class. It is neither possible nor desirable to completely conceal the wearing of an aid. Therefore, if the class is informed of the fact that "Johnny" is going to wear a hearing aid to enable him to hear better, just as "Susie" now wears glasses to make her see better, we have one step toward general acceptance. When Johnny finally arrives one day with the aids there will be much natural curiosity. If he permits (with the teacher's approval and supervision) the inspection of the aids and earmolds, he will find classroom adjustment relatively painless. This is also the ideal time to present a simple explanation of what a hearing aid is, how it works, and what it is expected to do for Johnny. On the other hand, if teacher and Johnny try to ignore or conceal the new aids, there may be many problems ahead.

Secondly, the teacher may help this child by arranging seating near the front of the class. The reason for this move is to enable the child to easily speech-read the teacher and to see the blackboard as advantageously as possible.

122

Thirdly, the teacher must remember to face Johnny when giving class assignments or explaining lesson details. Again, depending on the type and severity of the loss, the speech-reading may be the most essential element in communication with the child.

Finally, the teacher may be of great service by maintaining liaison (1) with the clinical audiologist (regarding the use and adjustment of the aids), (2) with the speech therapist (regarding lesson materials to motivate speech correction and/or development), (3) with the clinical psychologist (regarding emotional adjustment or behavioral problems), and finally, (4) with the parents (to enlighten regarding progress but also to direct for home-help).

Only through the early recognition of the problem, through the referral to the proper agencies and through the continued sympathetic management by the teacher, can we hope for maximum adjustment of the hearing impaired child to the hearing world.

SUMMARY

Hearing loss in children may be conveniently divided into tive type of impairment is usually amenable to medical or sur- sensorineural type of loss or conductive type of loss. The conduc- gical treatment. A child with this type of loss is ordinarily a very good user of a hearing aid and is a relatively simple problem of rehabilitation. Referral of the child with this type of loss to the oto-audiological center will usually result in complete restoration of normal communication.

Children with sensorineural type of hearing loss present many more problems for successful habilitation. This type of loss might be due to either congenital or adventitious etiology. If the child has acquired good speech and language prior to the onset of the disease resulting in the sensorineural loss, he will probably be successfully rehabilitated. If the loss is congenital in origin, and if it is severe, then we cannot expect normal speech and language, but we may anticipate effective communication as the result of maximum habilitative measures.

The effective use of hearing aids must be related to the type and severity of the hearing problem. Most of the children with conductive hearing losses may achieve essentially normal communication through the use of hearing aids. In the sensorineural losses there are often problems of understanding and intolerance to loud noises and background sounds. If the loss is severe, normal speech thresholds cannot be anticipated. Hearing aids are recommended, however, even though speech sounds cannot be clearly transmitted by the aids. Even the profoundly deaf child with a small amount of residual hearing may benefit from the use of hearing aids in various ways.

A guiding principle in the use of hearing aids with children is to begin the use of the aids as soon as possible (whenever the diagnosis of hearing loss can be made) and that both ears be used for true binaural hearing whenever feasible. The clinical audiologist and the speech therapist have important roles to play in the selection of the hearing aids, in assisting with auditory training, and in giving instructions in lip reading and in speech correction.

The classroom teacher whether preschool, nursery, or elementary, has an important role to play in the early discovery of hearing problems in young children and in the referral of these children to the proper agencies.

SELECTED BIBLIOGRAPHY

Canfield, Norton, HEARING. Doubleday and Company, Inc., Garden City, New York, 1959. A discussion of the medical, psychological, economic and social problems of the hearing-handicapped.

Carhart, Ray, "A Practical Approach to the Selection of Hearing Aids," TRANSACTIONS OF THE AMERICAN ACADEMY OF OPHTHALMOLOGY AND OTOLARYNGOLOGY, Volume 50, 1946, 123-131. This article is concerned with principles and methods of hearing aid evaluations.

Gesell, Arnold, and Catherine Amatruda, DEVELOPMENTAL

DIAGNOSIS. Paul B. Hoeber, Inc., New York, N. Y., 1952. A valuable reference regarding growth and development of the child. This work includes a chapter on hearing and deafness in infants.

Glorig, Aram Jr., NOISE AND YOUR EAR. Grune and Stratton, New York, New York, 1958. This slim volume contains a thorough, easy to understand discussion of ear anatomy, basic audiometry and psychoacoustics.

House, Howard P., "Management of Congenital Ear Canal Atresia," THE LARYNGOSCOPE, Volume 63, Number 10, October 1953, 916-946. This article is concerned with the surgical correction of congenital ear canal atresia.

Johnson, Eddie W., AN ELECTROENCEPHALOGRAPHIC STUDY OF FRUSTRATION IN DEAF AND NORMAL HEARING CHILDREN (unpublished Doctor's dissertation, the University of Southern California), 1955. An investigation into the responses of deaf and normal hearing children when confronted with frustration.

Morkovin, Boris, THROUGH THE BARRIERS OF DEAF-NESS AND ISOLATION. The Macmillan Company, New York, New York, 1952. This book contains many practical suggestions for helping hearing-impaired children. An excellent orientation for parents and teachers.

Myklebust, Helmer, AUDITORY DISORDERS IN CHIL-DREN. Grune and Stratton, New York, New York, 1954. A comprehensive manual for differential diagnosis.

Myklebust, Helmer, YOUR DEAF CHILD. Charles C. Thomas, Springfield, Illinois, 1950. A book written expressly for the parents of young deaf children.

Newby, Hayes A., AUDIOLOGY. Appleton-Century-Crofts, Inc., New York, New York, 1958. A comprehensive text and reference book on audiology, its principles and practices.

O'Neil, John J., and Herbert J. Oyer, VISUAL COMMUNI-CATION FOR THE HARD OF HEARING. Prentice-Hall, Inc., Englewood Cliffs, New Jersey, 1961. A new approach to lip reading methods and materials.

Sortini, Adam J., "Speech Audiometry Testing for Pre-School Children," THE LARYNGOSCOPE, Volume 63, Number 10, October 1953. A discussion of the basic methods of speech testing for small children.

E. W. JOHNSON, chief clinical audiologist for the Otologic Medical Group of Los Angeles; Instructor, School of Medicine, University of Southern California. Member of the American Speech and Hearing Association. ASHA certification in hearing. B.A. 1939, Gustavus Adophus College, St. Peter, Minnesota; M.A. 1953, University of Southern California; Ph.D. 1956, University of Southern California.

NOTES

1. The American Standard Reference Zero for normal hearing for pure tones is based upon mean values for 12,000 audiograms for individuals considered to have normal hearing. This study was carried out by United States Public Health Service in 1935 and 1936. The Audiometric Reference Zero is in terms of 0.0002 dynes per square cm.

THE BLIND, PARTIALLY SEEING, AND COLOR WEAK

Robert M. Frumkin and Miriam Zisenwine Frumkin
State University of New York (Oswego)

When one comes to the realization that about 85 percent of the contacts of normal persons are made through the medium of vision, one then gains some insight concerning the impact defective vision might have on various aspects of human behavior. The educational achievements, and the psychological and social adjustments of individuals might all be influenced, therefore, by defective vision, depending on the degree and nature of the impairment.

Birdwhistell and others have noted the significance of vision in nonverbal communication.[1] The kinesic (nonverbal) aspects of communication dependent on vision are so important that normal socialization is often, if not always, endangered by defective vision. It has been suggested by Birdwhistell, for example, that about one-third, and, in some cases, as much as two-thirds, of the *meaning* of ordinary verbal communications is conveyed through nonverbal (kinesic) behavior which must be seen in order to be interpreted.[2] That young children learn language through visual imitation as well as auditory imitation of adults and older children is evident to any alert adult who has reared or worked intensively with young children. And that they learn numerous other desirable (and undesirable) habits from visual imitation is likewise quite evident.[3] Much of the stilted nature of the language of those with defective vision and certain of their numerous mannerisms are directly traceable to the fact

127

that their visual handicap has prevented the kind of visual social interaction which the sighted individuals too often take for granted.

The purposes of this chapter are: (1) To summarize the research on three visual handicaps, namely, blindness, partial sightedness, and color weakness; (2) To make constructive suggestions for teachers, social workers, and other persons who have the responsibility of dealing with the problems of these types of unusual children, the blind, the partially sighted, and the color weak.

DEFINITION OF IMPORTANT TERMS

Blindness. It has been noted in the literature that blindness is a severe but inexactly defined degree of visual defectiveness. A complete inability to perceive light might be called absolute blindness. Practically, however, this is a useless definition because a much less severe degree than this makes it impossible for an individual to make adequate visual adjustments. The National Association for the Prevention of Blindness defines the blind child as one who ". . . has central visual acuity of 20/200 or less in the better eye, with correcting glasses; or central visual acuity of more than 20/200 if there is a field defect in which the peripheral field has contracted to such an extent that the widest diameter of visual field subtends an angular distance no greater than 20 degrees." [4] Visual acuity, the efficiency of the eye in terms of how well it sees, is expressed as a ratio between the distance which a blind person sees letters on a chart and the distance at which a sighted person can see them. Normal vision is 20/20 whereas blindness is generally defined as 20/200 vision with 20 degrees of peripheral vision or less after correction. The 20/200 ratio means that what a normally sighted individual sees at 200 feet can be seen by the blind person only if he is within 20 feet of the object or some letter on a chart. For the purposes of this chapter, and to avoid confusion over technical terminology, let us define *blindness*

128

as *a visual handicap which makes it relatively impossible for an individual to use vision as the main channel of learning.*

Partial Sightedness. Partially seeing individuals have been defined as having ". . . visual acuity of 20/70 or less in the better eye after the best possible correction and who can use vision as the main channel of learning." [5] The partially seeing might also include other children who in the opinion of eye specialists will derive benefit from the special provisions for the partially seeing. Let us define *partial sightedness* as *a visual handicap which requires special educational provisions but which nevertheless permits the individual to use vision as the main channel of learning.*

Color Weakness. The term "color blindness" is a misnomer. A more accurate term for the color blindness phenomenon is color weakness. *Color weakness* may be defined as *a visual handicap which is a result of a diminished sensitivity to certain portions of the spectrum and makes it impossible, difficult, and/or exceedingly dangerous for an individual to engage in certain activities and occupations which require normal sensitivity to colors perceived by normally sighted individuals.*[6]

SOME BASIC INFORMATION ABOUT VISUAL ACUITY

As suggested earlier, visual acuity refers to the efficiency of the eye, that is, how well it sees. Refractive errors, opacities of the cornea or lens, pathology of the retina, defects in the optic nerve, and other factors might all reduce visual acuity.

In studies of children in sight-saving classes it was found that refractive errors are of the greatest importance in producing a visual handicap.[7] By refractive errors we mean those errors in which the rays of light entering the eye are not properly focused upon the retinas.

The most common eye defects associated with refractive errors are myopia (nearsightedness), hyperopia (farsightedness), astigmatism, and asthenopia (eyestrain).

129

In myopia parallel rays are brought to focus in front of the retina when accommodation is relaxed. Myopia is considered by some eye experts to be a progressive disease which needs to be diagnosed early and checked regularly.[8]

In hyperopia the refraction of the relaxed lens brings rays to focus behind the retina. While it is not progressive, and tends to be reduced with age, too much near vision puts great stress on the eye muscles and results in fatigue and eyestrain for the hyperopic individual.

Astigmatism is a condition caused by defect in the lens of cornea which results in a difference in refraction in different meridians, that is, some rays focus before, some behind, and some on the retina. Uncorrected astigmatism causes a great deal of eyestrain.

Asthenopia also leads to reduction in visual acuity. Due to refractive errors and other conditions it is manifested by some of the following signs and symptoms: (1) headache and sick headache; (2) rapid fatigue of the eyes during reading, writing, and other close work; (3) pain in the eyes; (4) blurring of print; (5) feeling of sand in the eyes; (6) tendency to rub and press on eyeballs; (7) redness of the edges of the lids; (8) accumulation of bran-like masses on the edges of the lids; (9) double vision; (10) dread of light; (11) dizziness; (12) nausea; (13) floating spots before the eyes; (14) twitching of the lids; (15) a tendency to the development of sties in crops; etc.[9]

While simple or complicated refractive errors accounted for about two-thirds of children in sight-saving classes, about one quarter of these children had visual losses due to pathology of various parts of the eye. Among the more frequent types of pathologies associated with visual loss were: (1) cataracts (mostly congenital); (2) lenticular and corneal abnormalities resulting from injury or disease; (3) disease of the retina and choroid coat; (4) interstitial keratitis, a cellular infiltration of the deep layers of the cornea usually due to congenital syphilis.[10]

The various signs and symptoms of asthenopia or eyestrain are easily recognizable by the alert teacher, social worker, and adult dealing with children. Therefore the presence of any of these symptoms and/or signs should justify having special eye examinations made to determine the cause of the eyestrain and loss of visual acuity.

THE BLIND

Education. Using our definition of blindness, it has been estimated that about one out of every 5000 children in the United States of school age is blind.[11] In the 1954-55 school year there were about 7000 blind students in United States schools from grades kindergarten through high school.[12] About 85 percent of all blind children of school age receiving special education are attending residential schools for the blind, most of which are state supported.[13] The remainder are in schools for unusual (exceptional) children, or are integrated into or segregated in regular public or private schools.

Regardless of the type of educational setting a blind child is placed in, special methods of the education of the blind are of general significance. As Lowenfeld states: "Obviously, lack of sight necessitates certain adaptations in equipment and skills, particularly in the so-called tool subjects. Some standard procedures in this area are: braille reading and writing, the latter with stylus and slate or with a mechanical braille writer; typewriting, preferably from the third or fourth grade on; Talking Book use, as a supplementary reading medium to compensate somewhat for the slowness of braille reading; mental number work and use of an arithmetic slate as well as braille for computation; diagram drawings and use of solid, plane, and wire forms in geometry; maps either embossed or in relief for the teaching of geography. In the study of the sciences demonstrations and materials must appeal to the sense of touch, hearing, or smell if they are to be meaningful to the blind student. . . . Dramatic art activities . . . offer special opportunities for the correction of undesirable habits of posture, of standing and walking, of speaking, and various behavior patterns. Music is the art most widely associated with blindness . . . is recognized as perhaps the most important art activity of the blind." [14]

131

Industrial arts, from the beginning of the history of the education of the blind, has been significant because of its practical implications, that is, because such a large proportion of the blind are employed in such work as broom makers, chair caners, basket workers, weavers, carpet and rug makers, etc.[15] Physical education and recreation are also important parts of any good educational program for the blind.[16]

Lowenfeld lists five principles which are particularly important for the education of the blind: (1) *Individualization:* Classes for the blind should be kept small, 6 to 8 students on the elementary level, and up to about 12 on the secondary level. Considerations of the unique characteristics of each blind child is difficult or impossible in large classes. (2) *Concreteness:* It is only through touch that a blind child gains actual knowledge of the objects surrounding him, that is, knowledge of their shape, size, weight, hardness, texture, pliability, temperature, etc. Hearing has its greatest value as a means of receiving communications concerning objects. Concreteness in teaching helps the blind child to avoid falling into a pattern of unreality and verbalism which may prevent his realistic awareness of the world. Thus Eaton has been instrumental in developing a collection of "Objects of Beauty and Wonder from the Great Storehouse of Nature," a collection of objects enjoyable to the sighted and the blind. This collection, it is hoped, will encourage communication between the sighted and the blind in the appreciation and enjoyment of beauty.[17] (3) *Unified Instruction.* The blind child is at a disadvantage in not experiencing things and situations in their totality. The unit plan of instruction offers the best opportunity for unified instruction. Such units as the supermarket, the farm, the post office, etc., give blind children information which seeing children can be assumed to gain in the natural course of their growth. (4) *Additional Stimulation.* The teacher of blind children must provide them with opportunities for stimulating experiences which they cannot gain on their own. Field trips, study excursions, visits to museums, etc., help blind children by providing them with the stimulation which is commonplace to sighted children. How-

132

ever, it is essential that the teacher increase the blind child's ability to get about and secure stimulation by himself. As the blind child gets older, he should learn about all available aids in getting about, such as guide-dogs, human assistance, and coping with all means of transportation in his community. (5) *Self-activity.* Because a blind child cannot learn as do the sighted, through visual stimulation, training and guidance must meet and encourage the development of his maturing functions. The blind child must learn to do things for himself in order to avoid tendencies toward daydreaming, inactivity, and "blindisms" (awkward behavior patterns such as shaking the head rapidly, rubbing the eyes, etc.).[18]

Whether it be education for the blind in a residential school for the blind, in schools for unusual children, in segregated or integrated regular schools, or, even if it is home instruction, the general educational principles reviewed above are relevant. The general trend has been toward desegregating blind children both in special and regular schools. Integration of the blind in the regular classroom of regular schools seems the general goal which is encouraged by leaders in the education of the blind. The reasons for this stress on integration are basically of a psychological and sociological nature.

Personal, Social, and Vocational Adjustment. From a psychological perspective, it is essential that the blind child develop a concept of himself which is a healthy and realistic one. The blind child must be made to realize that he has a handicap but that it is a handicap which does not necessitate that he play throughout his life a deviant role, become an isolate, completely dependent, unemployable, etc. The individual's conception of his role and status is not rigidly determined by the degree of impairment of his vision. What is most significant is how he defines his role and status, what being blind means to him. So that blind children do not make a profession of dependency as blind adults, they must learn early in life the qualities of independence, self-reliance, etc., that make possible leading a relatively normal life in spite of the severe visual handicap that they must live with.

Sociologically, the adjustment of the blind child is significantly related to how his parents, teachers, peers, and the community in which he lives define his blindness and him as a blind person. Where parents overprotect the blind child he is almost sure to develop a strong pattern of egocentric behavior, to become skillful in manipulating others by trading on his handicap. Where the child is rejected he is likely to withdraw or react with strong aggression and hostility toward the world about him. Any program for the blind which segregates them, of course, in one respect always makes their adjustment more difficult. Segregation tends to increase the social distance between the blind and the sighted, to lessen communication and decrease mutual understanding, thereby tending to support outmoded myths and stereotypes about the blind which work against their becoming independent and well adjusted adults. There is too much of a tendency in our culture to pity the blind instead of trying to understand the nature of their handicap. This pity has taken the form of humanitarian programs which too often lead to greater rather than lesser dependence, increases rather than decreases the social distance between the blind and sighted, and tends to perpetuate stereotypes of the blind that interfere with their fullest participation in society.

One of the most important skills a blind child can learn is to travel, unaccompanied, or with the aid of a seeing-eye dog, from his home to various places in his community. His future occupational adjustment is, in large part, dependent on his developed independence and ability to travel around the community in which he lives with as little aid as possible. Although the blind are occupationally restricted by the nature of their handicap, the blind are found engaged in numerous occupations representing various levels of skills, training, etc. While a large proportion are engaged in the handicrafts, among the male blind are found a sizeable number of farmers, retail dealers, musicians and music teachers, clergymen, school teachers, and piano tuners; among the female blind, a fair number of seamstresses and fancy workers, musicians and music teachers, school teachers, and stenographers.[19] Once a certain independence in travel within the community is achieved, the employment and vocational adjustment of the blind are dependent on factors similar to those that influence sighted persons, plus the hazards that members of any minority group face. Basic to the vocational adjustment of the blind, therefore, is their development of skills and knowledge in some occupational field not dependent on vision for success, and their development of the skills and knowledge of traveling safely in their community with as little aid as possible.

THE PARTIALLY SEEING

Education. About one out of every 500 children in the United States of school age is classified as partially seeing. As early as 1802 it was recognized that partially seeing children should not be educated with blind children because: (1) they are sighted and their main channel of learning is through vision; (2) the majority of partially seeing children will never be blind (unable to use vision as the main channel of learning) ; (3) they are expected to live with normally seeing companions; (4) institutionalization should be avoided to prevent the stigma of blindness; etc. Unfortunately, however, there has been a small trend toward having organized classes for partially seeing children in schools for the blind. This is considered by some authorities as retrogressive, for it takes the responsibility for special services for the partially seeing off the local community and puts it on state supported institutions.[20] Placement of the partially seeing in special schools for unusual (exceptional) children is also another undesirable trend. Even segregated classes for the partially seeing in regular public schools is not best for these children because it tends, although to a lesser degree, to stigmatize them as "defective."

It is believed that the best educational programs for the partially seeing are those based on the one initiated by Dr. Robert B. Irwin in 1913. According to the Irwin plan, the child is enrolled in a special "sight-saving" class which serves as his homeroom. But he joins his normally seeing classmates in all classes except those requiring concentrated eye work. For con-

135

centrated eye work the partially seeing attend a special class-room with a teacher specially prepared to teach them. The most desired goal following from Irwin's efforts is integration of the partially seeing in regular classes of regular schools.[21]

One of the most interesting and valuable areas for educators to know about is that concerning the special classroom settings and curricular arrangements developed for the purpose of saving the eyes of the partially seeing and teaching them effectively.

Thus, it is suggested that: seats in the classroom should be arranged so that children do not have to face the light from the window directly; that the teacher shouldn't stand by windows when talking; that wall spaces should not be used for displays between windows; that working materials, tools, equipment, etc., be free from glare; that the level of illumination should not be too high; that every attempt be made to eliminate glare; that shadows be eliminated in working areas; that there be rest periods for the eyes; that writing which is large and clear be emphasized; that children use a soft, very black lead for pencil work and India ink rather than ordinary ink where it is called for; that if pens be used they should be those making a heavy rather than a thin line; that children should be trained to be as "earminded" as possible, that is, learn to be good listeners; that services of readers be employed in certain cases; that supplementary subject matter material be in large-type books to lessen fatigue; that dull, unglazed paper without lines be used by partially seeing children; preference should be given in reading assignments, to books with large, clear type and pictures; etc.[22] Any teachers will immediately realize that the above suggestions for the partially seeing also have practical meaning, in most cases, for the normally seeing who develop eyestrain and visual losses due to educational practices which do not take into account fundamental facts about the nature of the eye and the maintenance of its health. Thus, many will have taken note in recent years of the reduction of the size of the letters in textbooks, journals, and other reading matter, the construction of "modern" libraries in which glare and shadows produce eyestrain, poor lighting in "modern" classroom buildings, etc. Perhaps, educators

136

and scholars who use their eyes extensively should start an "eye hygiene movement" to help preserve the health of their eyes and the eyes of all people everywhere against thoughtless book publishers and school architects and industrial designers who design products which do not give human eyes the chance for healthful functioning they deserve.

Personal, Social, and Vocational Adjustment. The personal, social, and vocational adjustments of the partially seeing are similar in many respects to those of the blind. First, in his self concept the partially seeing child must learn to avoid defining himself as being blind. His main channel of learning, even though it might necessitate special educational methods and provisions, is through vision. He should not, therefore, hold the stigma of blindness. To avoid such a stigma it is best that the partially seeing child does not attend special classes in schools for the blind, or special classes in schools for unusual children, or even special classes in regular schools. It is best that he be integrated into the regular classroom in the regular school. Second, like every child, the partially seeing is unique and his handicap should be treated as a good teacher treats any special characteristic of each student. That is, for example, because of his special characteristic, that of having a visual handicap, he should not be required or encouraged to take such courses as mechanical drawing or stenography but rather encouraged to pursue areas in which his handicap will not be a severely limiting factor in his success. Third, partially seeing children should be prepared for and encouraged to enter occupations which are realistic in terms of their visual handicap. Many great people in the history of mankind were partially seeing individuals. They obviously did not permit their handicap to become an excuse for failure, dependency, and demoralization.

THE COLOR WEAK

Education. Little has been written on the education of the color weak.[23] Yet color weakness is a significant handicap in many occupations and many activities. In fact, not realistically accepting and reporting color weakness, has been basic in the etiology of many serious and fatal accidents. Thus, for example, Sweden was one of the first countries to make laws against hiring the color weak in the railway service. Many other countries have similar laws. Peters suggests that testing for color weakness should be a realistic and practical objective for every school and that the results of such testing be made a part of the permanent record of every student.[24] He believes the best type of test for his purpose is the pseudo-iso-chromatic plate kind of test. Such a test merely requires that the individual read various numbers or figures which appear among colored dots. These tests are easy to administer and to score, and are fairly reliable.

Personal, Social, and Vocational Adjustment. The personal and social adjustment of the color weak individual is closely tied up with his vocational adjustment. That adjustment can be significantly related to the kind of color weakness he has. Color weak students should not plan to enter the Navy, become an Air Force pilot, attempt to do interior decorating, become a chemist, enter the field of electronics where electrical components are color coded, become a television repairman when there is a transition to color television sets, be interested in fashion or becoming a make-up artist, etc. So far as is known, color weakness is a permanent thing. In certain occupations color weakness is extremely hazardous. It is against the law in most countries for color weak persons, for example, to be employed in the railway service in functions which demand normal color vision. In modern industrial nations color weak persons should not be permitted to drive autos, buses, trucks, or taxi-cabs. In the practice of medicine, nursing, and pharmacy many unnecessary deaths have been traced to the irresponsible disregard for a known color weak condition or lack of knowledge of such a condition. To ignore color weakness as an insignificant and meaningless type of visual handicap is to ignore a significant visual handicap that is, it is believed, more common than both blindness and partial sightedness. Yet the writers know of few schools which require color weakness tests. Here is a visual handicap, therefore, concerning which there is much to be done.

SUMMARY AND CONCLUSIONS

This chapter has summarized some of the important research done on three important types of visually handicapped children: (1) the blind; (2) the partially seeing; and (3) the color weak.

If each child with each handicap is thought of as a unique person with special characteristics calling for the special application of special educational methods, then we have come a long way in developing the kind of attitudes that make possible the best personal, social, and vocational adjustment of each of these unusual children.

The general trend, and the most desirable one, according to the experts on the education and socialization of the visually handicapped, is away from segregation, either in schools for the blind, schools for unusual children, or special classes in regular schools, and toward integration in regular classes in regular schools. In the integrated setting the visual handicaps are not ignored, they are simply given the same kind of special attention any special trait of significance to the education of a normal child should be given by an alert and competent teacher. Parents, social workers, guidance counselors, and various types of therapists responsible for the welfare of the visually handicapped should attempt to encourage in these children the same kinds of attitudes, values, and behavior patterns we encourage in normally sighted children. That is, the blind, partially seeing, and color weak, must learn to become independent, emotionally mature, responsible citizens. They must strive to develop their potentialities, taking into account the nature and limitations of their handicap without letting it become an excuse for a life of dependency, emotional infantilism, and civic irresponsibility.

As far as the blind and partially seeing are concerned, tremendous progress has been made in helping them to achieve greater independence and success in our society in spite of their handicaps. But there is much to be desired in locating and aiding the numerous color weak persons among us.

SELECTED BIBLIOGRAPHY

Abel, George Lee, RESOURCES FOR TEACHERS OF BLIND AND SIGHTED CHILDREN, American Foundation for the Blind, New York, 1953. A manual prepared for the use of teachers in public schools providing educational programs for blind children. It contains, among other materials, descriptions of devices and equipment used in the education of blind children and their sources of distribution.

Buell, Charles E., ACTIVE GAMES FOR THE BLIND, Edwards Brothers, Ann Arbor, Michigan, 1953. All about the physical education of the blind and partially blind. The author is director of athletics at the California School for the Blind. Those who think that the blind cannot participate in numerous types of athletics will be amazed at the range of physical activities the blind can and do engage in.

Chevigny, Hector, MY EYES HAVE A COLD NOSE, Yale University Press, New Haven, Connecticut, 1946. An adult sighted reporter became unexpectedly blind. Three years later he told the poignant autobiographical story of his blindness, In some extremely insightful passages on Negroes and prejudice, and on blind Negroes, he provides empirical evidence that "Were the whole world blind, there would be no race prejudice. There couldn't be." A book highly recommended for those who have prejudices toward blind and other minorities.

Chevigny, Hector, and Braverman, Sydell, THE ADJUSTMENT OF THE BLIND, Yale University Press, New Haven, Connecticut, 1950. A fantastically insightful work which demolishes many myths concerning the blind. The fact that the senior author is blind and the other sighted accounts, in part, for the great objectivity of this book. Contains a valuable bibliography.

Cruickshank, William M., and Trippe, Matthew J., SERVICES TO BLIND CHILDREN IN NEW YORK STATE, Syracuse University Press, Syracuse, New York, 1959. While this study is concerned specifically with programs for blind children in the state of New York, the findings and conclusions undoubtedly have many implications for numerous states in the United States, officials of which are seeking to implement programs for blind children and youth in terms of the best current thought and research. This work has numerous illustrations and figures, and 219 very informative tables. The appendix contains an extensive section on "New York State Law Pertaining to the Blind." In short, it is a goldmine of factual data on one state's services to blind children. Should be required reading for those interested in public and private programs for blind children.

Eaton, Allen H., BEAUTY FOR THE SIGHTED AND THE BLIND, St. Martin's Press, New York, 1959. An unusual book about the aesthetic responses of both seeing and blind persons to the wonder and beauty of the world about them. It aspires to encourage communication between the sighted and the blind in the appreciation and enjoyment of beauty. To this end the author has, with the aid of other persons and agencies, been forming a collection of "Objects of Beauty and Wonder from the Great Storehouse of Nature," a collection of objects enjoyable to the sighted and the blind. The collection includes such objects as follows: a Late Stone Age hand tool, Babylonian clay tablet with cuneiform inscriptions, a Pomo Indian ceremonial basket, an Eskimo carving of walrus ivory, a starfish, quartz, fossils, silk worm cocoon, wing of the Arctic Tern, etc. It is hoped that through the sharing of the joys of beauty that the sighted and blind will learn to appreciate and understand each other better. 45 meaningful illustrations.

Farrell Gabriel, THE STORY OF BLINDNESS, Harvard University Press, Cambridge, Massachusetts, 1956. The main portion of this book constituted the Lowell Lectures delivered at Boston University during November, 1953. A comprehensive and scholarly work, it is a good general introduction for anyone interested in gaining some understanding of blindness. Has a worthwhile collection of topical references.

Graham, Milton D., SOCIAL RESEARCH ON BLINDNESS: PRESENT STATUS AND FUTURE POTENTIALS, American Foundation for the Blind, 1960. Excellent, partially annotated, comprehensive bibliography on behavioral science research on blindness. Chapter VI, "The Young Blind," contains references to numerous research projects, books, monographs, dissertations (at the doctoral and master degree levels), and articles on pure and applied research on blind and partially blind children. There are 959 items in this up-to-date bibliography.

Hathaway, Winifred; Foote, Franklin M.; Bryan, Dorothy, and

Gibbons, Helen, EDUCATION AND HEALTH OF THE PAR-
TIALLY SEEING CHILD, Columbia University Press, New
York, 1959, Fourth Edition. The standard sourcebook for information on the education of the partially blind child, offering
a wealth of complete and authoritative material in this field of
special education. Contained in the appendixes is a valuable
chapter on "What the Teacher Should Know About the Eye
and Eye Hygiene," and also sections on "Suggested Equipment
for Partially Seeing Pupils," and "Vocabulary of Terms Relating
to the Eye," plus a topical bibliography.

Huffman, Mildred Blake, FUN COMES FIRST FOR BLIND
SLOW-LEARNERS, Charles C. Thomas, Springfield, Illinois,
1957. The author, a primary teacher at the California School for
the Blind, describes in detail the many procedures she uses in
managing a classroom of young mentally retarded blind children. This is one of those rare books in which a classroom
teacher has been able to analyze her procedures, her goals, the
group she is teaching, and the experiences provided. A valuable
work for teachers of young blind children of any level of intelligence. Besides containing an excellent bibliography and
meaningful photographic illustrations, it also includes annotated
copies of classroom tape recordings. Teachers and social workers
wishing to secure the original tape recordings for audio-purposes
may contact Dr. Berthold Lowenfeld, Superintendent, California
School for the Blind, 3001 Derby Street, Berkeley 5, California.

Lowenfeld, Berthold, OUR BLIND CHILDREN: GROWING
AND LEARNING WITH THEM, Charles C. Thomas, Springfield, Illinois, 1956. While this work is written primarily for the
parents of blind children it also contains a wealth of information
which is useful to teachers, social workers, and others who guide
parents or direct programs of education to meet the needs of
blind children. Dr. Lowenfeld, Superintendent of the California
School for the Blind, writes with great intelligence and understanding on the kinds of children he has the responsibility to
develop into self-confident, autonomous, and useful adults. Contains a small but helpful annotated bibliography, information
about educational facilities for the blind and organizations concerned with the blind, and an annotated list of periodicals dealing
exclusively or partially with the blind and partially blind.

Magary, James F., and Eichorn, John R. (Editors), THE

EXCEPTIONAL CHILD: A BOOK OF READINGS, Holt, Rinehart and Winston, New York, 1960. Although this collection of readings is devoted to an examination of all types of unusual children, Part VI, "The Child with a Visual Handicap," contains the following papers of interest on the blind and partially blind:

a. Berthold Lowenfeld, "The Child Who Is Blind";
b. C. Edith Kerby, "Causes of Blindness in Children of School Age";
c. Doris Gray, "The Blind Child in the Regular Classroom";
d. Hazel C. McIntire, "Education of Partially Seeing Children";
e. Anthony J. Pelone, "The Adjustment of the Partially Seeing Child in a Regular Classroom";
f. George A. Peters, "Color Blindness."

Norris, Miriam; Spaulding, Patricia J., and Brodie, Fern H., BLINDNESS IN CHILDREN, University of Chicago Press, Chicago, 1957. A report of a five year longitudinal study of the developmental patterns of 295 blind preschool children. It was concluded that, under optimal conditions, the blind child can develop into an independent, freely functioning individual who compares favorably with sighted children in his total adaptations. Contains a 78-item bibliography.

Pelone, Anthony J., HELPING THE VISUALLY HANDICAPPED CHILD IN A REGULAR CLASSROOM, Columbia University Press, New York, 1957. The school adjustment of visually handicapped children enrolled in regular public school classes is the subject of this practical work.

PEDIODICALS ON BLINDNESS

BETTER LIGHT BETTER SIGHT NEWS, Better Light Better Sight Bureau, 750 3rd Avenue, New York 17, N. Y. Published 6 times a year.

INTERNATIONAL JOURNAL FOR THE EDUCATION OF THE BLIND, 1867 Frankfort Avenue, Louisville, Kentucky. Published 4 times a year during the school year.

NEW OUTLOOK FOR THE BLIND, American Foundation for the Blind, 15 West 16th Street, New York 11, N. Y. Published monthly except July and August.

SIGHT-SAVING REVIEW, National Society for the Prevention of Blindness, 1790 Broadway, New York 19, N. Y. Published quarterly.

ROBERT M. FRUMKIN as an undergraduate majored in the physical sciences at Upsala College and as a graduate majored in the behavioral sciences at the New School for Social Research and the Ohio State University. Previous professional and related work experience include service in the U. S. Navy Hospital Corps, teaching the behavioral sciences at Hampton Institute and the University of Buffalo, research and statistical analysis for the Ohio State Department of Mental Hygiene and Correction, psychiatric social work at the Buffalo State Hospital, and consultant work for the New York State Department of Health and the National League for Nursing. Currently is teaching the behavioral sciences at the State University of New York (Oswego) and is research editor for the JOURNAL OF HUMAN RELATIONS. Author of books, contributions to books and encyclopedias, and more than a hundred articles in professional and popular periodicals. Biographic inclusion in WHO'S WHO IN THE EAST and WHO'S WHO IN NEW YORK.

MIRIAM ZISENWINE FRUMKIN as an undergraduate majored in elementary education and minored in the behavioral sciences at the Ohio State University and has been doing graduate work at the State University of New York (Oswego) in education. She has taught elementary education in the public schools of Columbus, Ohio, and those of Buffalo and Kenmore, New York. Co-author, with Robert M. Frumkin, of research articles in the OHIO STATE MEDICAL JOURNAL, JOURNAL OF EDUCATIONAL RESEARCH, and the JOURNAL OF HUMAN RELATIONS, as well as a short story entitled "Dan, the Candy Man," published in HIGHLIGHTS FOR CHILDREN, which was selected by the Voice of America for radio broadcasting to the countries behind the Iron Curtain.

NOTES

1. See Ray L. Birdwhistell, INTRODUCTION TO KINESICS, University of Louisville Press, Louisville, Kentucky, 1953; and, Jurgen Ruesch and

144

Weldon Kees, NONVERBAL COMMUNICATION, University of California Press, Berkeley, 1956.

2. Birdwhistell, OP. CIT.

3. See Clarence Leuba, THE NATURAL MAN, Doubleday, New York, 1954, especially the chapter entitled "Wild Children," 6-12.

4. Cited in James F. Margary and John R. Eichorn, Editors, THE EXCEPTIONAL CHILD, Holt, Rinehart and Winston, New York, 1960, 233.

5. IBID., 233.

6. See inter alia, George A. Peters, "Color Blindness," in Margary and Eichorn, OP. CIT., 279-280.

7. Edward T. Myers, A SURVEY OF SIGHT-SAVING CLASSES IN THE PUBLIC SCHOOLS OF THE UNITED STATES, Privately Printed, Philadelphia, 1930.

8. Arthur N. Alling, Discussion of THE PREVENTION OF EYE DISORDERS by Henry S. Miles, CONNECTICUT STATE MEDICAL SOCIETY PROCEEDING, 1922, 141-142.

9. See Guy L. Noyes, "The Relation of Sight and Hearing of Early School Life," UNIVERSITY OF MISSOURI BULLETIN, XV (Medical Series Number 5), 1914.

10. See Myers, OP. CIT.

11. Margary and Eichorn, OP. CIT., 233.

12. IBID., 235.

13. Berthold Lowenfeld, "The Child Who is Blind," in Margary and Eichorn, IBID., 255-256.

14. Lowenfeld, IBID., 251.

15. INDUSTRIAL ARTS FOR BLIND STUDENTS (Group Reports: No. 6), American Foundation for the Blind, New York, 1960.

16. See, inter alia, Charles E. Buell, ACTIVE GAMES FOR THE BLIND, Edwards Brothers, Ann Arbor, Michigan, 1953.

17. Allen H. Eaton, BEAUTY FOR THE SIGHTED AND THE BLIND, St. Martin's Press, New York, 1959.

18. Lowenfeld, OP. CIT., 252-254. On the nature and the etiology of "blindisms," see, inter alia, F. Park Lewis, "The Blind Child," OUTLOOK FOR THE BLIND, X, 1916, 5-9; Ralph V. Merry, PROBLEMS IN THE EDUCATION OF VISUALLY HANDICAPPED CHILDREN, Harvard University Press, Cambridge, Massachusetts, 1933 and J. M. Ritchie, CONCERNING THE BLIND, Oliver and Boyd, London, 1930.

19. See, inter alia, Harry J. Spar, "Some Special Aspects of an Adequate Vocational Training and Employment Program for the Blind," in Merle E. Frampton and Elena D. Gall, Editors, SPECIAL EDUCATION FOR THE EXCEPTIONAL, Porter Sargent, Boston, 1955, Volume II, 64-74.

20. See, inter alia, Hazel C. McIntire, "Education of the Partially Seeing," in Margary and Eichorn, OP. CIT., 266-269.

21. IBID.

22. Anthony J. Pelone, "The Adjustment of the Partially Seeing in the Regular Classroom," in Margary and Eichorn, IBID., 270-279.

23. The scientific name for color weakness is achromatropsia but therapists, and other personnel working with such handicapped persons prefer the term color weakness to achromatropsia or the popular term color blindness.

24. Peters, OP. CIT.

FILMS AND FILMSTRIPS

1. JOHNNY'S NEW WORLD, 16 minutes, 16-mm., sound, color. Explains need for early detection and treatment of children's eye problems. Source: National Society for the Prevention of Blindness, Inc., 1790 Broadway, New York 19, N. Y.

2. EYES FOR TOMORROW, 22 minutes, 16-mm., sound. Deals with eye health problems throughout life. Stresses the relationship with general health. Source: National Society for the Prevention of Blindness, *ibid*.

3. PROTECTING EYES AT WORK, 50-frame 35 mm. filmstrip, color, silent. For students in junior and senior high schools and vocational schools. Source: Text-Film Department, McGraw-Hill Book Company, 330 West 42nd Street, New York 36, N. Y.

4. GROWING INTO READING THROUGH THE USE OF BRAILLE, 25 minutes, 16-mm., color, silent. Presents many aspects of reading readiness for the blind through Braille means. Source: American Foundation for the Blind, 15 West 16th Street, New York 11, N. Y.

THE HARD TO REACH CHILD

Ruth Gasink Boyer

Richmond Professional Institute, Virginia

The "hard to reach" child is the one of whom the teacher despairs. He has average or better intelligence, he has no particular disability, but he does not learn. He fails to respond to the techniques usually successful in motivating children to participate in the classroom learning situation; he may just sit and stare out of the window, he may idle away his time while apparently working, or he may indulge in various minor forms of unacceptable behavior. His has been called a "learning" disability.

It is the purpose of this chapter to provide some practical helps to the teacher on how to reach this "hard to reach" child. He is not a child with a serious emotional disturbance, although the patterns of his behavior would still fall into the psychoanalytic categories of neurosis, character disorder, or psychosis, and the methods of handling him are based on this premise. Most of his relationships and adaptations to society are within the normal range, but his incipient disturbance shows itself through his refusal to learn.

The word "refusal" is used advisedly, in that this is the way you, the teacher, see it. And it is a refusal; but a refusal based on a troubled unhappiness making it too hard for the child to conquer the problems posed by the necessity of learning formal, academic matter.

The question, then, is how you can relieve this unhappiness

sufficiently to lift the soul-dampening burden which has robbed the child of his enthusiasm and motivation.

Before you can utilize specific suggestions with regard to what to do, you must first understand the "why" of what goes on. You must know, in general, what it is that causes some children to resist your best efforts, and how the child feels underneath this symptomatic behavior.

ATTITUDES AND MOTIVATION

There are as many specific reasons for a child's refusal to learn as there are for any other facet of his reaction to life, but there are some general tenets which it will be helpful for you to know.

Learning is an aggressive act. It means the child is stepping out into a world of his own; he is becoming an individual; he is reaching out for ideas he does not get from his parents, some of which may be in conflict with his parents' ideas. He is even going so far as to allow another person to become, in some aspects of his life, more important than his parents.

This is obviously a frightening step for a child to take. He must be very, very sure that his parents love him enough to want him to be independent; that they will continue to love him and consider him a valuable member of the family after he has become independent; and that they will allow him to return to them for continued dependency when he needs it.

Look around you, and see how many of your good friends, thoughtful, intelligent people, fall short of this in some respect! The wonder is not that some children are afraid to learn, but that so many dare to take this tremendous step.

What happens, then, to the child who is not this sure? He fears separation from his mother; he fears his anger toward her for the many ways in which she has failed him; and he decides, deep down inside the subconscious recesses of his mind, that the only way he can play it safe is to stay as he was, untutored and dependent on her.

148

Every child has a tremendous, deep-seated desire to learn. The teacher faced with a stubborn, recalcitrant non-learner finds this almost impossible to believe. But it is true. Only the child faced with complete lack of love and attention during his first months of life lacks the motivation for learning. This child either dies in infancy or goes early into an obvious psychotic withdrawal from life. The child who has matured to the extent of reaching the first grade with average intelligence wants to learn; that's why he has made the effort to learn the things necessary for survival during his first six years. The hard-to-reach child has made these first efforts with a passable degree of success, but has been stymied upon entering school because of the too-difficult, for him, shift from family and informal learning to strangers and formal learning.

Every child wants to behave. Children do not come into this world angry and disobedient. They want, above all else, to please the people on whom they are dependent, because this is the smoothest road to getting fed and cared for. As they mature, they learn to love in proportion to the degree to which they have been loved. When they are hurt, they hurt back, because this, too, is learned behavior. The child reaching school with a pattern of misbehavior is acting the way life has taught him, and he is caught in a vicious cycle from which he cannot free himself. He wants to do what you want, so that you will smile on him with affection; but he does not know how. Perhaps he has learned that misbehavior gets him some attention, rather than the lack of attention he got for behaving well. Whatever the reason behind it, he is stuck with his pattern unless some understanding adult can see below the surface, and know that this child, like every other, wants to please so that he will be loved.

There is no such thing as a lazy child. Laziness is a symptom, not a state of affairs *per se*. Anyone who has spent ten minutes watching children in free play knows that the amount of energy expended would leave an adult prostrated. When a child appears lazy, there is a reason. He may by physically below par, and this should, of course, be explored first. But he also may be a frightened child; frightened of the task of learning, frightened of his own aggressive drives and hostilities, or frightened of the strange situation and associates with whom he finds himself.

Some children are not ready for group experiences. Some children, because of their fears of independence, perhaps just their lack of experience with other children, may not be ready for the group situation. Perhaps they have been taught to be silent in the presence of others; perhaps they have been allowed complete freedom of expression and have no built-in controls. These children must learn not only academic matters, but the whole process of association with others. If it is forced upon them, they will retreat into complete silence or break loose into uncontrolled behavior. They need to be eased into group living, not thrown into it.

Most children have built up patterns of reaction not directly related to the situation at hand. All of us have defenses with which we meet life. Some of these are healthy, some are not. So it is with children. One child, when presented with a too-difficult task, will try to do something similar and acceptable but not quite so difficult; the next child will say he doesn't want to or that he won't. This does not at all mean that he really doesn't want to or really won't; it is simply his way of saying he can't.

Children have differing tolerance for relating to group activity. Most educational systems expect children to perform their tasks at the same time and in the same manner as other children in the group. Whether this system derives from habit or necessity matters little. What does matter is that some children are happy and productive only when they are doing exactly what the rest are doing, and some children are happy and productive only when they can reach out for individually creative heights. What is sauce for the goose is not always sauce for the gander, and to demand that all children participate equally in a given mode of expression is demanding that they all be constituted exactly alike, which they are not. One child may learn and be stimulated to learn more through the requirement that he recite orally the entirety of "Paul Revere's Ride"; another child may be driven to the depths of despair and withdrawal through the same

150

demand. We accept the fact that children have differing intellectual endowments; we must also accept the fact that they have differing emotional strengths and weaknesses.

One child's conscience is different in strength from that of another. A child's conscience begins to develop about the time he is five or six. Thus all children begin school with a mixture of ideas, most of them stemming from what they think adults expect of them. As they go through the grades, they develop more ideas as to what they, themselves, approve for their own behavior, and they develop this strength at completely different rates.

Cultural patterns make some children entirely unready for school, and other children ready in differing ways. At one school where all of the children eat in the cafeteria at noon, almost none of these children have sat at a table for a meal before beginning school. At another school encompassing mixed socio-economic backgrounds, one mother complained bitterly because the teacher was unwilling to toilet-train her child. In a school where most of the children came from backgrounds strongly defensive of American ideals, one child's religion forbade her to salute the flag. These are isolated examples, but indicative that in any school there will be children whose cultural orientations create special problems for them, and affect their ability and willingness to participate in the learning situation.

TECHNIQUES FOR HELPING THE NON-LEARNER

All of the materials we have discussed with regard to motivation and attitudes are related to the ability or inability of the child to extend himself to learn. It is not at all necessary that a teacher execute a complex psycho-social diagnosis on a child; but it is necessary that she look at the non-learner in the light of his individuality. It will reassure her if she can find out why he is not learning; but whether or not she can find out, there are certain basic techniques which will be helpful to her in getting him to involve himself in the process of learning.

151

As soon as you have spotted a non-learner, insist that he receive a complete physical examination. This should include complete eye and ear examinations, as well as anything else indicated. One delightful third grade girl stopped reading one day, and the consensus of opinion was that she was angry because of a special privilege her sister had received. Had it not been for the determination of the School Social Worker to find a better reason, the child would have died of a fast-growing brain tumor.

Believe, unequivocally, that the child wants to behave and wants to learn. This is very hard to do, but it is in keeping with the basic premise of our democratic society that a person is innocent until proven guilty. In the instance of belief in the child's desire to learn, you must never decide he is guilty of not wanting to learn; you may decide he is too disturbed to be amenable to the techniques available to you, in which case you will refer him to the School Social Worker, Psychologist, Counselor or other resource for more intensive work with the home or for direct treatment of the child's emotional problem.

Look with compassion upon the child who is not learning. See in his eyes the depths of his unhappiness, recognize in his naughty behavior his desperate fight for status. Let him know, very privately and just between the two of you, that you know how unhappy he his, that you are sorry with him about it, and that between you, you will find a solution. Don't be taken in when he says he doesn't care; the more he protests, the more he cares but doesn't dare admit it. Let him know that you expect him to learn, because that is why he is there, and that you expect to help him learn.

Give both reward and punishment, impartially and justly. Effort honestly expended must be rewarded; and effort withheld must be punished. Remember that we are now talking about the child who has the mental ability to learn. If he learns, he should be given approbation, approval, and grades as he deserves them. There is currently a practice from first grade through graduate school of withholding "A's" either because it's the first semester and "no one can do his best for the first grading period" or because "A" "is better than anyone can do." If either of these

152

fallacies were sound, "A" should be deleted from the list of grades. If "A's" are listed in your grading system, give them. If you don't give them, you are either being punitive or a poor teacher. Be generous with your reward; take credit for your good teaching. Likewise, the capable student who does not do the work should not be given a passing grade. He cannot learn to live with reality unless he is exposed to it.

Believe in a child's ability once it has been established. Many, many times competent psychologists have administered individual tests to children, found the children to be above average, only to have the teachers say, "Oh, but he isn't really that bright. He doesn't do that kind of work at all." True, he hasn't done that kind of work; and he won't as long as the teacher continues to believe he can't. It is the most natural thing in the world for the teacher to feel that a non-learner is dull; but it is a dreadful waste of the skill of experts and the tax payer's money for the teacher to refuse to take a new look at the child in the light of fresh evidence.

Respect the child's right to maintain his dignity. Talk about a child's problems to him when the two of you are alone, or to other concerned adults in the privacy of a planned situation. I wonder how many Congressional Libraries could be filled with the words of teachers who have ridiculed or otherwise exposed children to ignominy in the presence of others. If you expect to persuade him to learn, you must let him know that how he feels is important to you, and that you respect his dignity at all times.

Explore all reasonable possibilities for finding out why the child is having trouble. First of all, talk with the child himself. If you ask him with the honest intention of finding out what he has on his mind, you will be amazed at how helpful he can be. But you must be willing to hear things you don't like, such as, "When you yell at the kids, I get scared and can't think." Be fair: don't ask him unless you are willing to hear, and give thoughtful consideration to his answer once you get it. Talk with his parents. Many times they will tell you things which don't mean much to them but are extremely helpful to you. Use the resources of the specialists in your school if you can't get enough answers yourself.

The School Social Worker, especially, can get valuable information for you.

Tell the parents what they can do to help. Most parents really want to help. Their ideas of how to do it usually date from their own outmoded school experience, plus their own emotional problems, which gives, at best, a confused and loaded hodge-podge. Concrete ideas from you, given with reassurance and explanation are extremely helpful. To tell them simply not to try to teach Johnny to read at home is likely to mean to them that you don't feel they are competent, and they are insulted. But if you explain carefully how your method differs from the one which they know, they will understand; and if you further explain that parents usually get too upset and tense, resulting in a tense, hamstrung student, they can understand this, too. Sometimes you will want to lay it straight on the line. When a child comes to school repeatedly saying that his mother says he doesn't have to obey you, don't make the mistake of either believing or disbelieving him; but do tell the mother this is what he is saying. If it is true, she will be more careful; if it is not true, she will want to try to figure out with you why he says this. Either way, she will appreciate being told what he is saying; she will either want an opportunity to protect herself or to help the child. As long as you have presented the matter to her without criticism, simply as fact, you are in control of the situation.

Explore the child's interests until you can find some area in which he experiences success and pleasure. Once you can get this child participating successfully in some area of class experience, you are on the way; you can then move to related areas with comparative ease.

Let the child know that he has pleased you. Most non-learners are convinced that no one likes them, if for no other reason than that they do not like themselves. Thus you can be of great help to them if you will see to it that every day you say, "My, I liked the way you walked in so straight and tall," or something similar. You can find something positive about any child if you look long and hard enough; and as he becomes convinced that you like him, he will begin to like himself and be less afraid to learn.

154

Never tell a child that you like him because he behaves. This automatically means that you do not like him when he misbehaves, and it is essential to him to feel that you like him all of the time. Of course, you do not like his misbehavior, nor his refusal to learn; but you can still like him, as a person. *Never* say, "I like the way you did that, but . . ." Don't qualify your liking; let it be complete in and of itself. The "but" should come in another context, at another time.

Be sure he gets his share of treats. Most non-learners have been deprived of real affection for themselves as individuals, and to many of them the deprivation of food is synonymous with the deprivation of affection. Some of them have actually been deprived of food as well as affection, like the seven-year-old boy whose mother said, "No more rolls, honey. Mama knows how much food you need." Yes, she did know. What she did not know was that hidden under her apparent desire for his good was her own subconscious desire to keep him tied to her and to prevent his developing independence. She also supervised his bath, an indication that she wished to forestall his developing manhood as well as his independence. Faced with two indications that his mother wanted to keep him a baby, he was frightened of the aggressiveness of the learning process, and did not learn to read in spite of his superior intelligence. You can help this kind of child by recognizing the importance of food to him, and seeing to it, when there are treats available, that he gets his share. He may exhibit his fear by appearing to be greedy. If he does, try putting your arm around him with a good, solid hug when the treats reach him, and see whether this will help him settle for his share and reassure him, as well, that you, at least, want him to eat well and like him for it. Perhaps he will reveal his worry by being too careful not to get his share; then you must be even more sure that he has it and that he knows you want him to have it.

Don't force a child into oral recitation if he cannot do it. Many children can be encouraged to recite. If they do not respond to normal encouragement, let the matter drop. Then have the child recite to you, privately, or to one other child,

155

until he can open up. This method is particularly effective with the child who speaks in whispers, or perhaps doesn't speak at all.

Don't strip a child of his defenses. If a child says he won't or can't, don't go into a tizzy over his impudence. Rather, be gentle, and be understanding to the point at which you can say, "Well, maybe you can't right now. Sometimes these things are hard to do. But we'll try again tomorrow, won't we, and pretty soon it will be easy."

Always give the child the feeling that success lies close ahead. He won't know this is true, unless you tell him. He is too frightened to think he will ever learn; but if you are convinced of it, and tell him so, he, too, will begin to believe it; and with belief will come the potentiality.

Teach what the child is ready to learn. You already do this academically. With the non-learner, try to figure out also what he is emotionally ready to learn. If he can't learn the words right now, could he draw a picture of Dick? And if you print "Dick" under the picture, would there not soon be an association? And with one word learned, perhaps there would be the willingness to tackle another. But if he is deathly afraid of his mother's boy-friend whose name is Dick, let's hope you know this before you start, and can try a different word. There is another possibility: is the content of "Dick and Jane" simply too juvenile for a very bright child already deep in dinosaurs and space ships?

Allow, recognize, and encourage individuality. If he is so frightened that free art expression puts him in a panic, why not let him give a talk, or write a story about a picture? What's so precious about uniformity and one particular mode of expression? Conformity, when it serves a useful purpose, is good; but conformity which panics a child is devastating and harmful rather than helpful.

Expect that some children will not be able to give affection. These children will not function well in groups. Furthermore, they will be frightened by expressions of affection from either the group or you. Your encouragement must be quiet, subtle, non-demanding. The group will be more patient than you, because children intuitively understand these things. Don't push the

156

child into the group, nor the group toward the child. Watch the group closely, and you will get cues from them as to how this child can be reached.

Understand that you, as well as the parents, must be willing to let this child belong to himself. If learning is an act of aggression developing into beginning independence, you must forego the privilege of thinking of the students as "my children." They are not yours, nor are they their parents', really, if they are ready to learn. They belong to themselves, and to their own budding awareness of the delights of themselves as developing creatures. They will love you more if you can let them be free.

Help each child in the light of the cultural patterns which determine his behavior. If he refuses to eat in the cafeteria, perhaps he doesn't know how! If she won't go to the dance, are you sure she knows what to say when a boy speaks to her? If the first grader seems completely wild, don't assume he has not experienced discipline; perhaps he has not experienced freedom from it!

Remember that the degree of control you exert must reach all children in the class. You, because of your position, must of course act as conscience for the entire group to some extent. However, since some of the children in your group will have almost no conscience, and some will have overly active consciences, you must be careful that the controls you exert can be adapted by the individual child to his needs. If you say that *no one* may leave the room while you are gone, will the overdisciplined, overanxious bright child become more anxious, and wet his pants, never to forget the shame of it? The child with an over-active conscience is likely to be one of the hard-to-reach children, because his fear of self-assertiveness and competition make him afraid of the learning process. For him it is especially important that you do not accentuate his problem by being too rigid in your control of the group. Try to establish a firm but relaxed emotional climate which will allow the use of judgement to those who are capable of using it.

Let the punishment fit the crime. One of the most common offenses against this axiom is the punishment of the group for

157

the crime of one child. To engage in such a process is to be psychiatrically unsophisticated, because only the rare offender is reached. Some children with character disorders and apparent lack of conscience do respond to pressure of the group, and will behave better when the group, offended at being punished unjustly, insists that the child behave. But far more often, the child in question does not respond; and the hard-to-reach child, although not the offender, cringes at the unjustness of it and determines more strongly not to risk himself in the process of learning and group adjustment.

Let him know that the kind of work he does matters to you. Even the good student works better for and learns more from the teacher he likes; and whether or not he likes you depends a great deal on whether he feels he and his work are important to you. The hard-to-reach child feels that nothing he does is very important to anybody; if he is to learn from you, he must feel that every word he reads to you and every paper he hands to you is of vital importance to you and will be accepted with real appreciation, no matter how many mistakes it may have. Let him know that it makes you feel happy for him when he does well, and sad for him when he does not do so well.

Give him your undivided attention when you give it. If you can't give it, let him have a big smile with the comment that it isn't his turn right now, but that you will be back to him soon. Thirty seconds of undivided attention is far better than half an hour of begrudged, divided attention.

CONCLUSION

The child with the learning difficulty is a frightened child: frightened of himself, his environment, and the tremendous task of learning. To help him, you must be able to see his fear through all the over-laid protection; you must be thoroughly convinced that his desire to learn is greater than his desire not to learn; you must believe he can learn; and you must let him know that you believe he can learn, that you expect him to, and that you

158

will help him. Above all, you must use the recommended techniques only if you firmly believe in them yourself. A half-hearted try will result in sure failure; a determined try will give you better than a fifty-fifty chance; and success will make the whole world shine for both you and the child like a newly discovered star in the sky! Good luck to you.

SELECTED BIBLIOGRAPHY

Cruickshank, W. and Johnson, G., EDUCATION OF EXCEPTIONAL CHILDREN AND YOUTH, Prentice-Hall, Inc., Englewood Cliffs, New Jersey, 1958.

D'Evelyn, Kathryn E., MEETING CHILDREN'S EMOTIONAL NEEDS, Prentice-Hall, Inc., Englewood Cliffs, New Jersey, 1957.

Dinitz, S. et al., "Delinquency Proneness and School Achievement," EDUCATIONAL RESEARCH BULLETIN, V. 36.

Freud, Anna, PSYCHOANALYSIS FOR TEACHERS AND PARENTS, Emerson Books, Inc., New York, 1935.

Goldsmith, J. et al., "Changing the Delinquent's Concept of School," AMERICAN JOURNAL OF ORTHOPSYCHIATRY, V. 29, 1959.

Hartman, Heinz, Ernest Kris, and Rudolph Lowenstein, "Comments on the Formation of the Psychic Structure," THE PSYCHOANALYTIC STUDY OF THE CHILD, V. II, The International Universities Press, New York, 1946.

Havighurst, Robert, HUMAN DEVELOPMENT AND EDUCATION, Longmans, Green & Co., New York, 1953.

Johnston, Edgar G., Mildred Peters and William Eraiff, THE ROLE OF THE TEACHER IN GUIDANCE, Prentice-Hall, Inc., Englewood Cliffs, New Jersey, 1959.

Kaminkow, H. B., "Basic School Approaches in Preventing Juvenile Delinquency," UNDERSTANDING THE CHILD, V. 22, 1953.

Kaufman, Irving, EGO PSYCHOLOGY OF THE PREOEDIPAL PERSONALITY STRUCTURE: DIAGNOSTIC AND TREATMENT PRACTICE, Unpublished notes of Institute given at the Richmond Professional Institute of The Colleges of William and Mary, Richmond, Va., 1960.

Kornberg, L., A CLASS FOR DISTURBED CHILDREN, Bureau of Publications, Columbia University, New York, 1955.

Layne, W. J., "A Technique for Handling the Atypical Behavior Problem," SCHOOL REVIEW, V. 64, 1956.

Raskis, L. L., "Meeting the Reading Needs of Emotionally Disturbed Pupils," EXCEPTIONAL CHILDREN, V. 23, 1957.

Redl, Fritz, and William J. Watenberg, MENTAL HYGIENE IN TEACHING, Harcourt, Brace and Co., New York, 1951.

Spache, George, "Appraising the Personality of Remedial Pupils," EDUCATION IN A FREE WORLD, America Council on Education, 1954.

RUTH GASINK BOYER received a B.A. degree from the University of Minnesota in Sociology, and an M.S.S. degree from the Smith College School for Social Work in Psychiatric Social Work. She has had extensive experience in various kinds of social work, and seven years as School Social Worker in the Robbinsdale, Minnesota, Public Schools, during which period she also developed the Special Education Department. She is now Associate Professor of Social Work and Director of Field Work of the School of Social Work of the Richmond Professional Institute of the Colleges of William and Mary at Richmond, Virginia. She is a charter member of the National Association of Social Workers, and a past president of the Student Personnel Section of the Minnesota Education Association.

160

CHILDREN IN NEED OF INSTITUTIONAL CARE

Henry W. Maier
University of Washington

"What is past is prologue," a well-known quotation, is very apropos in our everyday approach to children with unusual complications. Yesterday's practices served as laboratories for today's approaches.

A child in our contemporary society is always viewed as part of a family. The family, that is, mother, father and in variant degrees siblings, assumes the major responsibility for a child's socialization and the transmission of "desirable" cultural values. As each child grows and develops his family increasingly depends and is asked to rely upon other societal institutions in its child-rearing effort. First, nursery schools supplement a child's gregarious experience with things and people. Later, schools enter with an increasing share in the partnership of bringing up children for a marathon of twelve to sixteen and more years. Other social institutions such as church, boys' or girls' clubs, community and recreation centers, supplement the child's development, wherever both the family and the community consider a special emphasis advisable. It is noteworthy that all these efforts—social, educational, religious, or character-building—occur with the clear understanding that the child is and continuously remains a part of the family. Most important, the family is recognized as his main resource for his socialization, his personal gratification and for identification. Furthermore, the family home stands for a place and a sense of belonging.

There are children, however, who require more than the

ordinary course of experiences for their successful development. They are children with *unusual* deviations in one or several aspects of their development. Consequently, they require additional and, at times, different attention and services than those available to children with more normal patterns of development. We find in our communities children with physical complications. These children tend to receive protective as well as corrective medical and nursing help or prosthetic aid, while emotional disturbances bring children to such therapeutic services as school guidance clinics, social work, psychotherapy, specialized nursery, play-group or camp programs. Children with unusual learning difficulties are also apt to secure special training opportunities through special programs or remedial teaching within the schools of their community. It is noteworthy that in one way or other each community mobilizes additional services in order to provide these children with *unusual* requirements the services they need. These services enable most of these children to remain within the "stream" of their own family, their peers, their neighborhood school and their community.

At the same time, however, we are aware of *special* programs for the blind, mentally retarded, delinquent or mentally sick children. These special programs are known as *Schools for the Blind, Training Schools, Correctional Institutions, Children's Wards,* and *Residential Treatment Centers.* We find these schools, "homes" or centers in our own communities and, more often than not, in far remote places in the less populated sections of our state. These programs were set up for "unusual children." Most of these programs have a long history[1] and reach back to a period when a child with the loss of sight was seen as a "blind child," a child with severe limitations in learning was pronounced a "mentally retarded child," and so forth. These children's unusual circumstances led their adult world to pronounce them as "unusual children." They were perceived as no longer within the ranges of acceptable variations in child development. In other words, one single deviation in the wide range of human functioning, such as the loss of sight, became the decisive variable of human growth and development. All other essential areas of

162

human functioning became defined as secondary and subordinate to the affliction. Society perceives and, therefore, establishes such a child as being *different* and consequently in need of a different course of life.

On the one hand we are tempted to proceed within the grooves of the previous practices, namely, to *categorize* children on the basis of their deviations, such as the historic classifications of blindness, deafness or mental deficiency. On the other hand, we operate on the premise that children, if at all possible, should grow up within their own family. If children happen to have unusual requirements, their specific complications need to be met through variations of and additions to the ordinary social, educational and medical facilities available to them in their immediate community. To illustrate, the former approach suggests dealing with these children as special entities, as unique classes of children in demand of special handling. The latter implies a challenge to deal with them first as children anywhere, and secondly, to concentrate all alterations in their peculiar life experience upon those steps which are absolutely essential in order that these children can develop into independent, effective citizens to the best of their potential capacities.

CONTEMPORARY CONCEPTS

Our contemporary knowledge and preferred practice can be summarized as follows: Human growth and development is a composite of many facets of human functions. No single function exists independently of the others and solely determines the course of human development. They are all supplementary to each other. Any one affects and, at times, can compensate for another one. Consequently, any one impairment can be in part compensated by others. No one functional deficiency or deviation can deny the fact that the child still continues to have the same wants, requirements and potential opportunities as any other growing and developing child of similar maturity. Children with severe deviations require special attention to the end that they can obtain with as little divergence as possible the same life experience considered as essential for all children of their community. It must be recognized, however, that the description, "unusual," constitutes a social definition and not the nature of the condition. Consequently, the success of special care and treatment programs for such "unusual" complications depends upon their public acceptance as an advisable and desirable effort.[2]

Who are then the children requiring institutional care?

What are the circumstances which are nowadays defined as decisive criteria for a child's removal from his home?

The foregoing presentation stresses the essential combination of "normal" home and community life experience supplemented by auxiliary services as the arrangements of choice for children with unusual developmental complications. Auxiliary services are to serve equally to rehabilitate or to compensate for the child's deviation and to enable the child to stay within his home and his community. Whenever this combination fails to meet the child's essential developmental needs it then might become advisable to weigh alternate plans. In some instances the home and community conditions point toward a change. Then a different home living arrangement such as *foster home placement* might be in order. To illustrate, in the case of actual loss of parents or a loss of their ultimate effectiveness, a new home arrangement, such as an adoptive or foster home, might seem advisable. In some instances, in the absence of urgently required auxiliary services, especially in small communities (i.e., classes in braille for the sightless or special classes for especially slow learners), foster home placement in a different community might be indicated. Again, all planning has to proceed with the full understanding that children with unusual circumstances demand *individual* rather than standardized arrangements.

In contrast, however, children for whom ordinary home and community life can no longer provide the care and essential experience they specifically need, and for whom auxiliary services within the community can no longer alleviate any of the intervening deficiencies, might be in need of a different form of living experience. Their unusual circumstances might lead them to

164

placement in one of the several institutional care and treatment programs. To re-emphasize, institutional placement becomes advisable when it appears that a child might be helped more effectively through *other* than family-living, rather than on the basis of any set classifications. Then, institutional group-living provides the "home base," while auxiliary services such as specialized therapies, education and social work, must be structured as essential service features of the institutional program.

TWELVE RANGES OF DEVIATION
AND INSTITUTIONAL PLACEMENT

In general, we can point to twelve groupings of circumstances which might imply the need for institutional care. In the discussion of these groupings which follow, it will be noted that, with the exception of the first one, the underlying circumstances point to separation from family-living within an open community.

1. Children and youth require immediate, but frequently only temporary detention, when they get into difficulties and find themselves so far outside of parental control that the community must convey to them that their social delinquency, or extreme lack of self-control, must be compensated by *immediate social control*. These include children persistently truant, in difficulties with the law, or frequently in conflict with the moral codes of their community. They might require a brief commitment to a local *Youth Detention Center*. A period of detention furnishes, first, the support and controls these children and their home situations seem to lack. Secondly, temporary detention can provide such children with opportunities to reveal their own confusions, and their family and neighborhood problems. Confinement then leads to an opportunity for appraisal of the underlying circumstances and planning of rehabilitation. Most important, detention is neither punishment nor treatment. It constitutes an intermediary step, a short-term period of stabilization evaluation and planning.

2. Children whose social and education diagnosis for self-

165

dependency in ordinary community life is so bleak that eventual institutionalization for their care and support becomes essential, require an institutional care program. Commonly, institutional, twenty-four-hour care becomes necessary at the point where neither home nor auxiliary services can render any longer the appropriate care unless home-life becomes so revamped that family-living ceases to exist. Children with severe conditions of mental retardation fall within this grouping. The degree of retardation or age limit for home-living cannot be established on any scale or by a blanket rule. In general, young children with even the darkest diagnosis can substantially benefit from the ordinary *personal* care inherent in a home situation for an extended period. The frequent contention that prolonged home-living makes it more difficult for the child to submit later on to permanent institutionalization is not borne out by our research and experiences.[3] To the contrary, as long as parental care can contribute to the child's development, he can gain much inner security and personal independence which will enable him to adapt more effectively and securely to the milieu of institutional living.[4] These children eventually require the protection and minimal social requisites provided by *institutions for mentally retarded children.*

3. Children whose rate of socialization and requirements for social training are so out of range that their growing-up process demands a miniature world, primarily adapted to their needs, should be evaluated for possible placement within an institutional care and training program. These youngsters' training is usually so cumbersome that every possible avenue of learning must be utilized and provided by specially trained and highly qualified persons, while simultaneously all stimulation and frustration which hampers opportunities for learning must be kept at a minimum. Again, these children can benefit from parental care as long as parental care (see situation 2 above) is neither thwarted nor frustrated by the complications inherent in their slow process of socialization. Their training can then become more beneficial in *training schools for retarded children.* The timing and length of around-the-clock care away from home

166

depends upon each child's particular circumstances. No ground rules can be drawn up.

The nature of an institutional experience has to become primarily that of social training, intertwined with personal care. Schooling and vocational training must serve to enhance each individual's personal competency. In other words, these children need a *temporary* life experience of personal care for their personal development. Vocational training becomes important at the point where training improves rather than mars their psycho-socio development.

4. Children with extreme neurological damage or functional breakdown, for whom our present-day medical and psychiatric knowledge and skills hold little promise for cure, require equally permanent institutional care at the point where their presence in the home will deny rather than encourage parental supportive and nurturing care. These children's peculiar behavior and attitudes frequently demand adult attention and care which can avoid a personal entanglement with their bizarre forms of living. Above all, they need the attention of caring adults who can fully devote themselves for definite periods. These children need the protection and permissive atmosphere which can be afforded within the wings of a *psychiatric ward* or a *residential treatment center*. They need a community with its own standards apart from the scrutiny and expectations of the community-at-large.[5]

5. Children whose self-dependence and regular development are so distorted by physical abnormalities that all life experiences have to be subordinated to special regulations connected with their disabilities frequently require the special program offered by a children's *orthopedic hospital* or *convalescent center*. Care and treatment, in these cases, is based upon a medical diagnosis. Placement, however, has to be anchored in a *social* diagnosis. The priority of medical decision must not deny the importance of other paramount developmental prerequisites. Therefore, institutional care becomes essential, first, if recovery is solely dependent upon it; secondly, if medical care within the home or on an outpatient basis becomes so cumbersome that it would negate the very security and stimulation a home could offer otherwise. If

167

continuous everyday parental care is no longer possible in the home, the essential ingredients of parental care have to be added to the nursing efforts in the medical program. Children with acute medical complications and in urgent need of medical care are still children. They continue to need similar care and experience as children need everywhere. Moreover, hospitalization does not occur on the basis of the type of disease or defect but rather upon an evaluation of the child's medical prognosis in relation to the psycho-social opportunities either in the hospital or in a home. Such an assessment has to occur periodically throughout the length of the child's treatment.

6. Children who are so severely withdrawn from all human relationships that they are no longer "tuned in" to the give-and-take of family-living, might be more readily served in a *residential treatment center*. Children diagnosed as *autistic* fall within this grouping. Such youngsters frequently appear as if they were retarded upon casual observation or an appraisal of their responsiveness to any one of our standard intelligence tests. Actually, however, these children have their basic deviation in their emotional make-up, in their communication with self in place of communication with others. They tend to find stimulation and satisfaction from their own sounds, rhythmic movements, and body. In contrast to mentally retarded children, these youngsters tend to recoil from most interpersonal contacts unless these contacts occur within a quality and timing of their choice. In other words, effective and personal care must occur within these children's sphere of activity and level of interaction, if at all. Their requirements can hardly be met by even the most giving and flexible form of family-living unless family-life ceases to be family-and-community oriented.

7. Children with unpredictable confusions about their relationships to adults frequently require other than a home setting. Such children, similar to those in the previous grouping (situation 6 above) deny themselves and their own, adoptive, or foster parents, the essential opportunities for relating effectively to each other. They are urgently in need of a group situation. A non-family-centered group setting can afford the necessary

168

protection, care and stimulation while demanding a minimum of close personal involvement. Simultaneously, their caring adults can help them bit by bit to gain new confidence in adults and adult authority in order that their previously warped or perverted feelings about adults can change from a frustrating distrust to a trusting dependency. These children are in need of an institutional program geared to their immediate social withdrawal as well as to changes in keeping with their improvement. Such a tolerant and fluctuating approach cannot be met by family-living, however urgent the needs of any one family member may be. Family-life necessarily must meet the expectations of various family members and those of the immediate community.

8. Children for whom family-setting symbolizes "failure," due to various unhappy experiences with family-living, reach a point where they might need a decisively different form of living. These are the children who may have traveled through many homes of their family circle, helpful neighbors, or foster parents. Frequent disruptions or a chain of unsatisfying (to the children) family experiences lead them to the point where they no longer sense it as safe and worthwhile to invest any personal attachment within any one family situation. These youngsters are in need of identification with a group and a setting with a variety of adults. For them it will be safer, and consequently more satisfying, to relate to and to depend upon peers and a program geared toward group care. Only within the safety of the group will they eventually establish a sense of dependency and a one-to-one relationship with one central person. The latter situation must ultimately occur in order that the child may identify and eventually relate differentially to others as an independent individual.

9. Children with unpredictable patterns of *outward* behavior can be equally designated as "emotionally disturbed." Yet, our experiences with them are quite different from those described in the above groupings in situations 6 and 7. These youngsters lack essentially in impulse controls. They require adults and a setting which can incorporate both controls and opportunities for expression which will afford them new successful life experiences. These children need more than ordinary parental controls and

permission (limits and outlets) which usually can be offered by a community-oriented family home. An institutional program can build-in these essential controls as part of its setting and personal handling of these children. Simultaneously, ample opportunities must be provided for a rich diet in daily experience in order that these children can express their feelings while finding opportunities to utilize more effectively, that is, less impulsively, everyday life experience.[6]

10. Children, and especially adolescents, in need of controls and psycho-social acceptance beyond those usually inherent in family settings, require institutional care. In this grouping we could place a vast percentage of boys and girls who make up the present-day population of our institutions for delinquents. Conflicts with the law, that is, insults to property, authority or community mores, mark these youngsters as offenders and statistically as *delinquents*. Their delinquent acts are provoking eye-catchers. Their case and/or gang histories, however, reveal youngsters urgently in need of acceptance and social controls. Frequently, their joint desire for acceptance has forced them into growth-denying gangs or brought them to self-defeating personal involvement with a partner of the opposite sex. Social controls can act as essential growth-producing ingredients, if they are combined with opportunities for experiencing a sense of worth-whileness. They need personal trust, interest-consuming activities and a promise for immediate success, in whatever constitutes for them their initial tasks. Again, an institutional program might provide tangible and genuine acceptance and controls to foster a sense of worthwhileness and self-control from within.

11. Adolescents are sometimes described as "belonging neither to their own home nor to anywhere else, but to themselves." Such comment describes the outward impression adolescents convey in contemporary America.[7] Actually, however, contrary to their apparent behavior, our adolescents are still very much anchored in their home life. They would find themselves very much at a loss and handicapped in their adolescent development if they were to lose their home base and the shadows of their caring adults. On the other hand, if, for one reason or other,

170

adolescents can no longer count on a close association with their home or these ties have been disrupted by confinement to a child-caring institution, they might be considered for a *group home*. At this stage of their development they are neither "in tune" nor should be requested to start anew in investing in the personal matrix of a "new" and different family situation at a time when their essential life struggle is that of separating from early family ties and in establishing membership in the social systems of their adult world (work group, reference groups and social partnership group). A *group home,* present knowledge suggests, seems more appropriate for them as their home base. A group home in one way is an institutional setting as repeatedly described in this chapter. In another way it is a home. It is socially structured; but clients and their central adults are committed to the immediate expectations of the surrounding social environment, not too unlike family-living.

12. Finally, children undiagnosable by traditional outpatient procedures might require a different form of study. Children for whom any combination of diagnostic case or group studies, medical and psychological tests, or psychiatric interviews, yields no conclusive information as to the circumstances underlying their deviations, might require periods of study and controlled observations within an institutional setting. Such an arrangement seems particularly advisable if the apparent difficulties find expression in interpersonal relations and in the children's incapacity to meet everyday life situations. For them rehabilitation depends first upon establishing a proper diagnosis. An institutional program prepared for such an effort might furnish the necessary clues. Institutional twenty-four-hour care and surveillance will afford an opportunity to study all aspects of such children's mode of living.

RANGES OF DEVIATION NO LONGER DECISIVE
FOR INSTITUTIONAL PLACEMENT

The foregoing pages highlight twelve groupings of children with unusual developmental phenomena which might require institutional care as part of the corrective effort. This listing does not include certain ranges of deviations which were once considered as grounds for institutional placement. To clarify their exclusion and to explain a contemporary trend, we shall mention these factors briefly.

Orphans and economically deprived youngsters once made up the main core of the institutional population. Today, homes for orphans serve other children even if they still carry their historic designation on their stationery. Orphans and other children without ties (social orphans) are either adoptable or can benefit from family living through foster home placement. Economic deprivations are substantially met through social security and other public welfare measures. They, like other children, have the opportunity of growing up in a family.

Moreover, the above listing purposely avoids such traditional classifications as "the blind," "the deaf and dumb," and "the mentally retarded," as well as "the unusually superior child." As stated before, none of these attributes alone define a child's need for institutional placement. Rather, institutional placement is a question of appropriate choice; namely, can institutional group care, or home living, combat more effectively the unusual complications?

Children from large families were once sent as a group to a children's home when their own family situation disintegrated and warranted their removal, as it was hoped thus to preserve the family. Experience has proved, however, that these children tended to lose more in ordinary life experience than was gained by holding the siblings together within the same institutional confines. Foster home placements can assure children from large family groups "normal" community experience without necessarily depriving them of frequent contacts with their brothers and sisters, if deemed advisable.

Finally, placing a child in an institution in case of emergency or as a "last resort," due to lack of alternatives, might be a necessity in extreme and rare situations. But such placements can never be listed as appropriate institutional placements. Throughout this chapter institutional care and treatment has been envisaged as a specialized facet, as a therapeutic tool of treatment for any one of the helping professions—medicine, social work, psychiatry, education. Institutional care and treatment, therefore, is no longer a traditional recourse of convenience but is rather becoming a diagnostically established resource of choice.

CONCLUDING SUMMARY

In a book dealing with the "unusual child" it might be advisable to point out once more that the descriptive term *unusual* defines the observer's classification of the child's condition rather than the condition *per se*. The very same conditions, such as mental retardation or behavior disorder, may establish any one child as a *child with unusual complications*. Yet these complications might not interfere with one child's ability to continue to benefit from home and open community life, whereas another child with similar complications might require other arrangements, such as institutionalization, in order to have a better chance to grow and develop to his best advantage.

To sum up, it is not the "unusual child" but rather the combinations of the child's personal situation and the opportunities offered within his immediate community, which will eventually determine if the child can benefit best from the ingredients of everyday life offered within an institution or within a family home.

SELECTED BIBLIOGRAPHY

Bettelheim, Bruno, LOVE IS NOT ENOUGH, The Free Press, Inc., Glencoe, Illinois, 1950. Descriptive account of the integration of rehabilitative care, programming and creation of a therapeutic environment for the treatment of severely disturbed young children. Special stress upon an unitary approach in the interpersonal relationship between child and his caring counselors and the overall institutional program.

Bowlby, J., MATERNAL CARE AND MENTAL HEALTH, World Health Organization, Geneva, Switzerland, 1952. Collection of classical papers and research findings on the implications of early institutional care combined with deprivation of personal attention of young infants.

Golden Anniversary White House Conference, FOCUS ON CHILDREN AND YOUTH, Golden Anniversary White House Conference, Washington, D. C., 1960. Summary of pertinent studies, reports and working papers of the nineteen fifties which serve as the foundation of the thinking and recommendations of the White House Conference on Children and Youth of 1960. (Pertinent to the chapter is the summary of Standards on Institutional Care of Child Welfare League of America—see pp. 36-37).

Gula, Martin, CHILD-CARING INSTITUTIONS, Children's Bureau, U. S. Department of Health, Education and Welfare, Washington, D. C., 1958. Review of historic development of contemporary practices and settings of child-caring institutions and an analysis of contemporary problems and unanswered questions posed for child care and treatment institutions.

Jones, Howard, RELUCTANT REBELS, Association Press, New York, 1960. Descriptive analysis of the various forms of institutional treatment programs currently existing in England and the United States, their underlying rationale and the range of clients they intend to serve.

Maas, Henry S. and Richard E. Engler, Jr., CHILDREN IN NEED OF PARENTS, Columbia University Press, New York, 1955. Detailed account and vivid discussion of a research project and its findings on the different communal (cultural) approaches to the care of children who need other than in-their-own-home care. Specially stimulating is its analysis of the impact of community attitudes for the opportunities for, as well as type and quality offered to, its children in need of substitute parental care.

Maier, Henry W., A HISTORY OF TRENDS OF CHILD-CARE IN CHILDREN'S INSTITUTIONS (Unpublished Manuscript), School of Social Work, University of Minnesota, Minneapolis, Minnesota, 1957. Account of the historic development and phases of child-care practices in institutional care in the United States from the beginning of the nineteenth century to the present.

174

Redl, Fritz, THE AGGRESSIVE CHILD, Basic Books, Inc., New York, 1958. Combined edition of Redl's previous publications, CHILDREN WHO HATE (1951) and CONTROLS FROM WITHIN (1952), which deal with the problems and questions posed by children with ineffective ego controls and their treatment within a therapeutic milieu.

Witmer, Helen L. and Ruth Kotinsky, PERSONALITY IN THE MAKING, Harper Brothers, Inc., New York, 1952. Integration of the working papers of the mid-century White House Conference on Children and Youth of 1950, and the implications of this accumulated knowledge for the understanding of the individual, his family, his community, and his social institutions. Special attention should be directed toward the material on personality development (Erik H. Erikson's concept) and the account of existing social services.

Witmer, Helen L. and Ruth Kotinsky, NEW PERSPECTIVE FOR RESEARCH, Children's Bureau, U. S. Department of Health, Education and Welfare, Washington, D.C., 1956. Edited proceedings of a working conference on problems in understanding adolescents, especially adolescents defined as "delinquents." Erik H. Erikson, Robert K. Merton and Fritz Redl served as the principal contributors. Erik Erikson's development of his concepts of "ego identity" and the "phychosocial moratorium" are especially pertinent for this chapter.

HENRY W. MAIER, Ph.D., Associate Professor, School of Social Work, University of Washington, Seattle 5, Washington. Fellow, American Association of Orthopsychiatry, Member of the National Association of Social Workers. Ph.D., University of Minnesota; M.S.W., Western Reserve University; A.B., Oberlin College. Formerly, he taught at the School of Social Work, University of Minnesota, as well as at the Department of Child Psychiatry and Child Development, Western Psychiatric Institute of the Medical School, University of Pittsburgh. His writings and research have been published in the AMERICAN JOURNAL OF ORTHOPSYCHIATRY, CHILD WELFARE, JOURNAL OF SOCIOLOGICAL RESEARCH, THE GROUP, THE INTERNATIONAL JOURNAL OF GROUP PSYCHOTHERAPY, and others. His special areas of concentration are social group work and institutional care and treatment. Prior to his academic career he worked on all levels of institutional care: classroom teacher for the mentally retarded, cottage parent, cottage parents' supervisor, social worker, and institutional consultant.

NOTES

1. At the time Horace Mann stood for widening the range of public education, Samuel Gidley Howe and others called attention to the fact that "the blind" were also educable. "Child saving" efforts for blind children and creation of special public schools for them became a combined undertaking. It is not surprising, therefore, that we inherited the following combination: *special, public schools* for children who happen to be either blind or deaf-mutes.

2. We can observe in such a development the change of public attitudes toward children with epileptic complications. Originally, this disease caused much concern and puzzlement. Children were confined to special institutions or sections of institutions reserved for "epileptics." More recently public acceptance of children having epileptic attacks has become widespread. Fewer questions are raised about their continuance of their regular school program within their community.

3. Masland, Richard L., Seymour B. Sarason and Thomas Gladwin, MENTAL SUBNORMALITY, Basic Books, Inc., New York, 1958.

4. Bowlby, J., MATERNAL CARE AND MENTAL HEALTH, World Health Organization, Geneva, Switzerland, 1952.

5. Robinson, J. Franklin (Editor), PSYCHIATRIC TREATMENT OF CHILDREN, American Psychiatric Association, Washington, D. C., 1957.

6. Redl, Fritz and David Wineman, THE AGGRESSIVE CHILD, Basic Books, Inc., New York, 1957.

7. Erikson, Erik H. "Ego Identity and the Psychosocial Moratorium," in Witmer, Helen L. and Ruth Kotinsky, NEW PERSPECTIVE FOR RESEARCH, Children's Bureau, U. S. Department of Health, Education and Welfare, Washington, D. C., 1956.

176

SOCIALIZATION OF THE ATYPICAL CHILD

Frederick Elkin
McGill University

Socialization, when applied to the child, refers to the process by which he learns the patterns of the society, or any group of which he is a member. It includes learning not only the expected ways of behavior, but the appropriate attitudes and feelings as well.[1] In what way, we ask, is the process of socialization unique for the atypical child? How is his psychological world different from others? How different are the roles of the family, school, peer group, and other agencies of socialization?

In this discussion, we include two types of atypical children: first, those who are atypical because of distinctive individual characteristics, often physiologically derived, for example, the deaf, crippled, mentally retarded, or gifted. Second, those who are atypical because of the distinctive characteristics of their families, for example, those whose parents are migrants, of mixed religions, mental patients, or adoptive. We are omitting those children who come from subcultures of such atypical groups as the Hutterites or orthodox Jews or those who, through accident or unique circumstance, are only temporarily hospitalized or set apart.

Although the varieties of deviance are many, atypical children have two characteristics in common.[2] First, others, in one way or another, consider them to be different, have different expectations of them, and treat them differently. Perhaps others organize special schools, have fund raising campaigns in their behalf, use

177

traditional expressions of sympathy or scorn, or avoid particular subjects of discussion. Second, the children, if they have sufficient mental capacity and awareness, come to know and feel that, in some particular deviant respect, they are different from others.

Thus atypical children have unique experiences not only because of the necessities of their particular deviance—a blind child lacks certain common visual stimuli, a child of a migrant family spends considerable time travelling, and the child of a mental patient is visited by a case worker—but also because they have different rights and obligations. Others, directly or indirectly, behave differently towards them and they, in turn, come to know and feel they are unique. The atypical child is not a "normal" child with a simple discrete difference. Rather, because of his particular deviance, he experiences a different complex of relationships with others and has a unique self image. How important this becomes of course varies, depending on the particular type of deviance, the attitudes of the society at large, and the treatment the child receives from others.

In this chapter we shall discuss—in so far as they are relevant to the atypical child—the values of the larger society; the distinct problems of socialization as experienced by the child himself; the role of such agencies of socialization as the family, school, and peer group; and finally suggestions which follow from our discussion.

VALUES AND THE ATYPICAL CHILD

We cannot understand our attitudes and behavior to the atypical child solely by studying our values. Our ideas of good and bad and right and wrong are too ambivalent and contradictory and their relationships to actual behavior too complex. Yet our values do often, directly or indirectly, affect our behavior to the atypical child, do serve as justifications for many of our actions, and are a necessary consideration in any proposed program of change.

Among the more prominent value complexes in our society

178

which directly affect our attitudes and behavior to the atypical child is that of health, beauty, and physical fitness in general. We publicize Miss America contests, choose high school beauty queens, idealize local and national sports heroes, stress the benefits of physical education and, in innumerable ways, emphasize the value of good looks and sound bodies. We cannot help but recognize and, to some degree, internalize these values. In so doing we implicitly disparage those who do not "measure up," those who are unattractive, have facial deformities, or physical handicaps of one kind or another. In day to day situations, these values underlie many of our reactions—we are pleased that our children are called handsome, we dread polio epidemics, we sympathize with the blind. We do not, in our society, as do some Italians, affirm the counter value that a deformed child is a "gift of God," a sign of God's trust in the family's strength and devotion.

A related complex of values in our culture derives from our "Puritan ethic." "God helps those who help themselves." We believe that individuals should be responsible, have high aspirations, and achieve to the best of their abilities. It is the duty of parents and other adults to teach such values. Applied to the atypical child, we expect him to accept his particular deviancy, to try to overcome any hardships it entails and, perhaps above all, not to waste time and effort by feeling and expressing self pity. We admire the deviant, the Helen Keller and Franklin D. Roosevelt who, despite handicaps, makes his mark in the world. The gifted child has a similar responsibility to make the most of his talents and abilities; it is wrong and unworthy of him to settle for mediocrity. This Puritan ethic, if sufficiently internalized, is a strong source of pressure and anxiety on the deviant child and those responsible for his welfare.

Another pertinent value in our society with a tradition that ranges from the David and Goliath story to modern westerns, is sympathy for the underdog. An accompanying value affirms that we should help the underprivileged, those less fortunate than ourselves. We manifest such values in our aid to disaster areas, support to underdeveloped countries, and contributions to Red

179

Feather campaigns. Applied to the atypical child, we contribute to charities for the orphaned, blind, and retarded. In everyday life we go out of our way to help the crippled child on the bus and avoid asking embarrassing questions. At times, our sympathy and desire to help may mingle with an attitude of pity towards the "poor blind" and "orphaned waifs," for whom childhood presumably is not the happy period we believe it should be.

Still another relevant complex of values focuses about conformity and social adjustment. We are concerned with the opinions of others, we wish to be liked and are reluctant to express idiosyncratic ideas or behavior. Many writers—in most recent years, David Riesman in *The Lonely Crowd* and William H. Whyte in *The Organization Man*—have shown the numerous areas of life pervaded by such ideas. Applied to children, we are concerned with their "all-around likeableness" and adjustment to peers. We do not want our children to be "characters," we wonder whether the child of a mental patient might be unstable and a harmful influence, we discourage our child from being too interested in isolating hobbies, we worry lest our child becomes a close buddy of a boy who wears a brace. Being different in itself suggests a stigma.[3]

THE ROLE AND SELF IMAGE OF THE ATYPICAL CHILD

A child has positions or *statuses* in many groupings and, for each, there is a different set of expectations or *roles*. As a boy, for example, he is expected to play with tools, not dolls; to shovel snow, play football, and not be afraid of worms. As a schoolboy, he is expected to do homework and pay attention to his teacher. So too are there expectations for position in the family, religion, nationality, age, social level, ethnic group and other statuses.

Learning roles necessitates the development of a *self*, the ability to view one's own behavior from the position of others, to be both subject and object. With a "self," a child can ask what is or is not appropriate for him as a boy, oldest brother, Cub Scout, Jew, or whatever other status he might possess. He can also be pleased or displeased with his behavior, thoughts, and character. In time, through a process best described by George Mead, he comes to feel the rightness of the appropriate behavior and attitudes for his particular statuses.[4]

Compared to other children, the atypical child has one extra status to learn, that associated with his particular deviance. He is a child with a "bad leg" or "bad heart" or he is adopted, or talented in music. For each of these statuses, there are expectations, rights, and obligations, and the child is rewarded and punished by others accordingly. The bright child is expected to do well in school and is reprimanded for getting only mediocre grades; the crippled child is expected to have difficulty carrying heavy packages and is complimented for getting up the stairs by himself; the boy with the rheumatic heart is given a jigsaw puzzle to play with and reproved for running around too much; the delinquent child is expected to be "bad" and his friends jeer him if he meekly obeys his teacher. Thus through the names given the particular deviance and the treatment the child receives, he learns in what respects he is distinct and what is expected of him.

At the same time, through innumerable remarks and gestures, seen or heard in the mass media, overheard in conversation, or expressed to the child himself, he learns the values of the society and the standards for children in general. The remarks may be casual—about a beautiful baby, a sturdy little chap, a girl whose eyes are just like Mommy's, a child who wins a musical competition, or a boy who is delighted with his new hockey skates—but they do indicate the values of beauty, health, talent, team sports, and the stigma of adoption.

The atypical child is likely to apply these values to himself, to ask how he measures up and to feel pleased or displeased with his own characteristics and development.[5] To generalize on the importance of a particular deviant status is of course impossible since this is just one of many statuses and each, depending on the circumstances, may become of greater or lesser importance, but the perspective of a self image remains a necessary consideration.

The roles and self images of many types of deviants have two common components—dependence and a sense of misfortune.

181

Atypical children, such as the hard-of-hearing, crippled, or children of mental patients, are necessarily dependent on others. The fear that atypical children might not only recognize this dependence but accept it as a right or depreciate themselves because of it, underlies the strong efforts of teachers and therapists to make handicapped children as self-reliant as their particular handicaps allow.

To be dependent, from another point of view, means to make demands on others. This may give a child a sense of power; but it may also, when he views himself from what he believes, rightly or wrongly, is the position of others, make him feel he is a burden—not a source of love, gratification, and hope, but an encumbrance, helped out of a sense of duty. A roughly similar situation may exist for the delinquent boy or the child in a foster home. For the gifted child, the situation may be reversed. He may see himself as relatively less dependent than others and, especially if he is spoken of with pride and called on to display his talents, see himself as an especial source of gratification.

The sense of misfortune—again, except for the gifted—is a closely related component. The atypical child may see himself as limited in his day-to-day activities, the groups to which he can belong, and his choice of a career or spouse; as humiliated and shamed even by those who want to help; and as a source of embarrassment to his siblings and others emotionally important to him. That some of these unhappy experiences may be necessary or helpful for his future life may not be understood and, even if understood, difficult to accept.

All children, the late Harry Stack Sullivan suggested, develop a system of self-security, a system of defenses—including patterns of relationships to others—by which they try to protect their ego and self esteem.[6] These patterns with others may center on avoidance, self-depreciation, subtle aggression, subservience, or of acting the "character." A type of defense especially significant for atypical children is suggested by the concept "reference group." A reference group is that group with which someone identifies, the group an individual uses as a standard for his activities and ideas.[7] The atypical child may have many reference groups associated with such statuses as religion, nationality, race, or attendance at a particular school. However, for many, the key reference group is that associated with his deviance. The reasons are understandable. By virtue of a selective interest and perception and his contacts in schools, doctors' offices and hospitals, he comes to know many who are or have been in positions like himself. With these children, in reality or fantasy, he has areas of common interest; feels better understood and less self-conscious, and expresses more spontaneity; is less often embarrassed and the object of pity, sympathy, or derision; is spared any pains of comparison; and can find models to emulate. The more important this reference group in the child's contacts and thoughts, the less important relatively are his other potential reference groups. We can see the importance of such reference groups in the associations of the deaf which include, besides informal groupings, churches, clubs, insurance societies, newspapers, journals, national professional and fraternal organizations, and athletic associations which periodically hold International Games of the Deaf.[8]

AGENCIES OF SOCIALIZATION

The Family. The family is the first agency of socialization with which the child has any contact and the most crucial. Here the child forms his first emotional attachments, finds his first models, and in general develops a base on which subsequent experiences act. And the family remains paramount while the child comes into contact with other agencies of socialization. The attitudes and behavior which characterize the socialized child—the language he uses; his moral values and loyalties; his knowledge of occupations, popular heroes and transportation facilities; his ability to use pencils, telephones, and tools; his awareness of dangers and the devices for influencing others—all have their beginnings in the family. We place primary emphasis in this chapter on deviance, but recognize its limited role in socialized behavior.

The relationships between an atypical child and his family are reciprocal. In the eyes of others, and the family members themselves, an atypical child stamps a family as atypical and atypical parents stamp a child as atypical. Both have statuses they would otherwise not have.

A family with an atypical child ordinarily has no recourse to automatic machinery and must itself work out solutions to its problems.[9] Some problems concern the atypical child directly. How, for example, is he to develop a sense of independence. Ordinarily this independence—the ability to do with less help from others and to make more of one's own decisions—comes about gradually, encouraged by maturation, broadening interests, and a widening circle of emotional attachments. However, the atypical child may have a more limited sphere of attachments and his dependency may last longer and be more intense. Another common problem focuses on long-run aspirations. The values which the family of a given social level has for its children —the professional career, the "good" marriage, or the hope that a child will achieve higher than his parents—may not be feasible. What too of standards of evaluation and methods of reward and punishment, or the means of encouraging normal development in non-deviant spheres. In day-to-day relationships—how are parents to explain the separations at hospitals, the cautions, the slurs and stares of others? The child does not readily understand the "deferred gratification pattern"—that a brace on his leg or rejection by a peer group now may make life easier in later years.[10]

Interrelationships within a family also present distinctive problems. There may be extra duties or at least an arrangement of jobs different from those in other families; family members may disagree on the priorities of unanticipated tasks; they may discuss certain subjects elaborately and studiously avoid others; they may develop a particular "front" before outsiders.[11] Perhaps siblings feel they receive too little attention, love, freedom, or financial help; or perhaps the deviance in the family embarrasses them before their friends.

In the community too, there are distinctive problems—taking long holidays or entertaining may be impossible with an unpredictable retarded child, going into town with a crippled child might

184

be an ordeal, relaxed feelings with unsympathetic relatives might be difficult for an adoptive family. Problems which seem trivial to others may be sources of family crises.

What makes these distinctive problems especially important in atypical families is that the ideas and feelings which accompany them, in all probability, are communicated to the child. Through hesitations, nervous movements, "tightening up," sudden relaxations, and other unwitting expressive gestures, the parents communicate their disappointments, guilt feelings, embarrassments, anxieties, and gratifications. Harry Stack Sullivan, and more recently Jurgen Ruesch, have shown how subtle this type of communication can be.[12] Thus the child, no matter what may be the intention of the parents and siblings, is likely to become aware of the emotional meanings attached to his deviancy.

For family members to recognize the problems is only a partial answer. Often the day to day problems are so pressing and the medical and financial demands so exacting that parents can do only what is immediately and objectively necessary. Long run questions are left to resolve themselves.

Peer Groups. Peer groups have several important functions in socializing the child—they give him experience in egalitarian type relationships; teach him popular culture and aspects of our culture ordinarily taboo; and especially, through the support members give each other, help him become independent of his parents and other authority figures.

The peer group activities of the atypical child, however, are often limited. Atypical children with certain disabilities must stay away from others to avoid infections or the over-expenditure of energy. Some, for example, the epileptic, immigrant, or blind, perforce spend considerable time alone or with their families. And often, the atypical child's peer group activity is limited because the peers refuse to acknowledge him as an equal or because the child, with or without good reason, is unhappy and withdraws.

When the atypical child is among his peers, in the neighborhood or at school, he is not always gently treated. Peer group members, seeking targets for their hostile feelings or seeking to impress their friends, may mimic the accent of the immigrant child, call the lame boy "slow poke," or the deformed child "a big ape." Even when the behavior of others is not malicious—for example, not inviting the crippled child to a dancing party or choosing him last for a team competition—the child feels he is rejected. Thus to view himself from the position of the peer group is often humiliating. And contributing all the more to the wounds may be the attitudes of the child's parents, and the child himself, who have internalized the values of social adjustment and good peer group relationships.

How the child reacts to peer group relations—the degree, for example, to which he withdraws, or seeks the companionship of adults or deviant reference groups—depends of course on many variables. Did the family acknowledge the deviance when he was young and, if so, how did they define it? Have peer group members ever matter-of-factly accepted his deviance? To what degree does he find gratification in hobbies and school work? Does he know others who are similarly deviant? To be considered too is the child's stage of development. Certain periods, perhaps when he enters school or during adolescence, may be especially critical.

The School. The school in our society has important functions for any child—it teaches him our culture and intellectual heritage; it upholds respect for authority, knowledge, and achievement; it encourages politeness, propriety, and proper language; and it prepares him for an occupation or career. The school also —and herein lies its special significance for the atypical child— helps the child to develop personally and socially through extending his range of contacts.

The selection of a school is no problem for most atypical children; those whose parents are adopted, mentally deficient, divorced, migrant, etc., go to the public school; those who are blind, retarded, and deaf, if feasible, attend a segregated school. For certain other children, for example, the crippled or mildly hard of hearing, a choice may be available. The differences between the two types of schools point up certain pertinent sociopsychological problems.

In the public school, the deviant child is unique by virtue of

186

his deviance. The child who doesn't hear well may sit in the front of the room, the crippled child may be excused from gym class, and the child of divorced parents may have forms signed only by his mother. Others know that the child is deviant. The teachers may be sympathetic but are neither especially trained to handle a deviant, nor are they in a position to give him very much attention. So the child, to a great degree, is left to the mercy of his peers who, as we have noted, may or may not be kind and understanding.

In contrast, in the segregated schools, the teachers may be especially trained and the facilities and activities especially adapted. The children themselves may differ in age, sex, religion, social level, and other characteristics, but what sets them apart is their particular deviance—they are all more or less in the same position and do not feel very different because of their deviance. Nor is there any "unfair" competition. But the school for these children, in contrast to those who attend public school, is a special situation and may be strikingly different from the situation at home or in the neighborhood where each is an individual deviant. The long run significance of this difference on a child's self image is an important research question on which, unfortunately, we have little information.

Innumerable other agencies such as hospitals, church groups, special camps, volunteer charity associations, and welfare agencies may have important roles in giving the atypical child new perspectives for viewing and judging himself. Some of these agencies, such as hospitals and camps, involve a separation of the child from his family and take over certain parental functions, a situation which may be quite traumatic for the child.[13] On the other hand, these new settings may also give the child the opportunity to extend his range of interests and knowledge of people, form new friendships, and in various ways test his personality expressions and capabilities. And of especial importance, the atypical child may develop close emotional ties with particular "significant others"—perhaps a social worker, physiotherapist, or camp leader —who not only help the child break his family dependency ties but also give him new models of behavior.

CONCLUSION

We know much more about the physiological and psychological development of the atypical child than we do about his socialization. Pertinent socio-psychological research is still in its infancy. Nevertheless, our perspective which focuses on the meaning the deviance has for the child and its relationship to other aspects of social development, suggests some directions that merit serious consideration. We recognize first of all that an atypical child *is* a child and is brought up in a given culture. Like other children in the society, he develops gradually, following a sequence of age-statuses; he is socialized into the patterns and ways of life of his groups; he learns the expectations of behavior for his many statuses; and he learns his statuses and the accompanying values through the definitions, rewards, and punishments of others and through emotionally identifying with significant individuals. His particular form of deviance gives him one extra status which may, depending on the circumstances, be of greater or lesser importance.

The atypical child, like all children, is not a pawn to be manipulated by surrounding adults. He perceives and remembers selectively, actively defines his experiences, and inextricably intertwines his feelings with his attitudes and behavior. Adults cannot simply impose their plans; if they are to understand and effectively help, they must both recognize the child's right to a subjective world and take it into account.

Our perspective also suggests that a child, within the limits of his age, understanding, and developing personality, should be offered a sufficient range of materials to learn about himself, his position in the world, and the characteristics of this world. If he is to develop his potentialities and function adequately in his social groups, he needs to work through, with honesty, his relationships to others and to himself.

Finally, perhaps above all else, we require a sophisticated knowledge about ourselves—about the relativity of some of our values, the subtleties of our communication, and the effects of our own anxieties on our attitudes and behavior.

188

SELECTED BIBLIOGRAPHY

Barker, Roger G., Wright, B. A., Myerson, L., and Gonick, M. R., ADJUSTMENT TO PHYSICAL HANDICAP AND ILLNESS: A SURVEY OF THE SOCIAL PSYCHOLOGY OF PHYSIQUE AND DISABILITY, Social Science Research Council, New York, 1953. The authors present a review and critique of several hundred studies concerning the adjustment to physical handicaps and illness.

Bell, Norman W. and Vogel, Ezra F., eds., A MODERN INTRODUCTION TO THE FAMILY, Free Press, Glencoe, Illinois, 1960. The readings in this volume include reports on unemployed families, and on retarded, emotionally disturbed, and brain-damaged children. They are presented in a coherent theoretical context.

CHILDREN AND YOUTH IN THE 1960'S, Golden Anniversary White House Conference on Children and Youth, Inc., Washington, D. C., 1960. This volume consists of a series of survey papers prepared for the Conference participants. Up-to-date information is given on problem families and on various types of atypical children.

Goode, William J., AFTER DIVORCE, Free Press, Glencoe, Illinois, 1956. Goode's study is based on interviews in Detroit with divorced women with children. Some of the ideas expressed about children might be applied to children of atypical families in general.

Jaco, E. Gartly, ed., PATIENTS, PHYSICIANS AND ILLNESS, Free Press, Glencoe, Illinois, 1958. This volume of readings linking behavioral science to medicine includes a number of articles on the social psychology of the handicapped and the ill.

Parsons, Talcott, THE SOCIAL SYSTEM, Free Press, Glencoe, Illinois, 1951. In chapter X, Parsons analyzes illness both as a psychological disturbance and a deviant social role. Many of the ideas are applicable to the atypical child.

Wright, Beatrice A., PHYSICAL DISABILITY—A PSYCHOLOGICAL APPROACH, Harper, New York, 1960. Dr. Wright brings together, in a most interesting and readable style the available data and relevant theories on the psychological aspects of disability.

FREDERICK ELKIN is an Associate Professor of Sociology at McGill University, Montreal, Canada. He was born in the United States and took his academic training at the University of Chicago (Ph.D., 1951). He has also taught at the University of Southern California and the University of Missouri. He served in the U.S. Army (1942-1945) and on the research staff of the Motion Picture Association of America, Hollywood, California (1947-1950). He has participated in research conducted by the National Opinion Research Center and has served as project director and consultant for the Defence Research Board, Canada. He is a member of the American Sociological Association, Eastern Sociological Society, and the Canadian Political Science Association. He is the author of THE CHILD AND SOCIETY (1960), has written chapters for CONTEMPORARY SOCIOLOGY and MASS CULTURE; and his articles have appeared in the AMERICAN SOCIOLOGICAL REVIEW, AMERICAN JOURNAL OF SOCIOLOGY, JOURNAL OF ABNORMAL AND SOCIAL PSYCHOLOGY, SOCIAL FORCES, PUBLIC OPINION QUARTERLY, JOURNAL OF EDUCATIONAL SOCIOLOGY, SOCIOLOGY AND SOCIAL RESEARCH, PHYLON, and HOLLYWOOD QUARTERLY.

NOTES

1. Elkin, Frederick, THE CHILD AND SOCIETY, Random House, New York, 1960.
2. We use "deviance" in the sociological sense of varying from the norm. No stigma is intended.
3. For a good general discussion of values in American society see, Williams, Robin M., AMERICAN SOCIETY: A SOCIOLOGICAL INTERPRETATION, Rev. ed., Knopf, New York, 1960, Chapter 11. For a recent study of attitudes to physical disabilities see Richardson, Stephen A., Goodman, N., Halstorf, A. H., and Dornbusch, S., "Cultural Uniformity in Reaction to Physical Disabilities," AMERICAN SOCIOLOGICAL REVIEW, XXVI, 1961, 241-247.
4. Mead, George H., MIND, SELF AND SOCIETY, University of Chicago Press, Chicago, 1934.
5. For a report which illustrates the importance of self feelings see MacGregor, Frances C., "Some Psycho-Social Problems Associated with Facial Deformities," AMERICAN SOCIOLOGICAL REVIEW, XVI, 1951, 629-638. That self images may change in a therapeutic setting is shown in Rosengren, William R., "The Self in the Emotionally Disturbed," AMERICAN JOURNAL OF SOCIOLOGY, LXVI, 1961, 454-462.

6. Sullivan, Harry Stack, THE INTERPERSONAL THEORY OF PSYCHIATRY, eds., Perry, H. S. and Gawel, M. L., Norton, New York, 1953.

7. See Merton, Robert K., and Kitt, A., "Contributions to the Theory of Reference Group Behavior," in Merton, R. K. and Lazarsfeld, P. F. (eds.), STUDIES IN THE SCOPE AND METHOD OF "THE AMERICAN SOLDIER," Free Press, Glencoe, Illinois, 1950; and Shibutani, Tamotsu, "Reference Groups as Perspectives," AMERICAN JOURNAL OF SOCIOLOGY, LX, 1955, 562-569.

8. "Research Needs in the Vocational Rehabilitation of the Deaf," AMERICAN ANNALS OF THE DEAF, CV, 1960, 349.

9. Recent discussions of family crisis and uncertainty are discussed in the following articles: Farber, Bernard, FAMILY ORGANIZATION AND CRISIS, Society for Research in Child Development, Indiana, Serial No. 75, XXV, 1960. Davis, Fred, "Uncertainty in Medical Prognosis, Clinical and Functional," AMERICAN JOURNAL OF SOCIOLOGY, LXVI, 1960, 41-47. That the adoptive family may also feel "handicapped" is brought out in Kirk, H. David, "A Dilemma of Adoptive Parenthood: Incongruous Role Obligations," MARRIAGE AND FAMILY LIVING, XXI, 1959, 316-326.

10. For a brief review of this concept, see Schneider, Louis and Lysgaard, Sverre, "The Deferred Gratification Pattern," AMERICAN SOCIOLOGICAL REVIEW, XVIII, 1953, 142-144.

11. See Goffman, Erving, PRESENTATION ON SELF IN EVERYDAY LIFE, Doubleday Anchor Books, New York, 1959.

12. Ruesch, Jurgen, DISTURBED COMMUNICATION, Norton, New York, 1957.

13. The following recent reports show the roles of the hospital and social work agencies as family substitutes: Greenblum, Joseph, "The Control of Sick-Care Functions in the Hospitalization of a Child: Family Versus Hospital," AMERICAN JOURNAL OF HEALTH AND HUMAN BEHAVIOR, II, 1961, 32-38; Weinstein, Eugene A., THE SELF-IMAGE OF THE FOSTER CHILD, Russell Sage Foundation, New York, 1960.

COMMUNITY SERVICES FOR THE UNUSUAL CHILD

Ross E. Fearon

State Department of Education, Augusta, Maine

PRESENT STATUS AND TRENDS

A broad definition of community services for the unusual child would encompass all services that deal with the child. However, in this chapter discussion of these services will be limited to services which meet the following criterion:

> *Community services can be considered as those supportive services, either publicly or privately sponsored, operated, and supported, that are ancillary to the major established institutions such as the public schools, the state hospitals, and the state institutions.*

Basically there are three major institutions of near universal public service for the exceptional in our society; Education through the public schools, Medical Care, Treatment, and Training through state, public, and private hospitals, and the Corrective through state institutions. All community services for the unusual child can be broadly classified as supportive agencies for one or more of these major institutions.

In many instances the community services must play a major role instead of a supportive one. This is a result of the failure of the major institutions to provide service to a particular population segment or geographical area within our society. Many times this is a lack of foresight and leadership on the part of the

192

major institutions, but more often it is the failure of our society to recognize and provide for the needs of its individual members. Here the community services fill a vital gap in the continuum of services in our society. However, the community agencies can be most effective if they are free to function in a supportive role rather than assuming the major burden of a basic service. The role of the community service should be to augment the basic service, refine that service, to personalize the impact of the major institution, and to provide for the individual needs of the unusual child within the dynamic environment of the local community.

Within the terms of the above definition we will look at the services offered by clinics, day care centers, evaluation units, guidance centers, counseling services, rehabilitation centers, sheltered workshops, and other services which are related to the training, education, treatment, adjustment, and community integration of the unusual child.

Since the turn of the century there has been a continually expanding growth of such services. Much of this growth has paralleled the increasingly successful attempts to provide universal public school education, greatly aided by the gradual recognition that auxiliary services must be available if we are to achieve this goal of education for all of our children. Many children brought into the public schools in the name of universal (compulsory) education are found to be unable to benefit unless special provisions are made and special services are available. There are still many school systems in the United States that require exceptional children to attend school, but make little or no provision for the services needed to allow these children to properly benefit from their school experience. There are other school systems in this country that exclude the unusual child from public school experience. They believe in education for the "normal" while the "abnormal" are excluded from school as being "unable to profit."

Schools are becoming more and more aware of their responsibility to adequately provide for the universal population in matters of education, and this concept *includes* the exceptional.

In doing so they have increasingly adopted and adapted services that have had their origin in private sponsorship or in public demand. In many cases privately organized groups have had to demonstrate that these services could be offered, and that the services were a vital factor in the child's development, before the services were accepted as a function of the schools. Many groups have almost made a practice of demonstrating the feasibility of such services by beginning the services, successfully operating them, and then demanding that the public schools adopt and continue the services. This procedure has not always resulted in the best services for the child, but it has resulted in services. Prompt attention, action, and leadership on the part of the public schools would have resulted in more realistic services in some instances.

However, one should not suppose that all services for the unusual child will eventually become a responsibility of the public schools. This would not be the most realistic use of such services in terms of the philosophy and structure of the public schools, nor a rational approach to a solution of the problems presented by the unusual child. The public schools have been delegated the responsibility of education within a broad field, with many implications for those involved in this area. But, many problems of the unusual child must find resolution within other disciplines and through other resources. The public schools can aid in this resolution but they should not have the total responsibility.

The age limit acceptance of responsibility of the public schools has been gradually undergoing a change, but the time is not yet foreseen when this responsibility will be thought of in terms of life span. The public schools are still basically thought of as having a terminal responsibility within stated limits of age, function, and purpose. The age limit responsibility may continue to change, but definite limits can be, will be, and should be placed on the function, the purpose, and the role of the school. The unusual child often needs services beyond the actual, accepted, and projected scope of public education. And the unusual child

194

all too often becomes the unusual adult with the need for services continuing into adulthood.

Community services should be thought of in terms of life span services which may be initiated at any time in the life span when the need arises, for whatever period of time they may be necessary. This is not now, nor should it ever become, merely a public school problem. This is a problem of our society which requires cooperation among the resources of our total society to meet and resolve this many faceted problem.

Government in a democracy is traditionally slow to move and to adapt to change. This is equally true at all levels; federal, state, and local. Primarily for this reason people have organized to provide services which are needed by particular groups, but which are not available from government sources: e.g., the major institutions. Successful private services have had little difficulty in justifying their existence or the public need. In many instances the organized groups have succeeded in transferring the responsibility for these services to government support. In most cases this has occurred in the area of basic service which the major institutions were originally unwilling to render. The major institutions must bring themselves to service for all the elements of our society that *must* have service if they are to participate in our society. No one institution should be expected to do this, but a coordinated approach to the problem is indicated. This would leave the community services free to basic service in terms of the local need and the local environment.

There is a great need in many areas of the country for a coordinating agency for community services. And there will be further needs as the major institutions extend their services to elements of the population who are now in need of services and who have none. Also, we can expect a continual growth of community services. We are now faced, many times, with a partial or even complete lack of communication among and between the major institutions and the community services. This results in a lack of recognition, duplication of services, lack of awareness, and poor or nonexisting coordination between services on all levels. One other major result is increased cost for poorer services.

Some areas have been fortunate in developing an overall coordinating agency, but this is by no means a general practice yet. Some states have begun moving in this direction by superimposing structures on the framework of the major institutions. These structures have usually been interdepartmental in nature, on a high level. It will take some time for the results of this practice to filter down to the lower levels. However, this is a long needed move in state government. This move does not seem to have resulted from an awareness within the major institutions. Rather it seems to have resulted from a recognition by service groups that overall direction, leadership, and coordination is essential for integrated, functional, and economic service.

To assure that necessary services are provided without unnecessary duplication and waste it will be necessary to establish coordinating agencies, at least on the state level. Legislators, state officials, and department heads within our state governments are not moving in this direction as fast as they should. Duplication of services, of function, and poor use of public funds has resulted in some cases. In other cases there is no service and a lack of awareness to the needs of the people. It often seems that we are much more interested in spending money for correctional and custodial services than we are in putting our best efforts into prevention and the proper utilization of the resources of our total society.

To attain our goals in the area of public service a concerted effort is needed to broaden the scope of our services and to coordinate the efforts of all agencies concerned with the problem. We are not likely to achieve this end by mere acceptance of the goal and the expression of agreement among the existing agencies. We have had examples of this many times before. This problem can only be solved with the establishment of a new agency along with a new pattern of organization for public services. The most logical solution would be to establish the following organizational pattern for public services.

The direction of and participation in the utilization of services would be the most important contribution of the coordinating agency. Overall direction is necessary to effectively utilize available services. Much work needs to be done in reshaping the direc-

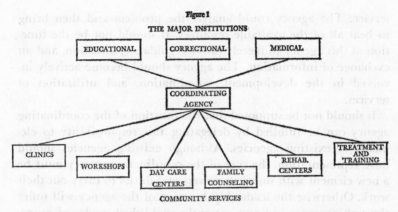

Figure 1

THE MAJOR INSTITUTIONS

EDUCATIONAL   CORRECTIONAL   MEDICAL

COORDINATING
AGENCY

CLINICS   WORKSHOPS   DAY CARE
CENTERS   FAMILY
COUNSELING   REHAB.
CENTERS   TREATMENT
AND
TRAINING

COMMUNITY SERVICES

Figure 1. *This figure does not include all the community services now available. It only serves to illustrate the pattern of organization and responsibility.*

tion of existing services and redefining their objectives. The coordinating agency, having access to the knowledge of the total program, would necessarily provide leadership in this respect. To provide for the most functional, economic, and needed utilization of services, one agency must assume the responsibility for direction.

Public information on the scope and function of these services, and their existence and application is essential to the alleviation of many of our problems. This information is not readily available to those in need since there are few agencies who know the full range of services available. Referral and passage of information between services is often confused or lacking. The coordinating agency would also aid in the improvement of services presently available as well as helping develop new services when and where they are needed.

The coordinating agency should not only act as a means of communication and provide for the integration of services, but this agency should serve as the major source of referrals. This would provide one basic source to which people could turn for assistance with any problem requiring some type of special

197

service. The agency could analyze the problem and then bring to bear all of the available resources. It should not be the function of this agency to merely provide guidance, direction, and an exchange of information. The agency should become actively involved in the development, coordination, and utilization of services.

It should not be supposed that the function of the coordinating agency can be fulfilled by delegating this responsibility to elements of existing agencies. Although existing agencies should have representation, the core of the coordinating agency must be a new element with sufficient powers and duties to carry out their work. Otherwise the leadership function of the agency will suffer through preconceived and presently established modes of operation already well structured in existing agencies.

Other agency functions could be developed as the needs arise. It is important that serious consideration be given to the establishment and scope of these agencies. We are in great need of a survey of our present facilities, public and private, with a view to more equitable distribution, better utilization of financial and personnel resources, and improved service for public needs.

DIVISION OF SERVICES

Community services can be considered as having five general phases. These phases can be classified in terms of major areas of coverage; Evaluation, Treatment, Education, Training, and Counseling. These are broad areas of coverage and encompass many smaller and specific divisions of service. Although there are existing facilities operating within one major phase of service, it is not unusual to find two or more phases within one facility.

There are degrees of service connected with each phase which depend on the availability of space, personnel, equipment, and financial resources. Other considerations governing the amount of service offered are the existence and scope of other services in the area and the type of population segment to be served. Older, more established facilities are generally apt to offer a wider range of services. However, they reach this period through a growth process that is responsive to local needs. It takes some time to become established as well as to adjust to the needs of the environment.

In order to better understand the use of community services we will look briefly at the various phases and the function of each. This will be a look at the organizational structure of each and not a study of the actual operation. It is difficult to generalize successfully about services which have been established and are operating to serve peculiar needs.

Evaluation. The primary task of evaluation units is that of diagnosing the basic exceptionality, remedial defects, and allied conditions. It is also part of the evaluation process to provide direction for disposition of the case as well as a preliminary prognosis. There may be other complimentary services associated with this task, but the basic function is stated here.

Primarily there are three basic subdivisions within the realm of evaluation. They are medical services, psychological services, and social services. There are evaluation units which do not have all three services. But, the inclusion of these three services would provide adequate coverage for the majority of cases. Social services often fulfill more than one function by providing referral services, counseling services, and liaison with other phases of community service.

Thorough and proficient evaluation is an essential need of any community service. It is not necessary that every community service have evaluation facilities. However, it is impossible for a community service to operate efficiently without access to evaluation.

There are many specialized types of evaluation services as well as those large in scope. Evaluation units usually function as clinics in conjunction with a hospital. This practice ensures access to good medical facilities. Some clinics specialize in one area providing full evaluation in this area; e.g., speech, hearing, and orthopedic clinics.

Treatment. Treatment with regard to community services primarily means medical care. This may or may not be a division of evaluative services. Many times clinics will refer the case to other sources for treatment. It is impossible to provide treatment without evaluation of some kind. There has been a large growth of centers in this country providing comprehensive service. Some of these began as evaluation and treatment centers and gradually added the full range of services.

Treatment is a highly specialized area and many times the best may be none too good, with a view from the patient's outlook. Advances in technology and new knowledge are gradually making inroads on the incidence rates of some exceptionalities. Much research is still needed in the great majority of areas. It is to the treatment centers, in part, that we look for this research. Facilities for controlled conditions are usually much better there than elsewhere.

Education. Education in the context of community services usually means a highly specialized type which is difficult to maintain within the framework of the public schools. Education in this respect would be concerned with areas such as the blind and the deaf. However, there are some school systems which have moved in this area. In many systems the emotionally disturbed, the juvenile delinquent, the cerebral palsied, and others are segregated from the general schools. There can be and is some serious discussion of the role of education with respect to the above named and other segments of the population. However, volumes could be devoted to opposing points of view.

In many instances education is provided through community services because the public schools refuse to recognize responsibility. The educable mentally retarded and the physically handicapped have been and still are excluded in many areas in the face of general recognition that they should be educated in the public schools.

Community services should not have to carry a burden that is rightly the property of the public schools, or of any of the major institutions. Many of the school systems must review their philosophy of service for the unusual and make a greater effort to broaden their services. This is not to say that the public schools

200

must serve all the exceptional, but in many cases a revision of policy is needed.

Training. The community services role in training is a large one. Many of the unusual need highly specialized training to participate effectively in the community. And many of these cases have a prognosis for marginal efficiency. Some of the referrals have received public services and failed to adjust successfully. Community services provide a source of long term training and are often backstopped by sheltered employment if placement fails.

Public services generally conceive their role to be a transitional phase between a disabling condition and productive participation in society. Thus, those with a marginal prognosis are often dismissed as not being a feasible case. Many times this is a result of the concept of "producing results." Sheltered employment or highly supervised participation becomes the responsibility of community services for these people.

Other concerns of community services are for those who are below or beyond the accepted public service age limits. Examples of this are homes and services for the aged and pre-school experiences for the mentally retarded. In some areas group experiences for the severely mentally retarded are placed in this category in contrast with areas where they are a public school responsibility.

Another classification of training would deal with such specialized areas as vocational training, rehabilitation services in part, and physical and occupational therapy. Training services often operate apart from other phases although close contact is retained.

Counseling. This is a rather broad field in itself as well as being intimately a part of other phases. Counseling goes hand in hand with each of the previous phases, but, at times, it is a complete service in itself. Guidance and direction are fundamental needs for the unusual. Referral services are often another responsibility of counseling. The follow-up work of counseling services is a valuable step in working with the unusual. Interpersonal relationships are at the heart of services and it is to this area that counseling makes its greatest contribution. It is extremely important that the unusual receive a constant flow of services and counseling provides direction for this pattern. Counseling can also do much to smooth relationships between agencies.

Family counseling services, guidance centers, and youth helping agencies are just a few of the many established counseling services. The counseling phase is most apt to touch on the full range of the unusual through a life span period.

Important to all of these phases is the realization of the inter-relationship of all services. There is a need for cooperation and joint responsibility. It is to this end that we must address our efforts if community services are to meet the need. There is a continual dependency among all phases on each other, and we must explore avenues of improved communications to ensure better and more complete services.

UTILIZATION OF SERVICES

One of the first steps in any program for the unusual is the process of locating and defining the function of available services. Teachers and/or school administrators may want to establish a card file if this information is not available from other sources. One way of doing this is to use 5" x 8" cards listing the following information:

Name of Facility
_____

Type of Service Offered
_____

Days of Operation and Times
_____

Staff Available
_____

Additional Information
_____
_____

The amount and scope of services available from other major institutions should not be overlooked in this survey. However, many sections of the country have directories for their area, and the teacher should be certain that a directory is not available before attempting to compile this information. If such a directory is not available, it would be a worthwhile project for any group to attempt compiling this information and distributing it to those people who are in need of this data.

After finding what services are available, the next move is to survey the student population to determine the needs. There are many different methods of surveying student groups both through inductive and deductive means. It is essential that teachers know the composition of the student body with respect to exceptionalities if services are to be realistic.

With the knowledge of what services are available and the need for service, teachers can plan a program of aid for the unusual. Much consideration will have to be given to both local and state policy in this respect. Programs should be framed within existing regulations whenever possible. It may be that it will be necessary to work for changes in policy that do not adequately reflect the prevailing conditions.

Referral procedures are usually not standardized in areas where services are now. Those teachers operating in areas of long standing services will find that referral is not a problem. However, the following form is a sample of the information that should be available when a referral is made. Some agencies will have their own form, but it is a good idea for teachers to develop forms such as the sample below to collect what is fairly common referral information.

Referral Information

GENERAL INFORMATION

Referred To	School
Teacher Reporting	Grade

School Reporting

Student's Name

Address   Phone

Father's Name

Mother's Name

Address, if different

Marital Status   Married   Divorced   Separated

Number in family   Language at home

Student's IQ   M.A.

Date of test   Name of test

Person doing test

General Education Level   Name of test

General Home Background

Are there any unusual factors which may be influencing the child?

HEALTH

Days Present

Days Absent

General reasons for absences

_____

_____

_____

General Health during the past year

_____

_____

Speech Defect   Yes   No   If so, what

_____

_____

Hearing Defect   Yes   No   If so, what

_____

Vision Defect   Yes   No   Glasses

What is pupil's coordination?   Very Good   Good   Fair   Poor   Very Poor

General physical appearance   Very Good   Good   Fair   Poor   Very Poor

Personal appearance and
    cleanliness   Very Good   Good   Fair   Poor   Very Poor

Any major health problems?

_____

Any major deviations in height and weight?

_____

Physical conditions that might influence school performance

_____

_____

_____

SOCIAL AND EMOTIONAL

Please qualify answers when possible

Emotional stability	Very Good	Good	Fair	Poor	Very Poor
Cooperation	Very Good	Good	Fair	Poor	Very Poor
Acceptance by others in group	Very Good	Good	Fair	Poor	Very Poor
Attitudes toward school regulations	Very Good	Good	Fair	Poor	Very Poor
What is pupil's usual disposition	Very Good	Good	Fair	Poor	Very Poor
What is pupil's response to success	Very Good	Good	Fair	Poor	Very Poor
What is pupil's response to failure	Very Good	Good	Fair	Poor	Very Poor
What is attitude toward school and other property	Very Good	Good	Fair	Poor	Very Poor
What is pupil's attitude toward self	Very Good	Good	Fair	Poor	Very Poor

In what areas are pupil's longest and shortest spans of attention—designate both

Arithmetic Language Spelling Reading Social Studies Health Art Other

Does pupil share with others	Yes	No
Does pupil play fairly	Yes	No
Does pupil anger easily	Yes	No

Does pupil like or dislike school and why _____

_____

Family Conflicts _____

_____

Nervous Habits _____

_____

What does pupil say about the family

_____

_____

What are pupil's marked dislikes and fears

_____

How does pupil meet new situations

_____

What are pupil's typical activities with classmates

_____

Pupil's usual play activity and its relation to others

_____

_____

In what situations does pupil most frequently become upset

_____

What does pupil do when upset

_____

_____

What is pupil's attitude toward others   Negative   Positive

_____

_____

_____

207

The teacher should work closely with the family in developing services for the unusual. This may be done through other agencies or directly by the teacher. If the teacher is to be involved in the service for the child, then the teacher should work with the family. It is quite important that the teacher have first-hand knowledge of the environmental context of the child. Many times services have less than their desired impact, or even fail, because this information is lacking. And, in many areas, it is a regulation that services cannot be initiated without the parent's permission.

One of the more difficult tasks of the teacher is to keep from becoming personally involved. Services may be much more effective if the teacher uses detached judgement rather than emotional involvement. It is true that the teacher must have some feeling toward the child to initiate action, but feeling should not be the dominant factor.

Counseling sessions with all those concerned is an important participation role for the teacher. Even if the teacher is not directly involved in the service being given, attention should be given to staying abreast of the case. It is not the teacher's job to refer and forget. Continued assessment of the child's progress often will produce insights which are applicable to other problems.

Participation by the teacher in community service can be a highly educational experience. Not only can the teacher contribute her learning and experience, but much can be taken back to the classroom from various sources. It may not be possible for the teacher to take a leading role, nor is it necessary. The interchange of ideas will prove to be a stimulating experience. Many other disciplines offer much for the classroom teacher in application or adaptation of their advances.

Two major items stand out for the classroom teacher: (1) Know your students. (2) Know the services available. With these two steps the teacher can go a long way toward better adjustment for the unusual in her class, and more effective community participation for all.

208

SELECTED BIBLIOGRAPHY

Abraham, Willard, A GUIDE FOR THE STUDY OF EXCEPTIONAL CHILDREN, Porter Sargeant Publisher, Boston, 1956. An excellent reference for guided study in the field.

Cruickshank, William M., Editor, PSYCHOLOGY OF EXCEPTIONAL CHILDREN AND YOUTH, Prentice-Hall, Inc., Englewood Cliffs, New Jersey, 1955. Survey of exceptionalities with much to offer in personality understanding and guidance.

Cruickshank, William M., and Johnson, G. Orville, EDUCATION OF EXCEPTIONAL CHILDREN AND YOUTH, Prentice-Hall, Inc., Englewood Cliffs, New Jersey, 1958. Educational survey of provisions and practices for the exceptional.

Frampton, Merle E., and Gall, Elena D., Editors, SPECIAL EDUCATION FOR THE EXCEPTIONAL, 3 Volumes, Porter Sargeant Publisher, Boston, 1955. One of the better surveys of the area offering many insights and much constructive material.

Hayes, E. Nelson, Editor, DIRECTORY FOR EXCEPTIONAL CHILDREN, 1960, Porter Sargeant Publisher, Boston, 1960. A handbook on services available throughout the country.

Henry, Nelson B., THE EDUCATION OF EXCEPTIONAL CHILDREN, Forty-Ninth Yearbook of the National Society for the Study of Education, University of Chicago Press, Chicago 37, Illinois, 1950. An overall view with a look to future needs and provisions.

Mackie, Romaine P., Dunn, Lloyd M., and Cain, Leo F. PROFESSIONAL PREPARATION OF TEACHERS OF EXCEPTIONAL CHILDREN: AN OVERVIEW, U.S. Department of Health, Education, and Welfare, Bulletin 1959, Number 6, Government Printing Office, Washington, D.C. Survey of teacher preparation and desirable personal qualifications.

National Committee on Sheltered Workshops and Homebound Programs, SHELTERED WORKSHOPS AND HOME-BOUND PROGRAMS: A HANDBOOK, The Committee, 15 West 16th Street, New York 11, New York, 1952. A highly useful handbook for anyone involved in this area.

Woods Schools, HELPING PARENTS UNDERSTAND THE EXCEPTIONAL CHILD: PROCEEDINGS OF THE 1952 CONFERENCE, Publications Office, The Woods Schools, Langhorne, Pennsylvania. Proceedings of a conference with many implications for services.

Woods Schools, SERVICES FOR EXCEPTIONAL CHILDREN: PROCEEDINGS OF THE 1956 CONFERENCE, Publications Office, The Woods Schools, Langhorne, Pennsylvania. Emphasis on services now as well as research implications for the future.

ROSS E. FEARON: born 1931. Attended Public Schools in Maine. Graduated Northeastern University A.B. 1954. Ed. M. Northeastern University 1959. U.S. Army 1955-57. Teacher, junior high school. Teacher special class for retarded children. Coordinator of Special Classes. Acting Director, Education for Mentally Retarded Children, State Department of Education, Augusta, Maine.

EDUCATION OF THE PARENTS
OF EXCEPTIONAL CHILDREN

Stanton D. Plattor
Plainedge Public Schools, Long Island
and
Emma E. Plattor
Plainview Public Schools, Long Island

Every child, whether gifted, handicapped or normal, is a product of many interacting forces. The success with which a child grows into a mature and self-reliant member of society is, to a considerable degree, the result of the maturity and adjustment of his parents and their ability to provide for the individual needs not only of their children but of themselves. The realization of any child's potential is a function of the attitudes which his parents bring to his growth and development. As research continues into the role of the parent in the education and adjustment of the unusual child, it becomes increasingly obvious that a vital need exists for assisting these parents to understand and accept themselves as well as the specific behavior which their child's exceptionality manifests.

While a child is born with a certain heritage or potential, the exploitation of these innate aptitudes depends upon the steady and supportive strength which the child receives from his parents. Minimizing the emotional conflicts of the parents will aid in maximizing the effectiveness of the interaction between parents and child. Since it is primarily in the home that the child learns to cope with the difficulties of growing up, the successful adjustment of the unusual child to his own condition, to

211

his family and to the community in which he lives is rooted in the successful adjustment of his parents to him.

Although well recognized for some time, the importance of the home environment is receiving increasingly greater emphasis in the thinking and planning of those responsible for the education and training of the unusual child. The roots which guide this child's reaction to educators, social workers or peers are, for good or ill, firmly implanted in the home. The mere factor of deviance requires that the unusual child obtain his sources of satisfaction in greatest measure from his parents; thus his dependence upon his parents is increased a thousandfold. Few parents are adequately equipped, either through expectation or training, to cope with the advent of exceptionality in their child. Often such deviance may signify the thwarting of many hopes, dreams and ambitions. Considerable training may be required to prevent transmitting this reaction to the child.

Whether the deviance takes the form of giftedness or handicap appears to make little major difference in the parents' need for help in learning to live with the unusual child. The differences may be of kind, may require variations in technique, may call for specialized types of training and adjustments. This does not alter the fact that the depth and intensity of the parents' need for help varies more with the personality of the parents than with the type of deviance present in the child. Where the exceptionality takes the form of a handicap, it seems to matter very little as well whether this appears at birth or as a result of a later injury or disease. The parents' need for guidance in understanding and accepting their child overrides the what, when and how of the child's difference from the norm. The difficulties experienced by many wounded service men and their families in adjusting to scars, amputations and disfigurations merely underscore this fact.

Most parents develop along with their children, experiencing successes and failures, joys and sorrows, pain and pleasure, secure in the knowledge that the successes, joys and pleasures will usually far outweigh their antitheses. This is far less often the case with exceptional children; however, this need not necessarily remain so. The parents' reaction to both fate's kindnesses and buffetings is to a large measure conditioned by what they have been taught to expect and the manner in which they have been taught to cope with situations and events. Unfortunately, all too little emphasis is placed, in the training of young people in our culture, on those skills which will enable them to function effectively as parents. The preparation for parenthood of a child who is "different" is virtually non-existent.

Since "trial and error" parenthood often leaves scars on even the most normal of children, there appears little room for argument about its inappropriateness in dealing with the unusual child. Early awareness of, and attention to, the special physical, emotional and intellectual needs of the unusual child is obviously necessary for each of these children, whether gifted or handicapped, has needs even more unique than the most unique needs of the nonexceptional child. The more readily the parent realizes these needs; the more effective the development of the ability to deal with them without doubt and uncertainty; the greater the opportunity for the exceptional child to develop to his maximum potential with the least residue of unhappiness and and frustration.

It is extremely important for the unusual child to participate in the social life about him; yet he often finds great difficulty in maintaining even the simplest relationships with adults or peers. The very nature of the child's handicap may create a situation where the social adjustment of the parents becomes confused. Anxiety or shame concerning the child may inhibit the parents' normal contacts and may even create withdrawal from participation in family group activities. Assisting the public to understand the behavior of the unusual child, as well as the requirements of the parents of these children, is of paramount importance. Much remains to be done in this endeavor.

A report describing the sentiments of parents concerning their contacts with professional people working with their exceptional children was presented several years ago during a conference on the Pre-Adolescent Exceptional Child, held by the Woods School in Pennsylvania.[1] Responses given by these parents to several pressing questions were presented. Significant among these were the following:

WHAT DOES THE PARENT DESIRE
FROM THE PROFESSIONAL?

(Professional in this case included the specialized fields of medicine as well as psychology and social work.)

Professionals should be honest with parents . . . where an accurate prognosis can be made, it should not be withheld, but care should be exercised in breaking the news; the process should not be prolonged; it should be done with friendliness and sympathy; the parent should be given all available information and acquainted with all known resources.

WHAT DOES THE PARENT EXPECT
FROM THE EDUCATOR?

It should not be left to parents to bear the burden of arousing the community . . . it is the educator who should be in the vanguard in promoting community interest in the problem. We believe the task of awakening the public can be handled with greater authority by educators. It is up to the educator to prove to the community that expenditures for education and training are not only the duty of a civilized community but are good economy.

WHAT DOES THE PARENT EXPECT
FROM THE COMMUNITY?

They want their child to be treated as all children are treated, with due recognition, of course, of the child's differences. And they want as nearly a normal life as possible for the family, recognizing that it can never be really normal because of the handicapped child. They want a chance for their children to develop within their limited capabilities, and to lead as useful a

214

life as possible. It would seem to us that if parents, educators and other professionals exercised their respective responsibilities to the fullest, we could have better facilities and services for the children in the community.

Too often, parents hesitate to admit, even to themselves, that their child is different. Such refusal to face reality may be followed by a period of "scape-goating" or trying to find someone or something on which to blame the problem. These are normal aspects of parent development and must be dealt with patiently and realistically. To help parents accept their unusual child as he is, with a minimum of false hope and wishful thinking, involves a clearly explained, straight-forward evaluation of the nature and meaning of the exceptionality. Such an exposition may require considerable repetition and reinforcement before a real understanding and acceptance are achieved.

Parental anxieties and frustrations can be channelled into vast resources of energy to assist the professional person in dealing with the unusual child. When parents have been adequately reassured of their own ability to train their child, these resources may be tapped. A basic need of the parents is the acceptance of the knowledge that exceptionality need not inhibit their child's leading a full and useful life to the limits of his potential. Adequate information, interpretation and guidance concerning the specifics of the deviation will help to assure them of this fact. Parents must be assisted to realize and to fulfill their role in the professional planning necessary to construct a society which will recognize and adequately provide for the needs of exceptional children.

Educators of exceptional children must, perhaps more than in other fields of education, work extremely closely with parents. No service for these children can truly be successful unless the total family constellation is integrated toward helping the child adjust to his environment. Family members must develop an understanding of the reciprocal nature of the family relationship. Living together must be accepted as a "give and take" situation, in which the needs of each member of the family are carefully considered. As children pass through varying stages of maturity, emphases shift. Parents must develop a flexibility which will permit them to reorganize their approaches to these changing conditions.

It is most advisable that parents achieve an understanding of any program of services being provided to the child outside the home. This is particularly necessary when departures from normal educative procedure are considered or are in existence. Parents who understand and accept, for example, the program in their child's school can assist the school immeasurably by applying its goals to the routines of living at home and in the community. This in turn minimizes conflict and confusion for the child. Obviously, this is a highly individualized matter. Educators as well as parents must recognize that a "master plan" can be drawn up only in very general terms. With each child and each set of parents it is necessary to retain the flexibility and individuality so essential to successful education. This goal of individualization, transmitted to parents, will guide them to the realization that provision for unusual children must be tailored to their personal needs to at least as great an extent as for their more normal counterparts.

Assisting parents to accept realistically their child's potential, limitations as well as strengths, is a fundamental aspect of parent education. Depending upon the type of deviation, parents may set their "expectation level" either way above the child's capacity to perform or considerably below what he can do when properly motivated. Since either extreme can be detrimental to the child's mental and emotional health, every effort to avoid extremes should be made. Careful evaluation of the child's potential by professionals trained and equipped for this responsibility; full sharing of the results with parents; development of a joint plan for exploiting the full gamut of the child's abilities in all areas are absolute essentials.

Parental fears concerning their inadequacy to cope with their exceptional child must be overcome. There is nothing shameful about a child with a mental or physical handicap; yet many parents regard their child and his resultant deviant behavior in this way. On the other hand, there is no need for parents to experience feelings of shame or embarrassment as their gifted child progresses beyond them in an area of knowledge or skill. Most parents make errors occasionally in bringing up children; fear or brooding concerning mistakes causes loss of confidence and may breed emotional illness. These and similar concepts must be continually reinforced until fully accepted. Professional guidance must be available to parents in this endeavor.

TECHNIQUES IN PARENT EDUCATION

With advances of research and knowledge in the field, parents are seeking help at earlier stages in their child's development. The assistance which they are receiving is generally of a more objective nature than could previously be obtained. As literature concerning methods and techniques of parent education as well as information in the specific areas of deviation pervades the field, there has come about a more realistic approach to parent education coupled with a more widespread parental acceptance of the need for help.

Parents as well as professional people are discovering that a variety of techniques are now available or are in the process of development through which they can gain sufficient skills, insights and understandings to immeasurably increase their ability to help themselves as well as other parents toward acceptance and support. These forms of self help provide to parents the reassurance that they are not alone with their problems; that others have faced and found solutions to similar problems; that long-range programs for unusual children can be undertaken and successfully fulfilled; that approaches which others have utilized are readily available for modification to their own needs. As new attitudes develop, parents are able to see that the types of assistance available to their children through school and community agencies can be of value to themselves as well. With this realization generally has come a desire on the part of parents to affiliate with those organizations taking an active role in progressive

217

programs and legislation for exceptional children. This interest serves a twofold purpose: the central focus of the parents' problem is transferred from the exceptional child to the more objective overall situation. At the same time, interest is aroused and recruits are discovered who will work actively for the development of healthy and constructive attitudes toward the unusual child and his place in the community.

Various approaches have been explored and are being refined in an effort to develop the abilities of parents to communicate successfully with their exceptional children. As in any problem situation, final acceptance of the existence of a problem, leading to the desire to do something about it, implies comprehension of the problem itself. Comprehension implies that information has been received and that some understanding has been achieved. Understanding further implies that a learning situation has taken place.

The manner in which people learn has recently been the subject of extensive scrutiny and research. Frank[2] outlines four steps in the learning process. In order that a good learning situation may take place, some *involvement* must exist. The learner must become emotionally involved in the situation; he must see it as potentially meeting a need.

Once involved, the learning situation must *challenge* those behavior patterns which are blocking the learner's ability to undertake a course of action which will lead to a change in behavior.

Assuming that challenge generally implies threat, an effective learning situation must also offer *support*. It is relatively simple to involve and challenge a person with a program or technique offering ideas which differ from those which influence his operational behavior. However, unless the learner is supported to an understanding of the acceptability of these new ideas, they may well be rejected.

The fourth and most vital phase in this learning process provides within the situation itself *incentives to action*. Unless the learner applies what he has learned, the learning may be valueless. For parents, the learning situation must afford some

218

opportunity for trying out old attitudes and new ones, and for strengthening through practice those which work best.

Many parent education programs stress *comprehension* of a problem and therefore deal primarily with presenting and interpreting information. There are other programs which are not basically concerned with comprehension, but rather stress *acceptance* and the provision of a situation wherein parents can freely express their feelings. Many programs undertaken within the last several years have attempted to integrate the aspect of comprehension with that of acceptance through the use of varying techniques.

An informational program utilizing the technique of *mass media* makes the participant aware of a given problem and provides possible solutions. Books and articles may be read, lectures may be presented, films may be shown. Participation is generally limited; the role played by the members of the group is a passive rather than an active one. Mass media may be both challenging and supportive, as the more one knows, the more one's anxiety concerning the unknown is decreased. However, a resolve to action is not usually engendered; or if such a resolve is forthcoming, there is generally no incentive present to aid the participant in a desire to carry out such an action.

Professional assistance, placing the parent in a one-to-one relationship with a trained worker, is exemplified in the *home tutoring plan*. Here, the professional person makes regularly scheduled visits to the home, demonstrating training methods, working with the child, exploring goals and planning programs of care and education. The stress in this program is laid primarily on comprehension; the opportunity is usually not afforded for the parents to work through their feelings and attitudes. A major problem here is the fact that sessions are almost always held during the day, thus limiting the contact between the professional worker and the father. In cases where the child must be exempted from school, or where he is waiting for institutional placement, this individual contact with a trained person can be most supportive to the parent.

Classes for parents, also known as "Formal Study Groups" or

"Directed Discussion Groups," offer the participants an opportunity to explore a particular interest area under the direction of a trained leader. Again stressing comprehension, this technique requires a formal structure and a planned agenda. Some form of mass media may be included as one phase of the course of study. The problem to be examined is selected by the course planners; it is imposed by the leader upon the group with their approval. All discussion then centers about this particular subject.

Group Guidance Sessions, similar in many respects to Directed Discussion Groups, permit the parents to interchange ideas, attitudes, and prior learnings. A major difference exists, however, in that discussion topics in Group Guidance sessions are elicited from the members of the group, with no formal structure or agenda necessarily being present. A technique which stresses acceptance as well as comprehension, these sessions are directed toward the exploration of approaches to current, pressing situations rather than general phases of a problem. Directed Discussion Groups often limit the exploration of any given topic to one session; discussions in Group Guidance meetings may continue into several sessions depending upon the needs of the group. Opportunity is thereby afforded the participants to report on the outcomes of particular procedures discussed during the meetings, providing an "incentive to action."

A comparatively recent form of parent education is the *Free Discussion Group,* primarily concerned with creating an atmosphere conducive to the development of new and successful behavior patterns through group interaction and support. A leader is present but the majority of the time spent during the sessions is controlled by the participants. Points of agreement or disagreement on issues of importance to the group members are studied for action, thereby stimulating the persons involved toward some constructive behavior. In a discussion group of this nature, there actually exists a sample of any typical life situation; thus it is relatively easy to transfer decisions for action made in the group to social living.

Blodgett and Warfield[3] report the results of a study conducted at Sheltering Arms, a Research Center and Day School for retarded children in Minneapolis. A study group, planned and conducted by the faculty of the Sheltering Arms, met on a monthly basis for a period of three years and involved the parents of children attending the school. Topics for discussion were selected on the basis of importance to members of the school staff as well as to the participating parents. The results of this research indicate that the parents on the whole improved their methods in dealing with their unusual children, or at the least shifted attitudes; that they developed more concern with the broader aspects of the child's personality than the basic area of discipline, where much of the stress had originally been placed. In addition, parental interest expanded to the entire aspect of the exceptionality, rather than being confined to those aspects of immediate significance to their relationships with their own children.

RESOURCES IN PARENT EDUCATION

Recognition of the need for definite programs of assistance to unusual children has led to the formation of numerous organizations devoted to this purpose. Over the past few years there has been increasing emphasis upon developing specific programs of parent education within these groups. The general objective of these programs has been an implementation of the concept that guidance, begun early and made available to all, will develop a realistic and widespread acceptance of the problem of exceptionality in children. The rapid growth of these programs of parent education, within both lay and professional organizations, has been instrumental in giving impetus to further research and experimentation in this field.

Developing programs of parent education have been further stimulated by the encouragement of governmental agencies on the local, state and federal levels. Exemplifying these are the United States Department of Health, Education and Welfare; the Public Health Service; the National Institute of Public Health; Social Security Administration; Children's Bureau and Bureau of Public Assistance; the Office of Vocational Rehabilitation.

Voluntary service organizations fill a need in providing both information and service for educating and assisting parents of unusual children. These organizations not only serve as referral agencies but also provide extensive literature for the professional workers as well as the parents. While some of these agencies are concerned with the entire range of exceptionality, others are limited to such specific areas of deviation as the blind, mentally retarded or intellectually gifted.

Certain agencies are designed to provide general services for children and their parents; some have within their scope programs for the exceptional child as well. Among these are the International Council for Exceptional Children; Child Welfare League of America; American Council on Education; American Public Health Association. State Mental Health organizations provide many programs and services; these may be found in nearly all of the fifty states as well as Canada. Special organizations have been formed to deal only with specific problems of parent education, for normal as well as unusual children. Notable among these are the American Parents Committee; Child Study Association of America; National Committee for Parent Education; National Congress of Parents and Teachers.

Specific areas of deviation are treated by a variety of agencies designed for this purpose. While it is not possible to mention all of them here, a sampling from various areas will serve as an overview. The National Society for Crippled Children and Adults provides services in the general area of physical handicaps, including cerebral palsy, speech defects, brain damage, neurologically handicapped. In the area of specific physical handicaps, United Cerebral Palsy, Alexander Graham Bell Association for the Deaf, New York Association for the Blind, National Epilepsy League, National Tuberculosis Association, American Heart Association typify agencies which offer service. Such groups as the National Association for Retarded Children and the American Association for Gifted Children are spurring interest and research.

Schools for unusual children have provided much of the leadership in establishing programs of parent education. The Woods

School for Exceptional Children, a Pennsylvania institute, holds annual conferences on the Exceptional Child, which may be attended by both lay and professional people. Conference themes in recent years have included: "Helping Parents Understand the Exceptional Child" and "Counseling Parents of Children with Mental Handicaps."

The John Tracy Clinic, a California school for the deaf, publishes an extensive correspondence course for parents of deaf children. Included in this course are lesson plans, materials, activities, and suggestions for working with specific hearing defects. The school's philosophy concerning parent education is expressed in an introductory letter to fathers:[4]

"Any successful business means team work; any successful family is built on team work; this job of bringing up a deaf child —or any child, for that matter—requires team work on the part of every member of the family."

SOME SUGGESTIONS AND CONCLUSIONS

In order to provide the most effective service to parents of unusual children, each professional person must clearly understand and accept his own role in the implementation of the objectives of parent education. He must be ever sensitive to the particular needs of the parents with whom he is working if a successful program of educational experiences geared to individual interests and attitudes is to be developed. However, it is necessary for the professional person to recognize the limits of his responsibility. A fine line exists between the provision of inadequate services on the one hand and the usurpation of parental obligations on the other. This line will vary from parent to parent and will, moreover, shift as the individual parent achieves greater maturity and insight into his relationship with his unusual child.

Those responsible for parent education must work through and accept their own feelings concerning exceptional children in order that their work may be objective in scope. They must be constantly aware of what can and cannot be accomplished; of what can and cannot be changed. It will help to have as many professional people from various allied disciplines as possible involved in decisions concerning unusual children, for these decisions may have implications which any one person or discipline may not be in a position to realize. To this end, complete information concerning available resources within their own and neighboring communities should be at the fingertips of those involved in parent education.

It has been noted that parents should be acquainted with the philosophy under which their child is being educated, and the related facilities and professional services available. Further, it is necessary that parents develop an increased familiarity with those techniques, materials, and resources which are specifically designed for their child's deviation. Research findings in pertinent fields should be made available to parents where appropriate.

Each individual child requires careful study in order that the most accurate diagnosis may be made and the most effective long and short range planning may take place. Determining the degree of deviation and interpreting the situation with all its ramifications requires cooperation and patience. It is necessary that as detailed and accurate a history of the child's pattern of development as possible be made available. Both parents should be given an opportunity to discuss and explore their attitudes not only for purposes of clarification but also to avoid misinterpretations and misstatements between fathers and mothers.

Such assistance as has been described in this chapter should result in the provision of sufficient insight, knowledge and understanding among parents that they can ultimately help not only themselves but one another as well. While this is surely the most outstanding goal of parent education, there is potential danger in the fact that increased familiarity with techniques, resources and facilities may lead to an apparent parental sophistication or glibness which may actually mask incomplete understanding and acceptance. When parents are truly sympathetic with each other's problems they can offer each other that encouragement and support which will reinforce to the greatest possible extent those special services which the professional person can offer.

SELECTED BIBLIOGRAPHY

Abraham, Willard E., A GUIDE FOR THE STUDY OF EXCEPTIONAL CHILDREN, Porter Sargeant, Boston, 1955. An informational survey for parents and professional workers concerning the development of a course of study of exceptional children. Contains an extremely comprehensive bibliography in all areas of exceptionality.

Baker, Harry, INTRODUCTION TO EXCEPTIONAL CHILDREN. Macmillan, New York, 1959. An analysis of pertinent knowledge and latest research in the field. Provides good background material for those interested in parent education for exceptional children.

Blodgett, Harriet E., and Warfield, Grace J., UNDERSTANDING MENTALLY RETARDED CHILDREN, Appleton-Century-Crofts, New York, 1959. A consideration of various aspects of mental retardation and the roles of parents and professionals in the training of retarded children. Provides simple analyses of latest research in the field.

Brumbaugh, Florence N., and Roshco, Bernard, YOUR GIFTED CHILD, Henry Holt, New York, 1959. A practical guide for parents which includes devices for measurement of giftedness as well as advice for parents concerning their contributions to the child's maximum development. Presents effective ideas and materials for exploiting interests and hobbies.

Child Study Association of America, TAKING STOCK IN PARENT EDUCATION, Child Study Association of America, New York, 1953. An evaluation of methods and techniques in the field of parent education as described at the 1953 Conference held by this Association for workers in the field.

Frampton, Merle E., and Gall, Elena G. (eds.), SPECIAL EDUCATION FOR THE EXCEPTIONAL CHILD, Porter Sargeant, Boston, 1955-6. A comprehensive three-volume survey of the nature, problems and research in the various areas of exceptionality. Includes an extensive bibliography in each of the special areas, as well as a comprehensive listing of agencies and services available throughout the country in each of these areas.

French, Joseph L., EDUCATING THE GIFTED, Henry Holt, New York, 1959. A general survey of research findings, in the form of readings.

Gerard, Margaret Wilson, THE EMOTIONALLY DISTURBED CHILD, Child Welfare League of America, New York. An analysis, through various papers written during the author's career, of the diagnosis, treatment and care of emotionally disturbed children.

Heck, Arch O., THE EDUCATION OF EXCEPTIONAL CHILDREN, McGraw-Hill, New York, 1953. A consideration of the education of exceptional children, offering concrete guidance in such areas as parent education, the organization and administration of an educational program for these children, the provision of proper physical care.

Hutt, Max L., and Gibby, Robert G., THE MENTALLY RETARDED CHILD, Allyn and Bacon, Boston, 1958. An exploration of the internal emotional problems and external behavior of the retarded child, including emotional reactions of parents and their alleviation.

John Tracy Clinic, CORRESPONDENCE COURSE FOR THE PARENTS OF LITTLE DEAF CHILDREN, John Tracy Clinic, California, 1954. A valuable contribution toward the education and training of both parents and their deaf children. Includes lessons in lip reading, language and speech preparation, games and materials, and suggestions and comments from parents of other deaf children.

Martmer, Edgar E. (ed.), THE CHILD WITH A HANDICAP, C. C. Thomas, Springfield, 1959. A symposium of articles by specialists in the various fields of handicapped children, describing the characteristics of those who have specific handicaps as well as the roles of each of the specialists in working with them.

Norris, Miriam, Spaulding, Patricia, and Brodie, Fern, BLINDNESS IN CHILDREN, University of Chicago Press, Chicago, 1957. A careful analysis of the research methods and findings in the field, including case histories as well as good bibliography.

226

Papish, Martin F., "Understanding the Needs and Desires of the Parents of the Retarded Child," THE PRE-ADOLESCENT EXCEPTIONAL CHILD, Woods School, Pennsylvania, 1953. A discussion of the feelings of parents of retarded children concerning their contacts with professional people working with their children.

Woods School, HELPING PARENTS UNDERSTAND THE EXCEPTIONAL CHILD, Woods School, Pennsylvania, 1952. Conference proceedings devoted to a survey of recent trends in the development and significance of parent groups in the field of exceptional children.

Woods School, COUNSELING PARENTS OF CHILDREN WITH MENTAL HANDICAPS, Woods School, Pennsylvania, 1958. Conference proceedings concerning the scope and practice of parental counseling from the time of first knowledge of retardation to the time of using community or residential school facilities.

STANTON D. PLATTOR, presently Director of Pupil Personnel Services for the Plainedge Public Schools, Long Island, New York, holds a Bachelor of Arts degree in Education and a Master's Degree in Guidance and Counseling from Brooklyn College, New York. He served previously as Supervisor of Guidance for the Bureau of Guidance of the New York State Education Department, evaluating and supervising guidance activities in the public schools of nine counties in New York State. Prior to his service with the State Education Department, Mr. Plattor directed the Guidance Program for the Brentwood, New York, Public Schools; was Guidance Counselor in the New Hyde Park and West Babylon, New York, Public Schools, and was Teacher-Counselor in the New York City Public Schools. Articles by Mr. Plattor have appeared in the JOURNAL of the American Personnel and Guidance Association; EDUCATION, published by the New York State Teachers Association; THE SCHOOL COUNSELOR of the American School Counselors Association; and THE NATION'S SCHOOLS.

EMMA E. PLATTOR, presently Assistant Principal of the Mannetto Hill School, Plainview, Long Island, New York, holds a Bachelor of Arts degree in Education and a Master's Degree in Guidance and Counseling from Brooklyn College, New York.

227

She served previously as Supervisor in Test Development for the Division of Educational Testing of the New York State Education Department. Prior to this service, Mrs. Plattor coordinated the Guidance Department for the Plainview Public Schools, and served as Teacher Counselor in the New York City Public Schools. Articles by Mrs. Plattor have appeared in the BULLETIN of the National Association of Secondary School Principals, the EDUCATION DIGEST, the JOURNAL of the American Personnel and Guidance Association, EDUCATION, published by the New York State Teachers Association, THE SCHOOL COUNSELOR of the American School Counselors Association, THE SOCIAL STUDIES, and THE NATION'S SCHOOLS.

NOTES

1. Papish, Martin F., "Understanding the Needs and Desires of the Parents of the Retarded Child," THE PRE-ADOLESCENT EXCEPTIONAL CHILD, Woods School, 1953, 53-54.
2. Frank, Jerome, "How Parents Learn," TAKING STOCK IN PARENT EDUCATION, Child Study Association of America, 1953, 3-4.
3. Blodgett, Harriet E., and Warfield, Grace J., UNDERSTANDING MENTALLY RETARDED CHILDREN, Appleton-Century-Crofts, New York, 1959, 6.
4. John Tracy Clinic, CORRESPONDENCE COURSE FOR PARENTS OF LITTLE DEAF CHILDREN, John Tracy Clinic, California, 1954, 3.

EDUCATION OF TEACHERS
OF EXCEPTIONAL CHILDREN

Robert H. Mattson
University of Oregon

Programs for educating special teachers of exceptional children have traditionally been organized around specific diagnostic categories. Thus college and university training programs include distinctive training curricula for at least the following:

Teachers of the deaf
Teachers of the visually handicapped
Teachers of the physically handicapped
Teachers of the mentally retarded
Teachers of the socially handicapped
Teachers, or therapists, of the speech handicapped
Teachers of the gifted

Additional special categories, such as the brain-injured, warrant special curricula in some college programs.

There is no doubt a need for some curricular differentiation in educational programs for teachers of exceptional children; however, the author believes that a strong behavioral science background should be common to the education of all teachers of exceptional children, and that specialization courses are needed only to focus the application of general behavioral knowledge on special cases. Generally the necessary attention to application of behavioral knowledge in training special teachers can be accomplished in a sequence of three or four courses. A common pattern of specialization includes:

1. The psychology of the particular category of exceptional child
2. Curriculum and methods for the particular category
3. Practicum in assessment of the particular category of exceptionality
4. Student teaching

The essential point to be stressed here is not that such traditional specialization is undesirable, but rather that a strong basic behavioral science background is essential for all teachers of exceptional children. To emphasize the importance of a strong behavioral science background, this chapter includes:

1. An overview of the tasks common to teaching all categories of exceptional children.
2. An outline of areas of study common in the preparation of teachers of all categories of exceptional children.
3. A brief description of training in research and administration.
4. A description of representative in-service activities potentially useful to all teachers of exceptional children.

THE TASK OF THE TEACHER
OF THE EXCEPTIONAL CHILD

The "task" of the teacher of the unusual child is so complex that describing 'it' in a few words must necessarily result in extremes of abstractness. The following discussion is at best a frame of reference for the reader.

Two basic objectives of education of exceptional children seem rather distinctive and clear: (1) Reducing the deficiencies of the unusual child to maximize his well-being, and (2) Helping the child adjust himself and his world so that he can live efficiently even with his deficiencies. The focal concern of the above objectives is the individual child, and this concern must be the starting point in any attempt to define the task of teachers of exceptional children.

230

The teacher must identify the unusual child and must have thorough knowledge of him. The teacher must be able to assess the child's status, help the child establish goals, design and implement treatments likely to effect the desired changes, and evaluate the results. She must also be ready to provide or secure the courage and support the child needs to face the world with his deficiencies.

Assessing the Child. Although there is a justifiable tendency to separate technical assessment from teaching, the teacher of unusual children cannot escape the need to do the assessment basic to understanding the individual children he teaches. The teacher has to be able to satisfy herself with tentative answers to questions relative to the child's potential, his motivation, expectations, and courage, and the expectations and demands of the world on the child.

Knowledge of the nature of "normal" or modal children is basic to this kind of assessment. It provides reference points or a point of departure. This does not imply that everyone has to prefer the normal or modal child. The individual's preferences or standards for behavior may vary markedly from the normal, but the wise teacher will know when, and why, and how much variation exists between her standards and "normal."

Knowledge of the normal accrues to everyone in a variety of ways. The characteristics of human learning are such that we apparently seek constantly to identify that which is regular, or normal, or predictable. The pursuit of such knowledge appears to be inescapable, but teachers of the unusual child cannot leave its acquisition to chance. They must be highly self-conscious observers and interpreters of behavior. They must critically and unceasingly pursue knowledge of normal human behavior in every way available to them.

The teachers of unusual children obviously also need to systematically pursue knowledge of deviant or unusual human behavior. For many teachers this becomes a major task. The development of knowledge relative to distinctive categories of exceptionality has accelerated rapidly in the past decade, and keeping up with this expanding knowledge requires that effort be constantly applied to reading the professional literature about exceptionality, attending conferences, and even returning to college for workshops and summer sessions.

Acquiring knowledge of the normal and the unusual does not of itself accomplish the necessary assessment of an individual child; however, it is probably most important to the assessment procedure and requires the teachers' continual attention.

The actual task of assessing, logically relating information about an individual child to knowledge of the normal and the distinctively unusual, may actually take relatively little teacher time. This is particularly true if the teacher is supported with adequate psychological services which provide the essential information on each child.

Treating and Evaluating. Like all teachers, teachers of unusual children devote the majority of their time designing and effecting specific treatment programs for particular children. Establishing goals, planning lessons, selecting materials, and contriving experiences are the essentials; but as all experienced teachers know, the details are myriad and taxing in terms of time and labor involved.

Evaluation of results of treatment requires periodic reassessment of the child's status. Most teachers seem to depend for the most part on their own continuous subjective judgment of change, although some programs for unusual children provide for both assessment and evaluation through staff conferences involving the teacher, school psychologist, social worker, physician, and others with knowledge of the child.

Supporting and Adjusting the Child. Providing support for unusual children may be viewed by some as incidental to assessment and treatment. To some degree it is, but most children in special programs require additional support offered through counseling, group counseling, or indirectly through parent counseling. Teachers of unusual children spend varying amounts of time discussing adjustment problems with individual children, groups of children, and with parents. Even when professional staff members are employed to provide counseling, the teacher's rapport with her children ought to be such that she could not avoid supplying much of the needed support. To some degree, teachers helping to provide 'support' for exceptional children must become involved in administration and coordination of community services for exceptional children. However, the administrative function is not a primary task of teachers, and is therefore discussed in a later section.

The above discussion of the task of the teacher of unusual children is intended to emphasize the belief that such teachers must be highly cultured and competent behavioral scientists. They must have specific information and skill, but they must also possess the capacity and motivation to engender knowledge as they meet the unusual.

COLLEGE AND UNIVERSITY PROGRAMS FOR EDUCATING TEACHERS OF UNUSUAL CHILDREN

Quite adequate information is available concerning the nature of training programs for teachers of exceptional children. Mackie and Dunn[1] have provided thorough status information on training programs.

There also seems to be an abundance of authoritative literature describing ideal programs. Mackie, Williams and Dunn,[2] Frampton and Gall,[3] and Cruickshank,[4] present information about training programs, and also provide essentially a consensus of ideas relative to training programs.

A profound current need in teacher education, generally and particularly in "exceptional" teacher education, is research to describe the development of the distinctive characteristics of effective teachers. Surveys of teacher opinion, student opinion and expert opinion help to establish descriptions of effective teachers but do little to tell us how the teachers' skills are developed. We can be reasonably certain that all life experiences are related to success in teaching, but aside from selective recruiting there seems to be little that can be done systematically to provide adequate pre-college and post-college experience appropriate to developing effective teaching skills. For this

233

reason practically all literature related to the training of teachers of the exceptional child deals only with those experiences under the control of colleges.

Training for Classroom Teachers. There can be no doubt as to the necessity of systematic college programs designed to educate teachers of unusual children. The following outline delineating areas of study related to the previously discussed tasks of teachers of unusual children, is not intended to conform to any particular college program. Rather, it represents a summation of areas of study believed to be essential in educating teachers of unusual children. No attempt has been made to specify number of credit hours needed in a particular area of knowledge or whether or not a particular area should be pursued at the undergraduate or graduate level. It should be noted, however, that for some areas prior or concurrent experience with children is indicated.

I. Assessing the child
  A. Knowledge of the nature of children
    1. Humanities
      a. Literature
      b. Theatre
      c. Philosophy
    2. Biology
      a. General biology
      b. Human anatomy and physiology
    3. Sociology
      a. Institutions
      b. Marriage and family
      c. Group dynamics
    4. Anthropology
      a. Cultural anthropology
      b. Cultural dynamics
    5. Psychology
      a. Character and personality
      b. Learning or educational psychology (Prior or concurrent responsible experience with children)
      c. Developmental psychology

B. Knowledge of the unusual or exceptional
   1. Social Problems
   2. Psychopathology
   3. Psychology of group and individual differences
   4. Social-psychology of exceptional children in general
   5. Social-psychology of particular exceptional children
C. Knowledge of techniques of assessment
   1. Logic and scientific method
   2. Statistics
   3. Educational tests and measurements
   4. Group and individual tests
   5. Clinical procedures

II. Treating and evaluating
A. Techniques, methods of administration, and effects of particular treatments on normal children.
   1. Educational principles
   2. Educational curriculum and methods of instruction (prior or concurrent responsible experience with children).
   3. Supervised purposeful responsible experience with normal children.
B. Techniques, methods of administration, and effects of particular treatments designed to reduce the problems of exceptional children.
   1. Curriculum and methods of instruction related to particular categories of exceptional children.
   2. Supervised experience in planning and effecting treatment of exceptional children.
   3. Supervised experience in team evaluation of exceptional children.

III. Supporting and adjusting the child
A. Counseling

B. Play therapy, socio-drama (prior responsible experience with children)

C. Parent counseling (prior responsible experience with children)

D. Principles of social work

The foregoing represents a summary of areas believed necessary in minimum college preparation for teachers of exceptional children. Probably at least two full years of college enrollment are required to complete it; however, at least part of the program might be completed as general education requirements and much of it completed at the undergraduate level in most colleges. It should be recognized that most of the usual college general education requirements have not been included.

Questions regarding the desirability of preparation and experience in regular elementary or secondary education prior to preparation specific to education of exceptional children, cannot at present be answered with authority. There is very little doubt about the value of responsible experience with normal children; but there seems to be no substantial evidence to support the notion that preparation and experience in regular education is necessary. Expert opinion seems to be divided, although the majority probably prefer that teachers of unusual children have prior training and experience in elementary or secondary education.

TRAINING IN ADMINISTRATION

Teachers of unusual children often find themselves in positions which require administrative understanding and skill. The effective operation of a classroom program for unusual children may well require that the teacher extend her influence to help effect coordination of a wide variety of individuals, agencies and institutions serving children in her classroom. She may need to influence physicians, psychologists, social workers, rehabilitation workers, service clubs, recreation workers, and others concerned with the exceptional child.

In addition to the normal administrative demands of classroom operation, teachers of the unusual are often called upon by school administrators and community leaders for advice in establishing or modifying programs for unusual children. These is also an apparent demand for specially trained people to administer city, county, state, and institutional programs for exceptional children.

Information appropriate for the development of the administrative understanding and skill needed by teachers of unusual children is often incorporated into basic special education courses such as "Education of the Exceptional Child." However, many colleges and universities offer separate sequences of courses designed to maximize the development of administrative understanding and skill. Such sequences most often assume a background of training and experience in special education, and include such content areas as:

1. Legal-political basis for particular programs
2. Historical basis for particular special programs
3. Philosophical basis for particular special programs
4. Community organization as it affects particular special programs
5. Group dynamics and leadership as it is related to special programs

TRAINING IN RESEARCH

Programs leading to the doctor's degree and designed to prepare students to engender and evaluate knowledge related to exceptional children are offered by many colleges and universities. The specific content in doctoral study varies markedly from institution to institution, but will usually include:

1. Integrative theory in behavioral sciences
2. Research findings related to several categories of exceptionality
3. Research methodology
4. Statistics

Development of practitioner skill may be a secondary goal of a doctoral program and is likely to be a concomitant of all doctoral programs. Skill in assessing behavior is particularly likely to be improved with the study of research methodology and statistics, and in applying assessment techniques in a dissertation or thesis.

IN-SERVICE EDUCATION

In-service education may be utilized to upgrade services for unusual children in many different ways, but probably has its greatest utility as a force toward integration of various professional services.

Attention to the needs of exceptional children comes from a wide variety of quite independent individuals and professional groups:

> Educators (including 8-10 subgroups)
> Physicians (4-5 subgroups)
> Occupational therapists
> Psychologists (3-4 subgroups)
> Speech therapists
> Rehabilitation Counselors
> Nurses
> Social workers
> Parents
> Politicians
> Public administrators

Teachers on the job working with unusual children are likely to find themselves often frustrated because of lack of coordination and integration of the various individual and professional services to unusual children. Fragmentation of service to exceptional children is probably responsible for a great deal of teacher anxiety and tension. Various administrative approaches have been used to help reduce fragmentation of service but none have been consistently successful. Probably the best hope for inte-

238

grating service and thereby reducing the anxiety and improving the morale of teachers lies in in-service education programs which may be implemented within almost any administrative structure. Many kinds of in-service activities provide significant educational experience and have potential for helping to effect integration of services. The following types of in-service programs are only representative of the many possibilities.

Evaluation of Community Resources for Unusual Children. Studies of community resources, sponsored by private or public groups and utilizing the talents of all concerned professions, often pay big dividends in the development of cooperative relationships between separate professional groups. Individuals and groups involved learn a great deal about working with each other, and also acquire highly useful information about the community. A guide[5] for the evaluation of community resources published by the American Psychiatric Association in April 1949 outlines, in a very useful way, procedures for community study.

Action Research. Significant studies of particular problems in educating unusual children can often be conducted in local school districts through cooperation of many individuals representative of various professions. Again, integration of services may be effected as a concomitant of other learning which takes place. Stephen M. Corey[6] refers to action research as a process in which individuals and groups identify practices that need to be changed, try out more promising practices, and systematically test their worth.

Corey[7] states that research activity of any kind may involve team activity, but that in action research team effort is usually required. Certainly research efforts designed to improve educational practice as it relates to exceptional children requires team effort. Teachers, administrators, rehabilitation counselors, physicians, parents, and others will almost inevitably be involved every time an educational practice affecting exceptional children is initiated or modified.

Action research projects necessarily originate from local needs

239

and concerns. The following list of projects is a sample of the kinds of action research projects possible:

1. Transportation for physically handicapped children
2. Social and recreational facilities for exceptional children
3. Religious education for exceptional children
4. Pre-vocational education and guidance for exceptional children
5. Employment opportunities for the exceptional

The problems involved in meeting the needs of the exceptional are so complex and various that innumerable action research projects are needed in every program. It is difficult to have a conversation with a teacher of exceptional children that does not reveal concerns which are amenable to action research studies.

Professional Organizations. Numerous professional organizations provide very worthwhile educational experiences through local, regional and national meetings in which new information on exceptional children is disseminated. They also provide for meaningful and pleasurable professional fellowship. Many organizations include various professions interested in the exceptional among their members. Illustrative of the organizations teachers of the unusual child may find interesting and profitable are the following:

1. The Council for Exceptional Children
2. American Association on Mental Deficiency
3. American Public Health Association
4. American Speech and Hearing Association
5. American Psychological Association
6. National Rehabilitation Association

Many other professional, official, and volunteer organizations which may be of special interest to teachers of particular categories of exceptional children are listed by Frampton and Gall.[8] The above list includes only organizations which are clearly professional and which attract large memberships from various disciplines.

240

SUMMARY

The task of teachers of exceptional children is characterized as ordinarily involving assessment, treatment, and support of individual children; but may also frequently involve research and administration. The training of teachers of exceptional children is viewed as requiring: 1) a strong basic behavioral science background, (2) specialization in treatment and assessment of exceptional children, and (3) continuing in-service or self initiated education focused primarily on establishing cooperative inter-professional relationships.

SELECTED REFERENCES ON IN-SERVICE AND SELF-DIRECTED EDUCATION

Corey, Stephen M., ACTION RESEARCH TO IMPROVE SCHOOL PRACTICES, Bureau of Publications, Teachers College, Columbia University, New York, 1953. Corey makes a strong case for the importance of continual study by teachers of needs and problems in educating children. He also presents clear highly readable directions for action research.

Frampton, Merle E., and Gall, Elena D., SPECIAL EDUCATION FOR THE EXCEPTIONAL, Porter Sargeant, Boston, 1955, 374-437. This section of Frampton and Gall's well known work provides: a list of biographies for general use in special education, references, and lists of agencies.

Jenkins, Gladys Gardner, HELPING CHILDREN REACH THEIR POTENTIAL, Scott, Foresman, Chicago, 1961. This is a very useful resource book for teachers with a very realistic focus on basic needs of children.

Moustakas, Clark E., THE TEACHER AND THE CHILD, McGraw-Hill, New York, 1956. Moustakas provides a careful analysis of the nature and significance of teachers' relationships with children.

National Society for the Study of Education, IN-SERVICE EDUCATION, FOR TEACHERS, SUPERVISORS, AND ADMINISTRATORS, University of Chicago Press, Chicago, 1957. This yearbook provides a summary of important contemporary thinking on organization and implementation of in-service education programs.

Prall, Charles E., and Cushman, C. Leslie, TEACHER EDUCATION IN SERVICE, American Council on Education, Washington, 1944. Although copyrighted in 1944, the very thorough analysis of in-service education of teachers contained in this book is still highly valuable.

Suchman, J. Richard, OBSERVATION AND ANALYSIS IN CHILD DEVELOPMENT: A LABORATORY MANUAL, Harcourt, Brace, New York, 1959. Suchman's laboratory manual provides an excellent guide to developing skill in observing and analyzing child behavior.

SELECTED REFERENCES

Cruickshank, William M., and Johnson, G. Orville, EDUCATION OF EXCEPTIONAL CHILDREN AND YOUTH, Prentice-Hall, Englewood Cliffs, 1958, 125-139. Cruickshank provides a concise summary of competencies of teachers of exceptional children and stresses the importance of careful selection and training.

Gallagher, James J., "Advanced Graduate Training in Special Education," EXCEPTIONAL CHILDREN, Vol. 26, No. 2, 1959, pp. 104-109. This article summarizes the findings of The Council for Exceptional Children, Division of Teacher Education's study to establish minimum standards for advanced graduate training in special education.

Kirk, Samuel A., "A Doctor's Degree Program in Special Education," EXCEPTIONAL CHILDREN, Vol. 24, No. 2, 1957, pp. 50-52. Kirk in this article stresses the importance of selection, prior experience, and a careful articulation of specific programs of graduate study.

Lord, Francis E., and Kirk, Samuel A., "The Education of Teachers of Special Classes," NATIONAL SOCIETY FOR THE STUDY OF EDUCATION, FORTY-NINTH YEARBOOK, THE EDUCATION OF EXCEPTIONAL CHILDREN, Chicago, 1950, pp. 103-116. This article makes quite clear the basic issues involved in training teachers of special classes: recruiting, patterns of training, programs, and qualifications of teachers. Although the chapter was written in 1950, the content is still quite accurate.

Mackie, Romaine P., and Dunn, Lloyd M., COLLEGE AND UNIVERSITY PROGRAMS FOR THE PREPARATION OF TEACHERS OF EXCEPTIONAL CHILDREN, U.S. Government Printing Office, Washington, 1954. This U.S. government publication provides information on: the need for special teachers, training opportunities, college and university personnel, and illustrative college and university curricula in special education.

Mackie, Romaine P., Williams, Harold M., and Dunn, Lloyd M., TEACHERS OF CHILDREN WHO ARE MENTALLY RETARDED, U.S. Government Printing Office, Washington, 1957. This U.S. government publication includes information on needed competencies of teachers of the mentally retarded, opinions on the effectiveness of teachers of the mentally retarded, and development of competencies needed in teaching the mentally retarded.

Rabinow, Barney, "A Training Program for Teachers of the Emotionally Disturbed and the Socially Maladjusted," EXCEPTIONAL CHILDREN, Vol. 26, No. 6, 1960, pp. 287-293. Rabinow presents a very clear, well articulated proposal for training teachers of the socially maladjusted and emotionally disturbed which has implications for training teachers in all areas of exceptionality.

ROBERT H. MATTSON, Director of the Educational Evaluation Clinic and Assistant Professor of Special Education, University of Oregon (since 1957), received his B.A. degree from Montana State University (1949), M.A. degree from the State University of Iowa (1950), and D.Ed. degree from the University of Oregon (1959). He was Special Class Teacher, Kalispell, Montana (1950-1951), Director of Speech and Hearing, East Texas State Teachers' College (1951-1952), Coordinator of the Montana Center for Handicapped Children (1952-1957), and Director of Special Education, Eastern Montana College of Education (1952-1955). Has published studies in the ROCKY MOUNTAIN MEDICAL JOURNAL, OREGON SCHOOL BOARDS NEWSLETTER, and is the author of the EDUCATIONAL EVALUATION PROCEDURES MANUAL (University of Oregon, September, 1960).

NOTES

1. Romaine P. Mackie and Lloyd M. Dunn, COLLEGE AND UNIVERSITY PROGRAMS FOR THE PREPARATION OF TEACHERS OF EXCEPTIONAL CHILDREN, U.S. Government Printing Office, Washington, 1954.

2. Romaine P. Mackie, Harold M. Williams, and Lloyd M. Dunn, TEACHERS OF CHILDREN WHO ARE MENTALLY RETARDED, U. S. Government Printing Office, Washington, 1957.

3. Merle E. Frampton, and Elena D. Gall, SPECIAL EDUCATION FOR THE EXCEPTIONAL, Porter Sargeant, Boston, 1955, 252-284.

4. William M. Cruickshank and G. Orville Johnson, EDUCATION OF EXCEPTIONAL CHILDREN AND YOUTH, Prentice-Hall, Englewood Cliffs, 1958, 125-139.

5. Group for Advancement of Psychiatry, "An Outline for Evaluation of a Community Program in Mental Hygiene," American Psychiatric Association pamphlet, April 1949.

6. Stephen M. Corey, ACTION RESEARCH TO IMPROVE SCHOOL PRACTICES, Bureau of Publication, Teachers College, Columbia University, New York, 1954.

7. Ibid. 15.

8. Merle E. Frampton and Elena D. Gall, OP. CIT., 418-431.

VOCATIONAL REHABILITATION
ON FEDERAL AND STATE LEVEL

Ernest M. Gajary Kuhinka
Dickinson College

Vocational rehabilitation in the United States is open for a relatively free interpretation. The Constitution does not contain the term "vocational rehabilitation," and makes no direct reference to it; however, it does not reject it either. The "general welfare" and the "blessings of liberty to ourselves and our posterity" are the two clauses which certainly invite, rather than discourage, governmental interest in vocational rehabilitation.

The adjective "vocational" before the noun "rehabilitation" is misleading since the field of rehabilitation encompasses the entire span of an individual life of certain groups of the population; thus "vocation" cannot be so comprehensive that it would cover the young and the older age groups as well. There is hardly a time when one is not yet capable or is no longer capable of feasible occupational participation. Generally, the term vocational rehabilitation is placed in the frame of reference of one's employability. One's employability is understood as one's capacity to prepare for, enter into, and progress in a field of occupation in which he may find social, economic, and financial security as well as personal satisfaction.

There is, however, a group of people who are hindered by handicaps, disabilities, or age and unable to secure for themselves the blessing of employability. There are persons, for example, who either through a physical or mental disadvantage in comparison to others are unable to place themselves in the right place in the intricate web of the occupational structure of the nation which would bring the necessary satisfaction and security. Physically disabled persons, receiving attention from the nation, form another group. They are generally described, in terms of the medical doctor, as in need of physical restoration. Such a restoration will enable them to return, after a shorter or longer period of medical treatment, to the highest level of their physical ability. A third group is hindered in receiving proper employability because of older or younger age; included would be the mid-teens group. Those of our older citizens who are unable to work because of their disabilities generally receive cash disability retirement which will grant them a minimum of financial security. Younger and mid-teens persons who are handicapped, retarded, disabled or in any other way exceptional receive a different approach from the above-mentioned categories. Those of the young age group do not need rehabilitation for employment, nor retirement, but rather a special protection in their relationship with others and preparation for employment on the level of their potential ability.

All four groups are built around the problem of vocational rehabilitation, including research responsibilities, placement of the rehabilitated, and the like. All of these fields are very broad and diversified, and the question of employability is common to all four categories of rehabilitees. However, employability is not the necessary immediate need of a disabled person, since the training, counsel, or guidance may require first medical, social, or psychiatric services and as long as the rehabilitee, who is prepared for gainful employment, does not find suitable employment he is not considered rehabilitated. In most cases the criterion used to determine the termination of the rendered rehabilitative services is a successful placement in the field of employment where the rehabilitated is capable of securing for himself as well as for his dependents social, economic and financial security and personal satisfaction.

246

BRIEF HISTORY OF VOCATIONAL REHABILITATION

There were times throughout our past when American ideas of democratic government and individual liberty were perpetuated as interpreted by new techniques emphasizing ethical, humanitarian, and religious values rather than attempting to create economic chaos. In 1817, for example, the citizens of Hartford, Connecticut, subsidized a training school for the deaf. Another record shows the establishment of a hospital for crippled persons in Boston, Massachusetts, in 1833. The State of Michigan enacted a law to give specific treatment and hospitalization for needy persons who were suffering from chronic diseases in 1883, while the National Tuberculosis Association began its beneficent work in 1904.

Toward the end of the First World War public demand emerged for a program for the rehabilitation of disabled soldiers. Such a movement had not been constituted in the past even though we had suffered two great experiences of disabled soldiers in two wars. The Institute for Crippled and Disabled Men was started through the effort of the Red Cross in New York City in 1917 and further promoted by state legislation in 1918. However, the State of Massachusetts was the first that adopted the vocational rehabilitation law for civilians, just a month before it was ratified in New York. Other states followed the example of these progressive states and before the first federal law was passed in 1920 four more state programs in vocational rehabilitation were in operation and another six passed laws to establish similar programs. In the 1930's more and more states joined the rehabilitation program, and by 1938 all of the 48 states participated, including later Alaska, Hawaii, Puerto Rico, and Guam. All of these states and possessions acepted the principle that all of us are responsible for our disabled citizens. There are 87 state agencies, including specialized agencies for the blind, dealing with rehabilitative problems under the present federal and state programs. All of them are under professional control, using testing methods and refining their present operations, re-emphasizing the great value placed upon the dignity of the human individual.

The administrative organization of vocational rehabilitation as it could be summarized follows no regular pattern. In 37 states the State Board of Education and the State Board of Vocational Rehabilitation are the same. In 13 states there are separate boards of Vocation and Education. Of these 13 states 9 have no regular State Board of Education. In co-operation with the Labor Department they direct and recommend to the appropriate state agencies policies and procedures to promote the employment of the disabled, handicapped, and anyone who receives services through the public rehabilitation program.

This development, however, started as a new governmental responsibility with the signing of Public Law 236 by President Warren G. Harding on the second of June, 1920. Since the twenties we have a legalized program to restore disabled citizens. This legislation, called the Smith-Fess Act, received wide support not only from the two political parties, but also from numerous organizations who were connected with disabled persons, such as managerial and labor groups. This law was used as an experimental program for an undetermined period of time, but as so often happens with governmental programs it became more permanent through the Social Security Act of 1935. The next year the Randolph-Sheppard Act emphasized the needs of rehabilitation possibilities.

All of these legislative decisions helped the government to adopt and approve Public Law 113, best known as the Barden-La Follette Act of 1943, under the presidency of Franklin D. Roosevelt. This act was a turning point in the history of vocational rehabilitation since it provided for the first time medical surgery, hospitalization, and other treatments to eliminate or to restore physical or mental disabilities, or to rehabilitate the blind. After the enactment of this law the mentally retarded also became eligible for vocational rehabilitation on the same basis as other disabled. To defend this progressive law, the Kelly committee operated as a subcommittee of the House Committee on Education and Labor had accumulated a most comprehensive body of information for influencing legislation. At that time the National Association for Retarded Children was founded, a movement of parents and citizens who were determined to form a nationwide group to foster the welfare of the retarded, their families and friends. Since 1950 this Association has made great progress in the field of rehabilitation.

A new era in vocational rehabilitation began in 1954 when President Dwight D. Eisenhower signed Public Law 565, designed to improve and expand the nation's population resources by restoring disabled persons to productive employment. The same year the amendment to the Social Security Act enabled the state vocational rehabilitation agencies to be responsible in determining the disability of the applicants and also to check who would be eligible at the age of 50 (lowered to this age by a further amendment in 1956) for retirement benefits after becoming disabled. Thus the actual services for the rehabilitee are provided by the state and federal government administered by a grant-in-aid via the states to the local state offices of Vocational Rehabilitation. Further, the federal government gives the necessary leadership for programming rehabilitation.

This brief historical sketch of vocational rehabilitation re-emphasizes that the federal government provides encouragement and support for vocational rehabilitative agencies via the states. The government encourages support for health restoration, welfare services, and shares the financial costs of the program in steadily increasing proportion, aiding the temporarily or totally disabled persons as well as older-aged individuals, exceptional children, and the blind.

STRUCTURE OF VOCATIONAL REHABILITATION

Before 1943 vocational rehabilitation functioned as an educational and training operation. The federal government served the disabled via counseling and vocational guidance, but had no funds to restore via surgery, medicine, psychiatric counseling or any other form of physical assistance. The Second World War

249

greatly changed the attitude and the structure of vocational rehabilitation. The nation as a whole assumed a greater responsibility toward the disabled person than in the early twenties, when the idea of rehabilitation commenced. After World War II funds were designated to eradicate or reduce disabilities before the necessity for actual rehabilitation was undertaken whereby the disabled would then be re-educated for employment. The new program progresses along the lines of the three fields of health, education, and welfare; all of these are included in the Federal Security Agency. The new Barden-La Follette Act did not subordinate any of the offices but established a new bureau in the existing system of the Federal Agency, and called it the Office of Vocational Rehabilitation.

The Health Service concentrated on locating the causes which determine the disability of an individual. Further, this office prepared a program to cure the disease determinants in an ecological sense or via certain prescribed methods for treatment of the individual.

The Office of Education prepared broad programs in the field of vocational rehabilitation for all types of disabilities as well as educational programs for handicapped and retarded children.

The Social Security Administration provided financial assistance for the disabled as well as needy, blind, or retarded individuals. Further, it administered financial services to crippled children and proposed the enlargement of disability insurance, which in the nineteen-fifties became a reality.

The Office of Vocational Rehabilitation co-ordinated the rehabilitation services and administered a program to increase the health of disabled individuals. Further, research was conducted to create a better understanding of the problems involved in rehabilitation and to increase the number of rehabilitation centers.

FUNCTION OF VOCATIONAL REHABILITATION

The function of vocational rehabilitation has been a co-operative effort between state and federal government, ratified by federal statutes and partly by laws created by the state legislatures. The Federal Security Agency provides the leadership via the Office of Vocational Rehabilitation, which maintains nine regional offices and administers the financial side of the program.

The total expenditures of the last forty-one years indicate an increase in funds for rehabilitation. The increase does not include expenses for special projects. This upward trend illustrates the increasing support provided by the federal government. In addition to the existing funds for general expenditure, Public Law 565 stipulates additional grants for extension, improvement, demonstrations, and for the training of professional rehabilitation personnel.

The states, however, have received greater responsibility with the growth of rehabilitation programs. The State Board of Vocational Education has an over-all responsibility for both rehabilitation and education. In each state there is a separate agency for the blind. Further, there is a delegation of responsibility from the state level to the local, municipal or county level, but still the supervision is exercised by the agency which is responsible for the state rehabilitation program.

The number of persons rehabilitated under the vocational rehabilitation programs has steadily increased since 1920. The increase is particularly observable since 1943, the year of the adoption of the progressive Barden-La Follette Act. The increase is not only a numerical one; the quality has also become more progressive—necessitated not by the feeling of a charitable role but more by a sense of responsibility for the disabled. Rehabilitation services are provided without any tuition and include not only physical training and educational instruction for gainful employment, but also the mental adjustment required to accept personal differences. Therefore, medical service, vocational diagnosis, and training for employment were co-ordinated by the idea that the rehabilitee will be prepared for, enter into, and progress in the field of occupation in which he may find the greatest satisfaction and social and financial security. Large proportions of the rehabilitees were placed in the categories of skilled and unskilled workers, clerical and sales occupations, and service

251

workers. Professional and agricultural workers as well as family workers were placed in smaller proportion. This trend prevailed over a two-year period, indicating a stability in the occupations in which the rehabilitee was placed after rehabilitation.

EVALUATION OF VOCATIONAL REHABILITATION

Before the rehabilitees assume a position in the field of competitive labor, they are evaluated by different techniques. One of the most current evaluation systems was designed by The Behavioral Sciences Research Laboratory for Industries Limited, a sheltered workshop in Pennsylvania. The evaluation system was conducted under a grant from the Commonwealth of Pennsylvania, Department of Public Welfare, in 1961. This evaluation system was prepared on the principle that sheltered workshops as well as any other form of rehabilitation should use only one criterion on which progress in the training program could be measured and ranked according to scientific principles. This criterion may be used as a common denominator for all kinds of work participated in by the disabled, retarded, or normal. On the basis of such a denominator the comparison between normal and disabled work will provide the only way to understand the actual status of the rehabilitee who is prepared for actual work in the competitive field of labor. This method of work measurement already employed in Industries Limited is called the "methods-time" measurement in the field of industry—a system which applies predetermined time standards that have been established by careful research. It may be defined as a procedure which analyzes any manual operation into basic motions required to perform it and assigns to each motion a predetermined time standard which is determined by the nature of a motion and the conditions under which it is made.

The methods-time measurement is scientific in approach and is practical, as observed by The Behavioral Sciences Research Laboratory for any purpose related to work evaluation, or rehabilitation records which record the progress of the rehabil-

252

itee, because its application of a predetermined standard has been established by careful industrial research and used with great efficiency for a long time. In this analysis the method we use is that any work which is carried out will take a certain time to accomplish. Thus, the time it takes could be co-ordinated in time units, as one can see. However, the results of the rehabilitee, as well as those of a normal worker, will depend on the understanding of the performance the worker (rehabilitee) receives before the actual start of the work process. The method of the work process, therefore, must be established according to certain rules and understood by the trainee exactly and in great detail before the allowed time for completion can be determined. This fosters careful analytical work with emphasis on method and understanding. The time study men have also recognized that it would be confusing to use a large number of individual time studies, which in addition would produce a serious inconsistency.

REGISTER OF VOCATIONAL REHABILITATION

Using the above proposed work evaluation system, already operating with success, it would be possible to register scientifically the individual progress of any rehabilitee and therefore not depend solely on the concerted individual effort of the rehabilitation personnel. The accurate registration of the rehabilitee could be further registered by the state offices, who in turn could transfer the data at the end of each fiscal year to the authorities on the federal level. The availability of accurate information on accomplished work, as well as a register of anticipated future rehabilitees, would greatly facilitate the preparation of budgets for the coming years. The task of co-ordinating such research activity and evaluating the rehabilitation process is a challenging one, since it involves pioneering work in the field. However, such progress evaluation would be only one aspect of the responsibilities of vocational rehabilitation. There is another need in the field; namely, the register by regional subdivisions of potential rehabilitees. This will provide the necessary information of the future needs on the basis of state-wide knowledge. This register should include: (a) all children with an I.Q. of 75 or lower in public, private, or parochial schools; (b) all physically disabled persons in the files of physicians, including cerebrovascular, accidents, strokes, orthopedic and neurologic, cardiovascular, tuberculosis, mental illness, epilepsy, blindness, deafness, cerebral palsy, etc.; (c) it should assemble systematic information of potential rehabilitee participants; (d) agreement of each co-operating school district to notify the register of any cases where an I.Q. of 75 or lower is recorded, and when such a case is terminated; (e) physicians, after agreement with the necessary officials, will notify the register of disabled persons they administer; and (f) further, all caseworkers, county nurses, welfare agencies, etc. will automatically notify the register of any potential rehabilitation clients.

This state-wide register will provide a better operating definition for the rehabilitee than is in use today, as well as providing factual information. The register will reveal the following:

1. The relative distribution of the rehabilitees in various sections of cities, communities, as well as those served by the rehabilitation division.
2. Information regarding rehabilitation services available in any region wherein a prospective rehabilitee may reside.
3. Provide information concerning existing services or sources to parents, families, and friends of the rehabilitees.

With such data, as a base, each of the vocational rehabilitation centers can command actual coverage of all necessary facts vital to rehabilitation:

a. The over-all conditions within the region or area the rehabilitation centers serve.
b. Conduct continuous and systematic research of disabled, retarded, or handicapped individuals' behavior based on better general knowledge than is now available through official statistics.
c. Conduct evaluation on individual, departmental, and insti-

254

tutional levels and compare the different centers throughout the state.

d. Build up responsible budgeting of time based on factual information.

Such a register would permit the full cognizance of the advantages, the disadvantages, the rehabilitee costs, and the gains occurring from a particular course of action. Certain events cannot be solved upon their occurrence unless their coming has been expected and proper preparations have been provided. Factors such as length of training, tardiness, and absence will be kept in the personal files of the trainee, as well as the quality of the work, quantity of production, and those traits and characteristics which do not lend themselves to objective measurement, such as personality, dependability, judgment, and co-operation.

EXCEPTIONAL CHILDREN
AND VOCATIONAL REHABILITATION

If the register of vocational rehabilitation were kept up to date on a national level it would contain between four and five million exceptional children between the ages of 5 and 17 who would need special education. Such a large group of young people creates the responsibility for communities as well as for the nation (a) to give good basic general education to specialized teachers; (b) to offer services for the children; (c) to prepare them for some kind of occupation; and (d) to provide them a permanent place in society. The acceptance of these responsibilities by the community and the nation would reflect a public belief that it is a must—that exceptional children too may look forward to the "blessings of liberty" and to co-operate in the "general welfare" of the nation.

a. *General Education for Specialized Teachers:* Good will on the part of communities, states and national agencies is not adequate to carry out the responsibilities toward this young age group of exceptional children. The great need is to find thoroughly prepared teachers who could give the necessary training, following the principles of adapting materials to individual needs through constant evaluation, and freedom of choice on the part of exceptional children. A well-trained teacher is supportive in encouraging the handicapped child to achieve maximum adjustment to the demands of learning, vocation, and socialization. The community has responsibility for providing the handicapped child with the same opportunities for growth, development and social maturation as those available to other children. To determine the medical, social welfare, and educational services needed, however, it is necessary to know the incidence and characteristics of specific handicaps. This demands co-operation with the central register of vocational rehabilitation where systematic case-findings, reporting, and registration would be present.

At the present time only one-fourth of all handicapped children receive special services due to the lack of specialized and qualified teachers. The Office of Education estimated 100,000 qualified teachers would be needed to fulfill the requests of educational institutions. These teachers should be sensitive to the special needs of the handicapped and understand and appreciate the handicapped child's desire to do the things that other children are doing and help assist them to overcome frustration when they cannot participate in the simple activities of childhood.

The professional preparation of exceptional teachers is allocated to 122 colleges and universities. The major concentrations are centered around the Great Lakes and California. California has 15 institutions of higher learning offering at least one area of exceptionality, Pennsylvania and Illinois each have 11 and New York State 10 centers. The teachers are prepared for the visually handicapped, or for special health problems relating to crippling conditions, speech or hearing impairment, mental retardation and social maladjustments. Most of the students in these educational institutions acquired a Bachelor's degree (64%); one-third a Master's; and only a relatively small proportion of the students received a Ph.D. or equivalent in special education (3%) in 1953. The largest proportion of these degrees went to specialists in the fields of speech correction, mental retardation, and hear-

256

ing. Other areas of specialization were less popular, further emphasizing the need for more teachers of all phases of rehabilitation, including the socially maladjusted as well as gifted children.

b. *Offered Services for Exceptional Children:* Many of the families having exceptional children cannot cope with the problems of rearing these children and it becomes necessary for them to seek special health, education, and social welfare resources within their communities. These resources can be received through the (1) schools, (2) communities, and (3) federal aid.

(1) *The School:* The school often must act *in loco parentis* and this role places many responsibilities on the school administration. Among these responsibilities are the development of special classes for children with intellectual, emotional, or physical handicaps. For this reason public school administrators have sought to strengthen their staffs with psychiatric consultants, clinical psychologists, and school social workers.

Education is understood as a therapeutic process which effects change in the learner by giving him knowledge, skills, and experiences with which to cope with his environment. Psychotherapy grants the opportunity for the individual to understand his own behavior and will help him in discovering ways to come to terms with his personal environment. Exceptional children receive a great deal of attention through different testing, consulting, and social work services.

The schools which employ social workers emphasize the dual responsibilities of the educational institution: that of education and socialization. In public as well as in other schools no one single individual can assume all the responsibility; thus the social worker assumes major responsibility for the co-ordination of school casework services and the relation of the school with other health and welfare agencies in the community. Social work services are extended with greater emphasis toward children with serious difficulties, all applying the latest advancements, knowledge and skill of social work.

In some school districts the social worker has the responsibility of contacting families of disturbed children, serving as a mediator between the family and the school, arranging conferences, and staff consultations. If the problem is of great concern to the school staff they may hold conferences with the psychiatric consultant, who will explain to the staff the problem, offering feasible treatment plans and probable prognosis. Although the psychiatrist is available for diagnostic evaluation, interpretation of behavioral problems and treatment planning, therapy must be given by the school staff or a referral made to an appropriate social agency.

(2) *The Community:* A further professional service offered in some school districts is called the child guidance clinic which generally consists of a psychiatrist, clinical psychologist, and a psychiatric social worker. Most of these clinics operate on a community level. The psychiatrist has major responsibility for the administration and supervision of the clinic and for the treatment program, while the clinical psychologist administers and interprets psychological tests and other diagnostic materials. The psychiatric social worker will carry out the initial interview with the child's parents and works with them throughout the child's contact with the clinic. All community clinics assume responsibility for acting as an educational and consultant resource for parents, teachers, social agencies, community groups, and others requesting information relating to child behavior.

Community child guidance clinics are generally part of a statewide mental hygiene program and may be supported by state or local public funds supplemented by financial support from the Community Chest. These clinics maintain a place of great importance in the community because they are designed to discover emotional disturbances in children at an early age. However, the different social and health agencies, schools, parents, juvenile courts and other institutions on local, county or regional basis are overloading the clinics, which are generally poorly staffed. It happens probably because the function of the clinics is not clearly understood. Further, the interpretation of emotional disturbances in child behavior is poorly interpreted and in most cases overdramatized. This is of great concern, because it is not uncommon that a clinic staff of five is expected to serve a community of several hundred thousand population requiring diagnostic treatment and consultation over a larger special territory than the legal area in which it operates.

Another important organization which is helpful in the field of exceptional children as well as other community problems, such as child welfare and health, is the Community Welfare Council. This Council co-ordinates the interests of public and private agencies and that of professional interests in the field of social welfare needs and the effective use of resources. The agencies as well as individuals serve on the council on a voluntary basis. In many instances if the council is preparing a type of "self-study" or confronted with a complex problem with which they are unable to cope, outside experts will be consulted.

(3) *Federal Aid*: It is the belief that no child may develop into an emotionally secure individual who is compelled to live apart from his parents. Governmental agencies recognizing this premise have provided financial resources for families who may encounter difficulties in rearing their children through the Social Security Act of 1936. Title IV of the Social Security Act encourages the care of dependent children, enabling the states to furnish financial or other services to needy and dependent children in order to maintain family life and help to attain the maximum self-support and personal independence in the frame of reference of the family.

The Welfare Department processes the applications for Aid to Dependent Children and reports to law enforcement officials when assistance is being given to a child who has been abandoned by his parent (s) . Public attitude toward the ADC program and professional interest in this problem have provided assistance for the needy child, and strengthened family ties and encouraged self-support. Federal funds were again increased in 1957 to train more personnel for this mode of public assistance.

Title V of the Social Security Act authorized specific help for maternal and child health services, child welfare services, and crippled children. All states and territories promote the health and welfare of mothers and children, providing prenatal clinics for expectant mothers and health supervision for children of preschool age. New demonstration projects have been organized in many of the states to develop a pattern of services for children especially in the preschool age. Plans have been submitted to the Children's Bureau to expand the foster care program and to demonstrate the value of the homemaker service. The increase in the federal grants-in-aid make possible the employment and training of staffs and provide the skilled services needed by troubled children and their families.

Most of the states participate in the program for crippled children. These services have one objective: to locate children who need care, and to provide them with the means of physical restoration through diagnosis, medical or surgical treatment, and the alleviation of unfavorable social and psychological influences which hinder a rapid adjustment to a future life.

c. *Preparation for Gainful Employment:* Public school districts and private organizations have assumed the opportunity to expand their services for disabled youth and have applied for financial aid to state rehabilitation agencies and to the U. S. Office of Vocational Rehabilitation. In this way these institutions desire to establish training centers or sheltered workshops for retarded or disabled youth from 14 to 18 years of age.

Several grant-in-aids to these institutions stimulated the rehabilitation of handicapped youth through education. The young adults who were prepared for employment located their jobs directly through the school. Some of these exceptional young adults, however, needed additional services to those offered in the schools. A further preparation for vocation followed via the sheltered workshops, where the disabled person could experience not only prevocational preparation but also physical and psychiatric evaluation, treatment, on-the-job training, counseling, or personal adjustment before they were placed in competitive employment.

This financial assistance and the parent-sponsored community groups established the sheltered workshops. The Vocational Rehabilitation Act observes the effect of the training centers and sheltered workshops as education as well as rehabilitation. The MacDonald Workshop in Florida completed a pioneering study on the effect of vocational training while Industries Limited, a sheltered workshop in Pennsylvania, is progressing with an evaluation system which would enable state and federal agencies to properly estimate the effectiveness of the present work which is being conducted in the different sheltered workshops on an objective scale. This is of great importance since institutionalization in sheltered workshops requires large community and state finances to serve the handicapped.

In comparison to the other forms of vocational rehabilitation sheltered workshops are only at the beginning of their development and with administrative and training arrangements as nucleus, must look to the future for proper formulation. Nevertheless, their promise is great and it behooves us to think more realistically about plans to increase their number in a co-ordinated and logical location so that they may serve the disabled and handicapped youth at an employable age, thereby furnishing training for gainful employment.

d. *Placement of the Rehabilitated:* Schooling and preparation for job placement is one of the greatest undertakings both in responsibility and time involved. Throughout the schooling period employment is considered as one of the major objectives in curriculum building. Many schools provide training in some vocational skills through a unit course along with proper preparation for employment via counseling. These preparations culminate in selective placement. To place a handicapped individual on a job involves a series of professional services which include: (a) exploration of job opportunities; (b) evaluation; (c) job placement; and (d) postplacement counseling.

State Employment services and different employment agencies will supply all necessary referrals and professional guidance for sheltered workshops or other educational institutions that assume the responsibility of educating the handicapped.

Rehabilitation agencies use this information to plan their rehabilitative services, and with the new method of evaluation sheltered workshops are in a position to evaluate the handicapped production ability level. Placement through this method will no longer be a question of charity but actually a placement. Cooperating agencies should take into consideration that placement is not the termination of their work, but is followed up until the part-time experience of the handicapped in the competitive field of labor becomes a full-time job. During this transition period the social adjustment of the rehabilitee should also be followed up.

Vocational rehabilitation therefore should have a stake in postplacement services. If the rehabilitee employment is unsuccessful they should be returned to the sheltered workshops but only so long as they are unable to function independently in the community.

SUMMARY

This short essay comprises the brief history, the structure and the function of vocational rehabilitation, as well as evaluation in the field and the proposed register of rehabilitation. Discussing exceptional children, we emphasized the importance of the proper preparation of good teachers, the offered services, and work preparation for the gainful employment of the handicapped. In general, it has described the services available on local, state and national levels for the socially, physically, and intellectually handicapped. Government agencies take partnership in the communities' effort to help preserve family units and provide a hopeful future for the handicapped.

Handicaps and disabilities do not indicate that one should not attain social, economic, and financial security but rather that all persons should participate in the general welfare of our nation and should receive the blessings of liberty.

SELECTED BIBLIOGRAPHY

Allan, W. Sc., REHABILITATION: A COMMUNITY CHALLENGE (New York: Wiley, 1958).

Armstrong, W. Earl and T. M. Stinnett, A MANUAL ON CERTIFICATION REQUIREMENTS FOR SCHOOL PER-

SONNEL IN THE UNITED STATES (Washington, D. C.: National Education Association, 1953).

Burns, Eveline, SOCIAL SECURITY AND PUBLIC POLICY (New York: McGraw-Hill Book Co., 1956).

Cruickshank, William M., PSYCHOLOGY OF EXCEPTIONAL CHILDREN AND YOUTH (Englewood Cliffs, N. J.: Prentice-Hall, 1955).

DeFrancis, Vincent, CHILD PROTECTIVE SERVICES IN THE UNITED STATES (Denver: Children's Division, The American Humane Association, 1956).

DiMichael, S. C., PSYCHOLOGICAL SERVICES IN VOCATIONAL REHABILITATION (Washington: U.S. Department of Health, Education, and Welfare, Office of Vocational Rehabilitation, 1959).

Donnelly, Joan A., EMPLOYMENT OF THE PHYSICALLY HANDICAPPED—A BIBLIOGRAPHY (U.S. President's Committee on Employment of the Physically Handicapped, Washington: U.S. Government Printing Office, 1957).

Fredericksen, Hazel, THE CHILD AND HIS WELFARE (San Francisco: W. H. Freeman and Son, 1957).

Kessler, Henry, REHABILITATION OF THE PHYSICALLY HANDICAPPED (New York: Columbia University Press, 1953).

Mackie, Romaine P. and L. M. Dunn, COLLEGE AND UNIVERSITY PROGRAMS FOR PREPARATION OF TEACHERS OF EXCEPTIONAL CHILDREN (Washington: U.S. Government Printing Office, 1958).

Mackie, Romaine P. and L. M. Dunn, STATE CERTIFICATION REQUIREMENTS FOR TEACHERS OF EXCEPTIONAL CHILDREN (Washington: U.S. Government Printing Office, 1958).

Stroup, Herbert H., SOCIAL WORK: AN INTRODUCTION TO THE FIELD, 2nd ed. (New York: American Book Co., 1960).

Switzer, Mary E., VOCATIONAL REHABILITATION IN THE UNITED STATES (Washington: U.S. Government Printing Office, 1958).

Vasey, Wayne, GOVERNMENT AND SOCIAL WELFARE (New York: Henry Holt and Co., Inc., 1958).

Zietz, Dorothy, CHILD WELFARE: PRINCIPLES AND

METHODS (New York: John Wiley and Sons, Inc., 1959). Development of child welfare program and different services available.

ERNEST M. GAJÁRY KUHINKA, Director of The Behavior Sciences Research Laboratory, Carlisle, Pennsylvania, and Assistant Professor of Sociology at Dickinson College, received his B.A. from the University of Debrecen (1945), and his M.A. (1950) and Ph.D. (1952) from the University of Utrecht. He also attended the Graduate Faculty of the New School for Social Research in New York in 1956. Dr. Kuhinka is author of two books, and has written numerous articles, book reviews, and communications for leading national and foreign journals in the field of sociology. He conducted research for The Netherlands Committee for Research of the European Refugee Problem, The Hague; Catholic Institute for Socio-Ecclesiastical Study, The Hague; Provincial Country and Town Planning, Haarlem; Planning Institute for Sociological Reorganization of the City of Haarlem; and the Research Bureau of the National Council of Churches, New York. Dr. Kuhinka is a member of various professional associations on national and regional level and is well known through his research activities in the field of marketing, time measurement studies, rehabilitation, community development, and opinion. Presently he is directing research for local, state, and national agencies and associations.

PROVISION FOR THE UNUSUAL CHILD
IN WESTERN EUROPE

C. V. Russell
University of London Institute of Education

The welfare of the child from birth until it reaches adulthood
—and sometimes beyond—is admitted to be the responsibility of
the community at large. There is everywhere evidence of an
increasingly humane social consciousness which accords a new
respect to the individual and demands that each shall be enabled
to develop to the limits of his capabilities. This applies equally
to the sub-normal and the super-normal child.

In general, children are so heterogeneous in their characteristics and potentialities that it might seem desirable to plan for
each one an education uniquely suited to his particular needs.
However, this is neither possible nor desirable, for education
implies not only individual development but also the training
of different individuals to conform to the general requirements
of the society in which they live. At one level, this means the
development of an integrated personality able to mix freely with
his fellow men; at another level, this implies the provision of the
necessary skills to earn a living. Thus, there are positive advantages in educating diverse individuals in groups. But there must
be some restriction in the diversity or heterogeneity of any particular group, otherwise the educational process becomes ineffi-
cient and its purpose is frustrated. To take an extreme example,
it would be out of the question to try to train imbeciles and
university students in the same class.

Granted, then, that there must be a limit to the degree of heterogeneity, it might be suggested that any segregation of unusual children should be based on characteristics which (1) are stable and enduring; (2) can be accurately assessed; (3) have a major influence on educational progress; and (4) are acceptable to society. Here we come upon a major difficulty. There are few characteristics, apart from age and physical handicap, which meet all these requirements. For example, it is generally agreed that the deaf, the blind and the partially sighted, and those suffering from cerebral palsy should be segregated for special schooling under specially qualified teachers, though doubts may arise in deciding the degree of defect that requires such treatment. Homogeneous groupings based on other criteria, particularly those based on high mental and intellectual faculties, are liable to arouse intense controversy. Here the problem arises of reconciling the innate differences in human ability, as revealed by scientific investigations, with the concept of equality. There would seem, however, to be strong grounds for the special educational treatment of children at the two extremes of the intellectual scale, as far as this can be made compatible with a democratic interpretation of life.

THE MENTALLY SUB-NORMAL CHILD

From the various international investigations, notably that of the World Health Organization in 1954 and that of the International Bureau of Education in 1960, the fact emerges that there is a large number of mentally sub-normal children capable of learning and of adapting themselves to live in society, if given a suitable education, for whom no such individual instruction is provided, for the simple reason that the existing institutions, though excellent, are insufficient in number. For some countries it has been a matter of allocating slender resources to more profitable purposes. The economically under-developed countries, for example, facing the problem of mass-illiteracy, are obliged to concentrate on general education for all and cannot provide for a category of children who do not give returns in proportion to the expense involved in their education. Even in the more advanced countries such as Britain, France and Germany provision is inadequate.

In the United Kingdom the administrative responsibility for the welfare of youth is shared by the Ministry of Education, the Ministry of Health and the Home Office. In certain fields there is a very close overlap of administrative functions and this leads to some confusion, especially in the provision of special education. The education of children who are considered "educable" is the joint responsibility of the Ministry of Education and the Local Education Authorities, as is the education of all normal and especially gifted children. "Ineducable" children are referred by the Education Authority to the Local Health Authority which has the responsibility for "(a) providing suitable supervision for such defectives, and if this affords insufficient protection, taking steps to secure that they are sent to institutions or placed under guardianship; (b) providing suitable training or occupation for defectives under supervision or guardianship; (c) making provision for the guardianship of defectives placed under guardianship by orders under the Act." Apart from this the Home Office administers certain "remand" institutions for the re-education or rehabilitation of young delinquents and first offenders.

In order to limit the field it is proposed to exclude from the present study children in the lower reaches of mental sub-normality who are deemed to be "ineducable" or "non-recoverable" and for whom special provision in asylum or mental hospital is permanently necessary. This category includes, on the one hand, idiots and imbeciles and, on the other hand, the feeble-minded who suffer from a disability of mind which makes it "inexpedient that they should be educated in association with other children" owing to faulty habits or behavior. Practicing psychologists generally accept different intelligence quotients as characteristic of the three conditions although in law they continue to be defined in terms of the social ability and competence of the person concerned.

While it is relatively easy to recognize children who are seriously sub-normal—i.e. cases of idiocy or imbecility—the educable mentally deficient child is more difficult to identify. Cases of slight deficiency are often confused with slow learners or late developers, whose intelligence may be developed, whereas the mentally deficient suffer from a lesion of the brain which is permanent. In Britain the Education Act of 1944 recognizes ten categories of handicapped pupil, for whom the law requires "special educational treatment" in either special schools or in special classes at ordinary schools. The largest of these categories is the Educationally Sub-normal. Under the Act a pupil was defined as being Educationally Sub-normal (ESN) if his attainments were 80 per cent or less of those of an average child of his age. This applied *irrespective of the assumed causes* of such backwardness. In other words the ESN category included both the slow learner and the mentally deficient mentioned above. The Ministry estimated that some 10 per cent of the school population came under this wider definition. It was hoped that individual treatment of each case would help to distinguish the causes of backwardness and where possible effect a remedy. This proved to be an optimistic view, for in any event the intentions of the Act were largely defeated by a shortage of teachers qualified to deal with these children.[1]

As a sub-category of the ESN group 1.2 per cent of the school population were deemed to require day special or residential schools. These were pupils who, in the words of the Act, could be officially *ascertained* as Educationally Sub-normal. A child came into this category when his attainments were 70 per cent or less than the average and when no physical, sensory, emotional or other cause than apparent low intelligence could be found to account for his condition.

It is very important to note that prior to World War II such a child might have been *certified* as Mentally Deficient. He is now seen as belonging to a much larger group, all of whom require special attention. The whole concept of "mental defect" has been

268

removed from the school system. The term was retained for those excluded from the schools (usually those with an I.Q. of 50 or less). Even here there was evident a fresh approach to the whole problem of mental handicap and intellectual inefficiency. In recent years several investigations into the techniques of training mental defectives and the relationship of these techniques to occupational success have been reported, notably the work of O'Connor and Tizard.[2] In such a situation the border line between the "educable" and the "ineducable" becomes less easy to define.

As will be seen from the preceding paragraphs the intelligence quotient is a very widespread criterion of classification. This is a common practice in most countries in Western Europe. The procedure adopted in the County of Cheshire, England, may be regarded as typical. All Cheshire children are given a Moray-House group test of intelligence at the age of nine. At the same time they are given a Moray-House group test of attainment in Arithmetic and English. The Director of Education for Cheshire, reporting in THE SCHOOLMASTER 21st September, 1956, goes on to say; "By comparing the three quotients obtained by the children in these three tests . . . the primary school teachers can see at once if a child is backward in either of these basic subjects." Sometimes reading and reading comprehension tests are also carried out. Many psychologists, P. E. Vernon of the University of London Institute of Education among them, have pointed out the dangers of assuming that psychological tests can measure innate intelligence and therefore discriminate between the *dull* child, whose backwardness is irremediable, and the *retarded* child, who can be helped to work "up to capacity." Stott has put the matter succinctly; ". . . except for the most obvious cases of mental retardation, there is no quick and certain method of sorting out the children who merely need remedial tuition from those needing long-term treatment. The children's actual progress in remedial groups is the best means of such classification."[3] As indicated above, this view is very much in the spirit of the provisions of the 1944 Education Act.

The intelligence quotient, although useful as a general diagnostic tool, should not be the only factor to be taken into consideration. O'Connor and Tizard suggest six aspects of a subject's present condition which ought to be taken into account.[4] These are: (a) anatomical and physiological; (b) intellectual; (c) educational; (d) social (i.e. social competence); (e) occupational; and (f) temperamental or moral. In addition historical and family circumstances are important. Among these are the socio-economic status and occupational competence of other members of the family, the family history and the individual's own developmental and educational history. With the increase in the activities of the welfare state and the provision of free medical services every child will have undergone a medical examination on first entering school and will be subject to medical check at frequent intervals. This will be particularly true of the Scandinavian countries, where nearly all the new schools springing up in the towns have resident doctors and dentists and large well equipped inspection rooms. In Britain the Local Health Authorities run the school medical service, usually organized from some centrally placed clinic. However, in most countries these medical inspections are not sufficiently thorough to detect any serious mental deficiency. It is only after a certain length of time that the teacher and parents notice that the child cannot manage to keep up with his lessons. He has to repeat a grade and fall far behind the other children of the same age before anyone worries about his mental condition.

Guidance can often be obtained from the school record card and the medical records which are maintained for each child within the English School system. These are particularly valuable if the child transfers from one school to another, as they give continuity and help in the diagnosis of any troubles that may arise. The medical cards, in particular, give illuminating details of illness at vital ages (e.g. long absence at the age of 6 plus when most children are considered to be ready to learn to read); details of injury and surgical operations which may affect the child permanently. References to asthma, enuresis, sinus trouble, middle ear infection and so on, all tell their own story and have a bearing on the educational development of the child in question. In this connection it is vitally important to detect deficiencies in such children at an early stage, so that they do not waste their time in an unsuccessful attempt to keep up with instruction which is not within their grasp. Here we must rely to a great extent on the vigilance of the ordinary class-room teacher who will refer doubtful cases to more expert opinion.

EDUCATIONAL PROVISION

The trend in the post-war era has been to bring handicapped children "nearer to life," by considering the child in the setting of the family and the family in the setting of the community. Emphasis is on teamwork, in which parents, teacher, doctor, psychologist, and social worker, all play their part. This cooperation is essential in order to remove some of the misconceptions that have developed in the lay mind and the stigma attached to the field of mental handicap. Parents, in particular, need encouragement and guidance as to the best way of dealing with their handicapped child. What is often necessary is the reeducation of the parents, who are at a loss to understand their child's behaviour and have difficulty in admitting that he is not like the others. They must be helped to overcome their wounded pride and be led to understand that the child deserves to be educated and can, in spite of everything, be made a useful human being. In the give-and-take of family life the mentally retarded child is often left in isolation, because the other members of the family are impatient of the slower pace at which he thinks and do not take the trouble to bring him into their daily activities. Here, too, sympathy and understanding of his needs are necessary. Since the War a remarkable parent-doctor organization has come into being, called the National Society for Mentally Handicapped Children. It has had a profound influence on opinion. It has provided funds for research and financed the BRITISH JOURNAL OF MENTAL DEFICIENCY, as well as distributing pamphlets and technical literature to parents.

In principle, then, it would seem desirable that mentally sub-normal children should attend special classes attached to ordinary schools. They will thus not be separated from their families. Like their more fortunate companions they return each day to their families and, what is equally important, they remain in daily contact with normal children. This is the best way of integrating them into the life of the community and equipping them to play their part with normally developed adults later in life.

With the present shortage in the U.K. of teachers of all grades there is, however, a grave danger that the ESN child will be submerged in the large classes of 40 or more and that he will not receive the individual attention, of which he stands in need. On the other hand provision of special schools is limited and, in the circumstances, it is felt that only the most obvious cases can be transferred there. Some authorities even maintain that any child outside the narrow band of I.Q. 50-70 is, in fact depriving a more suitable applicant of a place. Under the prevailing conditions there is something to be said for this point of view. There is, thus, a considerable number of backward children who are considered, by whatever criteria of judgement, to be too bright for a special school but yet fall below the mental standard of the average child. Until this problem is tackled effectively at the primary stage, the English Secondary Modern School and the Comprehensive School will face difficulties which are almost insurmountable.[5] The ideal of at least one remedial teacher at each of these schools is unlikely to be realized in the foreseeable future. In this connection the work of the Kellerske Anstalt in Denmark might be mentioned. Schools often refer backward children to this institution. After a period of residential remedial treatment the pupil is able to return to a normal school. This implies a much more thorough investigation of the causes of the child's backwardness than is possible in an ordinary school by the administration of a battery of tests. This institution might act as a pointer to the future.

But what of the general education of the mentally sub-normal child? Most countries which provide special education start from the principle that mentally defective children need practical and concrete instruction, adapted to the pace of the individual, in order to stimulate their reduced mental functions and compensate for the shortcomings of their intelligence. Concrete education does not mean merely games and educational exercises, but above all handicrafts. Manual work helps those children in the lower ranges of ability, who are in general physically awkward, to coordinate their movements, and gives them an opportunity to carry out something successfully themselves. It is a means of giving them self-confidence and can also be the basis for their vocational training. There is also the question of social education. These children must be helped to adapt themselves socially and to live with others. To this end, use should be made of group work, playing together, sport and any other activity which develops mutual aid and fellowship, and a sense of responsibility towards society. Moral education and character training should not be neglected. Sir Cyril Burt, in *The Young Delinquent,* has long ago noted the connection between delinquency and mental deficiency. It is important, therefore, to give these children, who are weaker than others, a sound moral foundation as far as that is possible. In general, the mentally sub-normal child is a person who has little initiative, but who may compensate for this by well ordered habits.

THE MENTALLY SUB-NORMAL IN ADULT LIFE

As already indicated, mentally handicapped children can play a useful part in society, provided they are given the right kind of training and full allowance is made in the adult world for the difficulties under which they labor. It follows from this that some will stand in need of after-care for many years to come, perhaps all their lives. Others will be quickly integrated into the pattern of the daily life around them and will pass unnoticed among their fellow men. The difficulties of integration are less acute in periods of economic stability. In times of full employment it is relatively easy to place handicapped young people in jobs. The contribution which they make to the economy of the country can be considerable, as well as being of therapeutic value to themselves.

At the risk of stating the obvious, however, there is a limit to the field of useful work that can be carried out by mentally retarded youngsters. O'Connor and Tizard, in the work previously quoted, describe a survey carried out among a representative sample of leavers from all the *Secondary Modern* schools in Derby.[6] On the basis of their intelligence scores in the selective examination for secondary education, the boys were divided into two groups for low and normal I.Q. and paired according to social class and school. The mean I.Q. of the lower-intelligence group, the experimental group, was 70 with a range from 65 to 80. The mean I.Q. of the higher-intelligence group, the control group, was 99.5 with a range from 94 to 106. The sub-normal boys had had an average of 2.8 jobs in the two years between leaving school and call-up into the army and the normal boys had had an average of 1.5 jobs. The difference in the work record of the two groups is quite small. It is significant, however, that 12 out of 21 Sub-normal boys left apprenticed trades in which they had begun, whereas only 5 out of 29 normal boys left such positions. Presumably the demands of a skilled trade were too exacting.

Since full-employment inevitably affects any investigation of this kind, it is of interest to consider the post-school careers of pupils at a school for the Educationally Sub-normal in the County of Cornwall, where the figure for unemployment in 1959 was 7 per cent. Seventy-six boys and girls left the residential special school between July, 1953, and September, 1959, but only 57 per cent proved successful in employment. J. E. Collins, the County Educational Psychologist at this period, pointed out the close relationship between job-success and I.Q., but also noted the significance of a stable home background as I.Q. diminished.[7] Children with I.Q.'s of 70 or over were so satisfactory that they were not looked upon either by employers or fellow workers as mentally handicapped. About three quarters of the children with I.Q.'s of 65-74 were successful, and every one of the failures came from homes weakened by death or desertion. Children in this

274

I.Q. range appear likely to fail when there is a lack of economic and emotional stability in their home life. Success is much more remote when the I.Q. is below 55 and appears to be due to such chance factors as the kindness of an employer or the child's pleasant temperament. It is likely, then, that if work becomes scarce, the dull and the backward will fare badly in competition with brighter adolescents.

THE GIFTED CHILD—A SOCIAL PROBLEM

The major issues in education are seldom decided on grounds that teachers would call educational. We tend to think that the problems of developing and releasing talent of all kinds can be solved by the school. Actually, the solution is essentially political. It will depend entirely on the prevailing views on the nature of man and his place in society. In Europe, following a tradition that goes back to Plato, most countries were, in the past, and some still are, quite prepared to accept the principle of leadership through an intellectual *élite*. The function of the schools was seen as that of selecting and training *élite* groups. This may well be accepted as a valid point of view in a society with a firm class structure, served by a system of well established schools and a tradition of apprenticeship.

The educational pattern which emerged in 19th century Europe was one of overlapping categories of elementary and secondary education which served quite different groups of the community. A system of elementary schools gave instruction in the basic skills and other useful accomplishments. The literacy of the masses was valued largely as a means of producing a greater number of subordinate officials and employees of industry. In conjunction with the apprenticeship system they also trained craftsmen.

A limited number of secondary schools provided a highly academic education, in which the classical languages were prominent, leading to the Universities and the liberal professions.[8] The particular task of these schools was the preservation and transmission of the traditional elements of the national heritage and civilization. The true bearers of this culture were considered to be comparatively few in number and were destined to be the leaders of society. Attendance at a particular school was generally an indication of the social standing of the parents and, as a result, factors other than education determined the choice of a career. In this context, gifted children who might be identified among the social and economic groups, denied access to the best schools and universities, were granted scholarships without the need to alter the social structure or the school system. Thus, the "élitarian" form of society was preserved with only a very slight upward movement into the *élite* by other elements.

A system of education based on this ideology is wasteful of talent, because the process of identification and selection of the talented and gifted, however rigorous, is dependent on a very limited view of ability and allows factors other than educational ones to be crucial. It is obvious that a child from a socially under-privileged home has far greater obstacles to overcome in such a system than his counterpart from a well-to-do home. To counter-act these disadvantages, his talents must be the greater.

With the rise of political democracy, the efforts of the past 75 years have been directed, in many countries, to achieving social equality. Attention was naturally focussed on the schools. What had previously been regarded as the prerogative of the few, was now thought of as a basic human right. The underlying principle of the educational reforms of this period was equality of opportunity. Every child was to be given a chance, without social or financial discrimination, of obtaining a higher as well as an elementary education.

The first step was to bridge the gap between the vertical divisions of the elementary and secondary schemes of education, by enabling children of all classes to pass freely from one to the other. This was achieved by relieving parents of the financial burden of educating their children and by bringing the curricula of the two levels of education into line, so that there was a regular progression from one to the other. It is noteworthy, that most European systems retained some form of selection process for the secondary stage of education, usually after four to six years of elementary or primary schooling. The gifted youngster was the boy or girl who gained a place at the local grammar school or lycée.

In recent years there has been much discussion on the techniques used in this selection procedures, particularly in England where it is pointed out that the so-called 11 plus *selection* examination is an 11 plus *rejection* examination for about 75 per cent of the children in the age group. Every effort has been made to eliminate from the process factors which would favor children from a particular socio-economic level, by devising objective tests of intelligence and achievement. Nevertheless, public concern over the matter remains, and the dangers of creating two "cultures" have to be very carefully weighed against the possible advantages in intellectual acceleration of the academically talented. In other words, the segregation of the more able children into separate schools is no longer socially acceptable in certain quarters. The education of gifted children, in fact, presents problems which are exceedingly complex and many of which have not previously been encountered in their present form. They are sociological in nature, as they arise from a changing technology and a changing social organization.

An egalitarian society in which social barriers have been, or are in the process of being, broken down thus faces an acute dilemma. How can it develop the pool of talent within the nation without, at the same time, creating artificial distinctions among men? Is the grading of children, at an early age, according to their suitability for advanced secondary education, compatible with the concept of democracy? If everyone has a full right to the benefits of citizenship, including education, how can this be reconciled with the granting of special facilities to some and the exclusion of others? Do egalitarian ideals preclude special provision for the gifted, particularly as the social and economic rewards for the individual concerned are likely to be very great? Finally, is there not in this situation a grave danger of replacing the aristocracy of birth by an aristocracy of talent? These and other questions remain unresolved, except at the personal level.

In the present climate of opinion there is a manifest desire to achieve social equality, but existing social institutions which, in their structure, lag behind contemporary thought tend to militate against this. It is felt, for instance, that the present division in the education systems of Europe into academic and non-academic streams serves only to perpetuate the existing social divisions. There is an evident lack of faith in the techniques of selection which seem to favor those who already *have* to the cost of those who *have not*; or, in other words, selection procedures which favor children from a rich cultural background to the detriment of the culturally deprived. This point of view is summed up by Roger Gal: ". . . it is bad, from a social point of view, to divide young people into two classes before specialization for their vocations differentiate them in the normal way. Democracy can only tolerate inequalities determined by function and not those determined by birth or nature. Education should not accentuate the inborn differences, for it is essentially a social instrument—it has simultaneously an individual and a social objective." [9]

On the other hand, the need to develop talent of all kinds runs counter to the democratic idea. In a competitive world, survival as a nation will depend on the best use being made of all national resources, including human resources. Talented and gifted young people must be picked out, wherever they are to be found, and be given the necessary opportunities to develop their talents. The problem is not only to find qualified technicians in large numbers who will carry out fairly responsible jobs in industrial laboratories, but also the highly creative men who will rank as the world's leading scientists. It is doubtful whether such gifted people as the latter group can be helped to develop their full potential through an education geared to the needs of the normal or average children who are the majority in our school population.

Since World War II there has been a noticeable tendency, and not least among the highly industrialized nations, to regard education as a form of national investment and as an instrument of rapid industrial expansion. In the past decade industry has shown a distinct trend towards progressive rationalization and automation. Fundamental changes in the vocational training pattern are thus rendered necessary. Manual work is, to an increasing extent, done by machines. Therefore, systematic training in specific vocational abilities, manual skill and the traditional work-ethics, on the model of the former handicraft apprenticeships, no longer have any general relevance, for only one worker in three is today a skilled worker. On the other hand, there is a considerable demand for highly qualified technologists or "technical guidance" personnel, capable of analyzing a production program and of removing deficiencies. Apart from a knowledge of engineering such people must have a broad general education which will offer manifold possibilities for later development, and which will enable them to adapt their thinking to the new technical requirements, and to adjust themselves to new tasks. Versatility and a sense of responsibility for the whole plant will be equally important qualities.

At the present time there is a great deficiency in qualified personnel of all kinds. In Germany for instance, industrial output is 12 per cent below what it could be, if some 500,000 places in industry and commerce could be filled. This has meant that European industrial concerns have had to face the problem of identifying and developing talent. Two important trends are to be observed in their activity. (1) They will tend to widen the basis of selection of the talented and gifted as they look further and further afield, since the traditional sources do not meet the demand. This will ultimately be reflected in the school system. A large proportion of those rejected by the grammar schools or Gymnasia, etc. will be found capable of developing talents and gifts. In fact, it has recently been suggested in the UK, that the top 50 per cent of the 11 plus age group should, at least, embark on courses leading to the General Certificate of Education at the "O" level.[10] British firms have done much to extend the pool of talent by offering university scholarships in science subjects. Many organize the so-called "Sandwich course" in which able boys spend alternate periods of six months at the work bench and at university. (2) The requirements of a technological age will bring about changes in the traditional curriculum of the schools. This will in turn cause changes in the view of what constitutes talent and giftedness.

IDENTIFICATION AND EDUCATION OF THE
INTELLECTUALLY SUPERIOR CHILD

Half a century ago the gifted child was identified as the boy or girl (it was more likely to be a boy) who passed successfully through the secondary stage of education and obtained the necessary qualifications for entry to the university. Society was quite satisfied with the end-product and did not question this definition. Superficially the same is true today, but many changes have taken place which modify the total effect. Increased educational opportunity, not only in terms of greater provision at secondary level but also in terms of family allowances, free medical services, school meals etc., have meant a great increase in the number of children entering secondary school. The greatest increase is, perhaps, in Britain where 25 to 30 percent of the 11 plus age group enter grammar schools (including the corresponding grades of the comprehensive school) as compared with a pre-war figure of 10 to 12 per cent. In Germany the increase during the past decade has been from 17 to 25.5 per cent of the age group (combined figure for Mittelschule and Gymnasium.)

Selection procedures, too, have been modified. In the U.K. the purely academic entrance examination, based on what the child had learnt in the primary or preparatory grades, gave place to group intelligence tests, supplemented by various other devices. The latter included a supplementary individual interview and standardized attainment tests in English and Arithmetic, as well as a short essay. However, Grammer schools are naturally reluctant to accept pupils, no matter how bright the intelligence test shows them to be, who have not already acquired a good foundation in the basic subjects. The need to identify the children, not at the age of 11 plus on the basis of a single series of tests, but at a much earlier age and over a longer period, becomes apparent.

Teachers at the primary school are asked to keep cumulative record cards of the work and progress of each pupil from the age of 7 onwards. These are supplemented at regular intervals by standardized tests of both ability and attainment, partly to ascertain which of them appears to be definitely subnormal or super-normal, and partly to see that the child's school progress is keeping pace with his mental development.[11] Head teachers may make recommendations regarding the suitability of their pupils for grammar school education based on these records.

Naturally, questions about the validity of the 11 plus selection examination are often raised. A recent investigation, after following up two age-groups and applying supplementary tests three years later, reported that, of the various collections of tests and assessments that were examined, "a fair number were able to provide validity coefficients of 0.90 or more." [12] This means that "even the best methods at present in use are likely to involve wrong allocations for about 10 per cent of the candidates." These "wrong" allocations are, however, borderline cases. Those who were accepted and subsequently failed were not bad failures. The converse was also true.

Another criticism of the selection procedures, and of the intelligence tests in particular, is that they tend to pick out children of a particular type of culture and of a particular socio-economic class; in other words, that the tests do not measure innate ability unaffected by social background, as they were once thought to do. The Nuffield Student Selection Unit has recently published (1st June 1961) the results of thirteen years' research.[13] These show that a child's academic history is strongly influenced by the class into which he is born. The children of semi-skilled and unskilled workers are much less likely to pass the examination into grammar school than the children of professional or business men. This finding confirms the prior work in the same field by P. E. Vernon who states that in England "three times as large a proportion of children of the white-collar classes pass the tests as do children of manual workers." According to the investigation, the standards achieved by working class children show a progressive deterioration through the grammar school years, compared with those of the higher class. Once a pupil enters the *Sixth Form* (age groups 16 to 19 years), it seems that the selective effects of social class determinants cease to operate. These determinants have little effect in deciding whether a sixth form pupil applies to a university, and none at all, in determining whether he is accepted. So far as application is concerned the most important consideration is the desire, or lack of it, for a university education. The importance of personal motivation cannot be overlooked. The question arises whether certain groups in the community are more strongly motivated and therefore produce the greatest number of gifted children. T. Husen found that in Sweden a far greater number, proportionately, of the children of school teachers received university education than any other professional or social group, and school teachers are certainly not in the highest income bracket.

In Germany the selection procedure varies from province to province. In some it is similar to that carried out in Britain. In others there is a purely academic examination. Hamburg has been experimenting with a period of special observation lasting a week to ten days, during which the children are taught in small groups the normal subjects of the school curriculum. Their intelligence, capacity for abstract thought, ability to grasp new ideas and general suitability for a secondary school (Gymnasium) course are assessed by trained observers, made up of primary and secondary school teachers, usually working in pairs. It is noteworthy that no subjects peculiar to the secondary level of education are attempted; for instance, a foreign language or geometry.

The process of selection continues even after the child has entered the Gymnasium. As German educators are rigidly opposed to the idea of "streams" or graded classes, any single class will contain pupils of a fairly wide range of ability. On the other hand, promotion from one class to the next is not automatic as in England. Every child must reach the required standard in all major subjects before he can pass on to the next year's work. Assessment of progress is based on the teacher's marking and comment throughout the year. It is not uncommon, therefore, for a child to remain in the same class for two consecutive years. Failure to make the grade after repeating the year's work means that the parents must withdraw the child from the school. A considerable number of pupils leave the Gymnasium before completing the full course, and often only 20 per cent of those originally enrolled remain by the time the highest form is reached. This was described by one principal of a Gymnasium as a "constant screening process." Even so, it is said, that only 60 per cent of the pupils who sit for the *Abitur* (graduation or final leaving examination) actually pass. The leaving certificate gives the holder access to the next stage in the educational ladder—the university.

Here, too, social factors play a decisive role. Apart from the ability to maintain a child at school until the age of 19 or 20 years, a parent of good cultural background can do much to help his son or daughter, particularly in view of the very academic approach and wide field of study in the *Gymnasium*. The German authorities are perturbed by this wastage at the secondary level. Discussion has centered on the *Rahmenplan*, by which the educational system would be modified to give greater flexibility and to allow pupils to move more easily from one type of school to another. The proposals put forward to meet this requirement consist of a two year period of orientation to follow the primary years. This is called the *Förderstufe*. The object is to discover more accurately the talents and abilities of each individual child and to guide it into the type of education most suited to its needs. This period also forms a gradual transition from primary school to the more mature studies at the secondary stage. This plan has much in common with the Hamburg selection procedure, described above. Both are based on the principle that the child who learns most quickly, or makes the greatest progress in a given learning situation, has the greatest potential for continued or future achievement and that the best means of assessing potentiality is a school environment which enables the individual actively to explore his abilities through a varied program of interests and activities.

Another scheme recently announced by the German government outlines measures which have the object of simplifying access to higher education for exceptionally brilliant and deserving students who have not been able to finish their secondary education. These are exceptional cases, and out of 300 to 400 applicants only 20 or 30 have been admitted to the university without the secondary school leaving certificate *(Abitur)*. These candidates must show in an entrance examination that they are of superior intelligence, that they can express their ideas correctly, and that they have a certain amount of knowledge in the field which they wish to study, be conversant with present-day problems and know at least one foreign language. The candidates who pass this examination then enjoy all the rights possessed by regular students.

In France, the education system has also been criticized for being excessively selective. By its over-ambitious curriculum (certain concepts in mathematics and in grammar appear two or three years earlier in French education than in other European countries) and by its emphasis on abstract thought it eliminates many otherwise able and talented children. Of the total intake to the *lycée* 60 per cent never even reach the level of the *baccalauréat*. The selective examination has now been abolished and has been replaced by a two year period of observation (from 11 to 13 years) "which gives a better chance to the children and enables the teachers to remedy the deficiencies of earlier education, whether parental or scholastic."[14]

It will be observed from the foregoing, that there is dissatisfaction with the techniques of identifying gifted and talented children, but where the problem has been seriously considered in Europe, the solution has not been in terms of abolishing selection altogether, but rather in terms of postponement and of lessening the social effects of selection by allowing easy transfer from one type of school to another. The measures mentioned above are in this spirit, as are also the recent reforms carried out in Denmark and the British Education Act of 1944 which provided "secondary education for all" in a tri-partite division of Modern, Technical and Grammar School, each of which was to have complete "parity of esteem." There are also strong advocates of the comprehensive school. The London County Council has established many of these schools in its area. In general, educationists and politicians—we must distinguish between the two—have been more concerned with the average or normal child and far less so with the gifted and talented. Research, too, reflects this trend. In those countries, where a high degree of segregation of the more able children takes place, there are many more investigations into the effects of heterogeneous classes. In the United States the reverse trend is apparent.

CONCLUSIONS

Who then are the gifted? We would, in general, agree with the empirical judgements of educators on both sides of the Atlantic. At an early age gifted children can be recognized by their curiosity about the world around them, especially in the way that things work and in cause and effect, and by their quick understanding of and interest in the information that is given them. They remember what is said, and use more complicated phrasing than the average to explain what they have learnt. They sometimes teach themselves to read and take great interest in such things as clocks, calendars, encyclopedias, and dictionaries. They have to find out things and will concentrate for surprisingly long periods. They have above-average ability to reason, generalize, and deal with the abstract.

This last point is mentioned as typical of the older gifted child by Otto Woodtli in his work in the Swiss Gymnasium.[15] He points out that, to succeed at the Gymnasium, a child must possess exceptional intellectual ability. "The pupil must be capable of abstract conceptual thought and possess the ability to grasp scientific facts and to develop theoretical insight . . . he must penetrate the underlying fundamental principles and intellectual patterns: he must learn to elaborate and deal confidently with scientific ideas and concepts."

The Principal of the well-known Manchester Grammar School considers that the gifted child will thrive best on "a largely academic course of sufficient difficulty to give his unusual talents a stimulus and a challenge"; that such a child should not be denied "the opportunity of facing difficulties or of learning to work hard." He stresses that the approach should be that of seeking solutions to questions rather than of amassing facts.[15]

The selective secondary schools of Europe have generally met this "challenge" successfully. They have, on the whole, done rather well by the exceptionally gifted child. It is not on this score that they are criticized. Let Andrew Wilkinson of the University of Birmingham, England, have the final word.[15] "The English grammar school is a center of culture in a cultureless world. It provides a rich land of experiences from which gifted children may draw, out of which they may create. Creativity is to see how alike are chalk and cheese; to add two to two and make four million. In the last resort there is no training it— except by leaving the two and the two and the chalk and the cheese and a host of other things lying abundantly about."

SELECTED BIBLIOGRAPHY

Bereday, George Z. F. and Lauwerys, Joseph A., Ed., THE CONCEPTS OF EXCELLENCE IN EDUCATION. Year Book of Education, London and New York, 1961. A Survey on an international scale of the ideas held in various societies about the criteria of excellence and the problems, within that context, of educating gifted and talented young people.

Brain, Sir Russell, SOME REFLECTIONS ON GENIUS, London, 1960. A collection of Essays by an eminent neurologist on the concept of genius and the organization of man's cerebral functions.

Buseman, A., PSYCHOLOGIE DER INTELLIGENZDE-FEKTE, Mohn-Basel, 1959. A thorough study of all aspects of mental sub-normality.

Floud, Jean E., SOCIAL CLASS AND EDUCATIONAL OPPORTUNITY, London, 1956. An enquiry into the ways in which the educational system affects the process of social selection and the problems of providing equality of opportunity in post-war English education.

Furneaux, W. D., THE CHOSEN FEW, Oxford University Press, Oxford, England, 1961. An examination of certain aspects of University selection procedures in Britain.

Mallinson, Vernon, NONE CAN BE CALLED DEFORMED, London, 1956. A case study of a number of young people who are physically handicapped but who are of average or above average intelligence.

O'Connor, N. and Tizard, J., THE SOCIAL PROBLEM OF MENTAL DEFICIENCY, London and New York, 1956. An investigation into the stages and measures necessary in carrying out a process of orderly training, designed to lead the defective back to contented and useful life in the general community. Issues of a more theoretical or general nature have also been examined.

RAHMENPLAN ZUR UMGESTALTUNG UND VEREIN-HEITLICHUNG DES ALLGEMEINBILDENDEN ÖFFENT-LICHEN SCHULWESENS, Bonn, 1959. An outline of the proposals for the reform of the public education system of the West German Federal Republic issued by the German Commission for Education and Culture (Deutscher Ausschuss für das Erziehungs- und Bildungswesen).

Vernon, Philip E., THE MEASUREMENT OF ABILITIES, London, 1940, INTELLIGENCE AND ATTAINMENT TESTS, London, 1960. The first work describes the principles underlying the use of mental tests, scholastic examinations, of constructing tests, applying tests, and of interpreting the results both of tests and of examinations. The second reviews this field in the light of the most recent research.

Woodtli, Otto, BILDUNG UND ZEITGEIST, Berlin, 1959. Each generation has to make a reappraisal of the content and purpose of its education. The traditional values are no longer acceptable in the present spiritual and cultural state of the world. The secondary stage of education in the German speaking lands—Austria, Germany and Switzerland—must be given a new basis more in keeping with the spirit of the age.

RUSSELL, CLAUDE V., Lecturer in Education with special reference to teaching Modern Languages, University of London

Institute of Education; born in 1919; formerly Assistant Editor, YEAR BOOK OF EDUCATION; educated at Laymer School, Edmonton, England, and University College, University of London where he graduated in Modern Languages (B.A.). During World War II served in the British Army in the Intelligence Service with the rank of Captain. He contributed extensively in the field of comparative education, and made a special study of the Danish and German educational systems.

NOTES

1. TRAINING AND SUPPLY OF TEACHERS OF HANDICAPPED PUPILS. Her Majesty's Stationery Office, London, 1954.
2. O'Connor, N. and Tizard, J., THE SOCIAL PROBLEM OF MENTAL DEFICIENCY, Pergamon Press, London and New York, 1956.
3. Stott, D. H., AN ACCOUNT OF THE JAMES WYKEHAM EXPERIMENT IN THE TEACHING OF BACKWARD CHILDREN, University of Bristol Institute of Education.
4. O'Connor and Tizard, OP. CIT., 12.
5. In the United Kingdom the period of primary education is terminated by some form of selection procedure at the age of 11 years, by which the top 25% of the age group are drafted to the *secondary grammar school;* the remainder continue their education in a *secondary modern school.* In the latter school the ability of pupils will range from the ESN to the really bright (I.Q.'s 70 to 105). The *comprehensive school,* although non-selective in its intake, "streams" its classes or grades and is, in fact, a combination in the one campus of the "modern" and "grammar" schools.
6. See footnote 5.
7. Collins, J. E., "Employment of Educationally Subnormal Adolescents," FORWARD TRENDS IN THE TREATMENT OF BACKWARD CHILDREN, IV, 2, 1960.
8. Known in various countries as Latin School, Grammar School, Gymnasium, Lycée.
9. Gal, Roger, "Treatment of the Academically Talented in France: A Critical Assessment," YEAR BOOK OF EDUCATION 1961, Bereday, G. Z. F. and Lauwerys, J. A., Eds., London and New York, 1961, 275.
10. "Ordinary" or lower level of the leaving certificate taken at the end of the 5th year in the Secondary School.
11. Cf. The procedure of Cheshire County referred to in the present chapter.
12. Yates, A. and Pidgeon, D. A., ADMISSION TO GRAMMAR SCHOOLS, Foundation for Educational Research in England and Wales, 1957.
13. Furneaux, W. D., THE CHOSEN FEW, published for the Nuffield Foundation by the Oxford University Press, Oxford, 1961.
14. Gal, Roger, OP. CIT.

288

15. Lord James of Rushworth, "School and Society in the Education of the Gifted, A British Viewpoint'; Waddington, Mary, "Problems of Educating Gifted Young Children with Special Reference to Great Britain"; Wilkinson, Andrew, "The Role of the Mother Tongue in the Education of the Gifted"; Woodtli, Otto, "The Educational Aim of the Gymnasium in Switzerland," YEAR BOOK OF EDUCATION 1961, Bereday, G. Z. F. and Lauwerys, J. A., eds., London and New York, 1961.

INDEX